EDWARD THOMAS

A Poet for his Country

EDWARD THOMAS

A Poet for his Country

JAN MARSH

Paul Elek London

To my family

First published 1978 by
Elek Books Limited
54-58 Caledonian Road
London N1 9RN

Copyright © 1978 by Jan Marsh

ISBN 0 236 40122 X

Printed in Great Britain by
Unwin Brothers Limited
The Gresham Press, Old Woking, Surrey

Contents

Illustrations

Between pages 114 *and* 115

Acknowledgement is due to the following for permission to reproduce copyright photographs: Myfanwy Thomas (1); Don Eades (7); Timothy Poxon (3); George H. Browne—Robert Frost Collection, Plymouth State College Library, Plymouth, New Hampshire (8); the Trustees of the Rupert Brooke Estate (10); Imperial War Museum (12); Myfanwy Thomas and the Curators of the Bodleian Library (14); Myfanwy Thomas, Professor R. George Thomas and Oxford University Press (6).

Acknowledgments

Acknowledgment is made to the following for their kind permission to quote from copyright material:

Myfanwy Thomas: the poems 'P.H.T.', 'No One So Much As You', 'The Lane' from *Collected Poems* by Edward Thomas (Faber & Faber Ltd, 1936, new edition 1944; and W. W. Norton & Company, Inc); verse and prose passages from *The Diary of Edward Thomas, 1 January to 8 April 1917* (Whittington Press, 1977); verse by Edward Thomas from MS Notebook Vol. XIX (1897) in Henry W. and Albert A. Berg Collection, New York Public Library, Astor, Lenox and Tilden Foundations; *The Childhood of Edward Thomas* by Edward Thomas (1938); letter from Edward Thomas to Harold Munro, 15 Dec. 1914, MS in Poetry Collection of the Lockwood Memorial Library, State University of New York at Buffalo; letters from Edward Thomas to Robert Frost, 19 May, 15 Dec. 1914, 19 Oct. 1916, MSS in Dartmouth College Library, Hanover, N.H.; letter from Edward Thomas quoted in *The Life and Letters of Edward Thomas* by John Moore (1939); *World Without End* and *As It Was* by Helen Thomas (Faber & Faber, 1956 edition; published in USA by R. West); a letter from Helen Thomas to Janet Hooton; a letter to Helen Thomas from Franklin Lushington, 10 April 1917; Preface by Helen Thomas to *The Prose of Edward Thomas* (Falcon Press, 1948). Edward Thomas: Preface by Julian Thomas to *The Childhood of Edward Thomas*. Oxford University Press and Myfanwy Thomas: *Letters from Edward Thomas to Gordon Bottomley*, ed. R. George Thomas (© Oxford University Press 1968). David Higham Associates Ltd: *Edward Thomas: The Last Four Years* by Eleanor Farjeon (Oxford University Press, 1958), including letters from Edward Thomas to E. Farjeon, by permission of Myfanwy Thomas. Holt, Rinehart & Winston, Inc., the Estate of Robert Frost, and Jonathan Cape Ltd: poems 'Into My Own', 'The Road Not Taken', 'The Sound of Trees', and 'A Servant to Servants' from *The Poetry of Robert Frost* (Copyright © 1969 by Holt, Rinehart & Winston, Inc.); *Selected Letters of Robert Frost*, ed. Lawrance Thompson (© 1964 by Holt, Rinehart & Winston, Inc.); *Robert Frost: The Early Years* by Lawrance Thompson (© 1966 by Lawrance Thompson). Faber & Faber Ltd: poems 'The Whitsun Weddings', 'Talking in Bed', 'Water', 'Here' from *The Whitsun Weddings* by Philip Larkin (© 1964 by Philip Larkin); and 'Sad Steps' from *High Windows* by Philip Larkin (© 1974 by Philip

Introduction

When in 1915 Edward Thomas, newly enlisted in the British Army although over the usual age limit, was asked by a friend what he thought he was fighting for, he bent down and picked up a pinch of earth. 'Literally, for this', he answered, letting it crumble through his fingers.

He was not given to exaggeration. As his poems testify, the English earth was very dear to him. In 'Digging' he wrote

> It is enough
> To smell, to crumble the dark earth,
> While the robin sings over again
> Sad songs of autumn mirth.

and it is above all as a poet of the English countryside that Edward Thomas is known and loved. Not simply as a nature poet, for he loved and celebrated both the natural and human features of the landscape. Many of Thomas's poems emerged directly out of the country walks that he took through southern England and Wales, avoiding towns and main roads and observing country life keenly as he went.

One such poem is 'Haymaking'. It is midsummer, and the poem leads us along a country road:

> The smooth white empty road was lightly strewn
> With leaves—the holly's Autumn falls in June—
> And fir cones standing up stiff in the heat.

We note both the road in chalk country, before the coming of tarmac and traffic, and also the naturalist's knowledge of country things and their season. After listening to the birds in the hedgerow and looking at the swift flying overhead 'as if the bow had flown off with the arrow', the poem leads us gently down into a sloping field by the brook where the haymakers of the title are resting in the shade of a tree:

> The tosser lay forsook
> Out in the sun; and the long waggon stood
> Without its team: it seemed it never would
> Move from the shadow of that single yew.
> . . .
> The men leaned on their rakes, about to begin,
> But still. And all were silent. All was old,
> This morning time, with a great age untold . . .

This is the ideal England of landscape painting, but Thomas is also the poet of the unconsidered detail. Country beauty can be found in the most unlikely places—in the dusty, nettle-filled corner of a farmyard, for instance, or in the jam-jar 'Wasp Trap':

> Nothing on earth,
> And in the heavens no star,
> For pure brightness is worth
> More than that jar,
>
> For wasps meant, now
> A star—long may it swing
> From the dead apple-bough,
> So glistening.

Country people, and their lives and language, Thomas also loved—all those who lived in villages hidden up lanes and 'seldom well seen except by aeroplanes'. In 'Lob' it is the country tradition that gives the expressive names to flowers and birds and places, and that makes country speech both sweet and tough:

> 'He has been in England as long as dove and daw,
> Calling the wild cherry tree the merry tree,
> The rose campion Bridget-in-her-bravery;
> . . .
> He first of all told someone else's wife,
> For a farthing she'd skin a flint and spoil a knife
> Worth sixpence skinning it . . .'

There are, of course, many poets who have celebrated the English countryside and nature in its various aspects, though for me Thomas's voice is quite distinctive: his country verse could never be mistaken for anyone else's. There are rather fewer who have loved the English earth so dearly and directly that, though resistant to all other forms of patriotism, as Thomas was, they were willing to sacrifice their lives for its sake.

Describing his feelings at the outbreak of war in 1914, Thomas wrote:

> Something, I felt, had to be done before I could look again composedly
> at English landscape, at the elms and poplars about the houses, at the
> purple-headed wood-betony with two pairs of leaves on a stiff stem,
> who stood sentinel among the grasses and bracken by hedge-side or
> wood's edge.

What impelled Thomas to join the Army, which represented everything
he loathed, and go to war in France for the sake of a small purple-headed
plant by the side of a wood in England? Why was the country—as opposed
to his country—so important to him?

Was he, anyway, only a nature and country poet? Is his message always
unambiguous? In 'The Glory' he expressed acute unhappiness in the very
midst of natural beauty:

> Shall I now this day
> Begin to seek as far as heaven, as hell,
> Wisdom or strength to match this beauty, start
> And tread the pale dust pitted with small dark drops,
> In hope to find whatever it is I seek,
> Hearkening to short-lived happy-seeming things,
> That we know naught of, in the hazel copse?

Melancholy, or, as we should now say, depression, was for many years
a permanent feature of Thomas's life. Such moods were habitual, as he
recorded in 'Aspens':

> Whatever wind blows, while they and I have leaves
> We cannot other than an aspen be
> That ceaselessly, unreasonably grieves,
> Or so men think who like a different tree.

The depression had suicidal elements; Thomas dreamt often of ending it
all and on one fateful occasion took a revolver out into the woods to shoot
himself. When, after his enlistment, he faced the almost certain prospect
of death, it had few terrors for him:

> There is not any book
> Or face of dearest look
> That I would not turn from now,
> To go into the unknown
> I must enter, and leave, alone,
> I know not how.

To Thomas the country was both an inspiration and a reproach. As his father remarked sourly, as soon as Thomas could escape from his suburban home he went to live as far as he could from any railway, and sought to earn his living as a country writer. I shall attempt to show in this book that his melancholy stemmed from his inability to convey his delight in the country as vividly as he felt it, and that his inability arose from his tendency to idealise the country and from the unnaturalness of his writing, which was immaturely influenced by the Aesthetic Movement. Neither had much to do with the real world.

Ten years of actually living in the country, and a gradual shift in his mode of writing, turned Thomas from precious prose writer into a plain and lucid poet. His chief subject remained the same—the country—and it is this which forms the chief object of inquiry in this book. The questions I seek to answer are these. Why and in what ways did Thomas's love of the country influence his life and work? How did he come to terms with a less than ideal world, and how did his writing change in reflection of that growth in understanding? Why, without any conventional patriotic feeling, did he volunteer for what was almost certain death in the trenches? Finally, what kind of poet did England lose at Arras on 9 April 1917?

For one of the finest English poets of the twentieth century, and one of the most consistently popular with the reading public—his poems have not been out of print since they were first published—Edward Thomas has received curiously little attention from the academic world. The number of critical studies has been small; Thomas remains a poet more read outside than inside the universities—though when his work is academically discussed it is with admiration.

This critical neglect is due, I suspect, to the very lucidity which gives Thomas's poetry its quality and its popularity. He is a direct poet, and his verse is not obviously difficult to understand; thought is grafted seamlessly onto structure and image, and what he means he says. The result is often more complex than such a description suggests and the subtleties of meaning in the verse are sometimes hard to grasp, but the poems themselves are never mystifying and only rarely obscure; unlike some other modern poetry, Thomas's work does not use a private or public symbolism, nor employ an elliptical or perplexing style. It therefore does not require, nor will it bear the weight of much critical exegesis and interpretative analysis.

The lucidity of Thomas's poetry, as well as inhibiting the kind of critical treatment on which academic reputations are made, also creates a strange impression of timelessness, as if the poems existed in a world of their own. They are neither Victorian, nor Georgian, nor truly modern. When they are discussed, it is often in purely textual terms, without reference to the historical or literary context in which they were written.

By contrast with the poetry, there have been a comparatively large number of books dealing with Thomas's life—three biographical studies and at least three major editions of Thomas's letters to close friends (listed in the note on Sources at the end of this book). Much of the interest in Thomas's life has undoubtedly been aroused by Helen Thomas's brilliant, unforgettable memoirs of the passionate and turbulent relationship which was their marriage—*As It Was* and *World Without End*, both still in print today. A definitive biography of Thomas is currently being prepared by Professor R. G. Thomas of Cardiff.

In this study I have attempted to place Thomas's work in the context of his life as a whole. It is not intended as a biography, but as an account of the major concerns of Thomas's life and how these found their expression in his poetry; some biographical information was necessary to this. Of the major concerns of Thomas's life and work—firstly, his love of the English countryside, its landscape, inhabitants, traditions, natural features and immemorial aspect; and secondly, his individual sense of dispossession, dissatisfaction, unhappiness, which stemmed from his personality and situation—the first led him to the literal patriotism of love for his country, the second to a vain search for contentment, a sense of happiness, of 'being at home', and to his eventual acceptance of death. Both came together in his response to the war, when he began writing poetry and decided to enlist in the Army.

Having served a long apprenticeship as a writer in prose, during which time he was constantly searching for the right means by which to express his thought and feeling for the countryside, Thomas did not experience many failures when he finally took to verse. All his hundred and forty poems were written within two years, from December 1914 to December 1916, and they show little technical development. Thematically, however, some shifts are discernible, particularly towards the end of Thomas's life, when thoughts of death were becoming predominant. A checklist of the dates of the poems' composition, based on the careful notebooks Thomas kept, with dated entries, is given in William Cooke, *Edward Thomas: A Critical Biography* (1970). I have followed this chronology in general, though by no means exclusively, preferring to consider the poems in terms of the major themes of Thomas's life rather than in strict chronological order.

Thomas adopted love of the countryside and nature as the faith by which he lived, and this love, as well as his sense of yearning, was expressed, incomparably, in his poetry. But he was not alone in these beliefs, and it is an important part of my task to draw attention to the historical context of Thomas's life and work and to their closeness to the anti-industrial pastoral impulse to get back to the land, away from the city, to return to the abiding values of rural life and the close contact with nature which was a strong and pervasive cultural feature of urban and suburban life in the years between 1880 and 1920. There were many who dreamt of a country cottage and some, like Thomas, who achieved it.

At the same time, Thomas's career as a writer should be seen against its literary background. The years just before the First World War marked a shift in poetry and 'semi-poetical' prose writing away from the high, inflated rhetorical modes of the late-Victorian age and towards a plainer, more down-to-earth style, which could deal in realities as well as dreams. The emergence of Georgian poetry marked a change in this direction, which ultimately made the war poetry of Owen and Rosenberg possible. Thomas's achievement was to both reflect and transcend his age. To look at Thomas's poetry in the context of both his personal life and ambitions and of the ideas and poetic practice of the time is, I believe, not to diminish his work but to reveal its greater depth and strength.

I

Childhood and Youth

There are so many things I have forgot,
That once were much to me, or that were not
'The Word'

Edward Thomas was born in London on 3 March 1878, the first-born son of a Welshman who had come to London to take advantage of the expanding opportunities in employment offered by the commercial and imperial capital. Philip Henry Thomas was born in Tredegar of an ordinary working family; he had acquired an education and trained as a teacher. In London, he joined the civil service, working as a staff clerk in the Board of Trade, dealing with light rail and tram traffic. He married Mary Elizabeth Townsend from Newport in Monmouthshire. Both parents were thus first generation migrants, part of the great dispersal of population that accompanied mid-nineteenth-century economic developments. Other members of the Thomas family settled at Swindon in Wiltshire, finding work in the great railway workshops there.

Philip Edward, to give him his full name, was the eldest of six sons. His father was a stern figure whom it was not easy to love—'eloquent, confident, black-haired, brown-eyed', wrote Edward later. 'By glimpses I learnt with awe and astonishment that he had once been of my age.'[1] He could be affectionate, however, and read aloud to his sons when they were ill. To Edward, his mother was always the more sympathetic figure, and his later relationship with her was marked by great tenderness.

When Edward was born the family lived in Lambeth, one of the new suburbs then extending to the south of the river with the rail network, for office employees in the city and elsewhere. Subsequently the family moved to other parts of south London—first Wandsworth, then Clapham, and finally to Rusham Road in Balham. As he grew up, Thomas was conscious of the steady growth of the built-up area, as the open spaces where the children played gradually disappeared. This became a recurrent theme in his essays, where literary regret at the encroachment of town on country is combined with half-disclosed nostalgia for vanished childhood.

His own early childhood was happy and ordinary. It was a lower middle class childhood, spent largely in the street with groups and small gangs of other boys including his brothers, exploring, fishing, birds' nesting, climbing trees, building dens. He kept rabbits and pigeons too. At home he knew neither the rough intimacy of working class family life nor the polite control and distance of the upper classes. There was no nanny, for instance, but a maidservant to help Mrs Thomas with the housework, and some other help as required. Generally speaking, the Thomas boys must have led a free life, apart from school and the dreaded Sundays, when best suits had to be worn and running was forbidden. Edward always attributed his hatred of religion to the memory of those childhood Sundays.

The family was not rich but thanks to Mr Thomas's determined efforts to improve his position it was comfortable and secure. At first Edward was sent to a local Board school, which cannot have been long in existence, as the 1870 Education Act extending schooling to all children was little more than a decade old. It was, he remembered, a bleak place, smelling of chalk and echoing with young voices chanting their knowledge in unison. Some of the children were poor and ill-kempt. It was not long before Edward was moved to a private school, and to another, and then to Battersea Grammar School. His father also arranged private lessons in science and, later, Latin and Greek.

The workings of paternal ambition may be discerned here: perceiving that his son could and should benefit from the greater educational opportunities available, and being possessed of the means to them, Philip Thomas acted accordingly. Not satisfied with a grammar school, he next looked to a day place at one of Britain's finest public schools. At the age of fourteen, Edward was entered for a scholarship at St Paul's. He did not win one, but went anyway.

Joining the school at such a late age and surrounded by social and intellectual superiors, Thomas felt out of place and unhappy. He made no friends and found the academic work hard; lonely, he spent his lunch hours reading or watching games, occasionally walking alone by the river looking at the gulls and swans, 'sometimes in such wretchedness that I wanted to drown myself.'[2] Scholastically he was outclassed by boys who brought precocious analytical qualities to their work, where Thomas had only learnt to repeat the textbook; he later recalled being humiliated by this in a history debate.[3]

The move to St Paul's was no doubt dictated by Thomas senior's determination to see his son do better than himself—enter a profession, or take a career post in the Civil Service. For Philip Thomas was an able but frustrated man. Owing to his hard come-by but elementary qualifications, he had not been able to rise as high as his abilities warranted, and he remained a clerk. Some of his energies were diverted towards politics: he was a staunch Liberal, particularly after the party came to power in 1906, a supporter of fellow Welshman Lloyd George, and a firm upholder of Liberal policies on free trade, moderate social reform and home rule for

Ireland. In earlier days he was perhaps more of a radical, for Edward remembered being taken as a child to hear speakers like John Burns and Keir Hardie and, once, William Morris.[4]

He also remembered being dragged to different but equally disliked churches, as his father tried out different religious denominations. Brought up a Methodist, Philip Thomas was intellectually a free-thinker, that is an atheist, but he could not abandon the habit of worship nor the respectability that went with churchgoing Eventually he settled for the Unitarians, who had the least supernatural doctrine, until some time around 1910 when he took up with the Positivists. In Holborn a British follower of Comte had set up a Church of Humanity where the faithful gathered on Sundays to offer praise to their own version of the deity—'Our Virgin Mother, Humanity'. As is common among sects, the congregation was small and self-sustaining, and according to Philip Thomas it was at a crisis in its affairs that he was moved to offer his services as minister.[5] It is unlikely that this was a paid job, but it conferred honour and status, within a small circle. At home, Thomas's opinion had always prevailed, and he enjoyed political and philosophical discourse; in the pulpit he was in his element. He published a collection of his Positivist sermons or addresses in 1913 which reveal something of his character and motivation, as this extract shows:

> When I think of Positivism the image of a vast ocean encircling the globe comes before my mind; and I have spoken of individual Positivists as free to sail their own craft of all sorts and sizes upon its broad bosom, provided only they take the trouble to learn and duly practise the science and art of Positivist navigation. For my own part I declare that I could never accept a master who fettered me in mind or spirit. The master I love and follow is one who sets me free to make the most and best of whatever is within me—my own individuality and faculties.[6]

His family referred to him, at this stage of his life, as The Public Man. Perhaps some of his desires were satisfied. In 1918 he stood unsuccessfully as a Liberal parliamentary candidate.

According to his youngest brother, Julian, 'Edward was happy neither at home nor at school.'[7] As he reached adolescence, he began to rebel against his father's plans. He had already begun to write, stimulated by exploratory rambles with a friend in the countryside beyond the suburbs, and by his discovery of Richard Jefferies' *The Amateur Poacher*. This ends with the words:

> Let us get out of these narrow modern days, whose twelve hours have somehow become shortened, into the sunlight and pure wind. A something that the ancients thought divine can be found and felt there still.

In his cramped suburban home and classroom, these words acted as an inspiration to Edward, and he adopted them as a personal motto, thus early establishing the faith by which he was to live the rest of his life. That he knew little of country life as described by Jefferies was exactly the attraction; to him it was a perfect world:

> What I liked in the books was the free open-air life, the spice of illegality and daring, roguish characters—the opportunities so far exceeding my own—the gun, the great pond, the country home, the apparently endless leisure—the glorious moments that one could always recapture by opening the *Poacher*—and the tinge of sadness here and there as in the picture of the old moucher perishing in his sleep by the lime kiln, and the heron flying over in the morning indifferent. Obviously Jefferies had lived a very different boyhood from ours, yet one which we longed for and supposed ourselves fit for. He had never had to wear his best clothes for twelve or fourteen hours on Sunday. Enforced attendances at church and Sunday school could not have been known to him . . .[8]

The nearest Edward had been to country life was on holiday with his relatives in Swindon. Jefferies had been born a mile or so outside Swindon, which was an added attraction.

Despite his dismissive reference to Sunday school, it was there, as it happened, that Thomas began his literary career. The local Unitarian minister encouraged his essay writing—always in the style of Jefferies, as Thomas later noted, but based on his own walks and observation—and sent some examples to a children's magazine, where they were printed. This roused, Thomas recalled, his first 'faint ambition, both definite and indefinite, to do something in connection with learning or literature.'[9]

This desire began to grow when the minister introduced him to the writer and critic James Ashcroft Noble, newly arrived in Wandsworth from Liverpool. A man in his fifties, Noble had been an editor and had extensive contacts in the literary world. He read and admired some of Edward's essays, and placed them in the *Speaker* and the *New Age*, two cultured periodicals of the time.

This success, compared with the difficulty and dullness of school work, made Thomas decide that he would be a writer, instead of a civil servant as his father had planned. He began to insist on leaving school. Eventually his father agreed, on condition that he studied at home for the Civil Service entrance exam. But no sooner had Edward left school, at the end of the 1895 spring term when he had just turned seventeen, than he set off on the first of his many long walks, with a notebook in his pocket. The idea was Ashcroft Noble's, who had perceived that Edward's best writing came from direct observation, and advised him to extend his experience of the natural world a little further than the fields and commons to the south of the city. With this walk from London to Swindon as the basis, Thomas began a nature diary, opening on 1 April with notes on the heronry in Richmond Park. On the 12th he heard the cuckoo at Wimbledon, and on the 15th he set off for Wiltshire, arriving on the 18th.

He observed chiefly birds, and their nests, and wild flowers. Thus on 23 April:

Marsh-marigolds or 'bubble' in blossom with the dull-flowered lilac butterbur.
Ash-sprays out to greet the earliest sedge-warbler.
Coots laying in piled nests of drenched water-weeds and jointed 'mare's tail'.
Young dipper abroad at Coate Reservoir.
Cuckoo-flowers in the damp meadows.

By July he was back in London, noting 'Succory blossoming on dry wastes and stony road with docks and poppies; its petals lucent blue, notched at their narrow edge.'[10] In October there were gulls on the Thames at Hammersmith, and the last house martins. Over the winter Thomas went often to Richmond Park and Wimbledon Common, but in February 1896 he returned to Swindon, visiting Jefferies' birthplace at Coate Farm and the Iron Age forts above it on the Downs. He also began to do more than just look at nature; like Jefferies he became interested in the human inhabitants of earth, as revealed in this entry for 18 February:

Hedger cutting a hedge which had not been trimmed for more than forty years, and whose briers and thorns in a thick belt occupied half an acre in a small field. He meets with a fat sleeping hedgehog now and then, but it is getting late, and the creatures begin to breed and lose their fat. Their oil the hedger holds a sovereign remedy for hoarseness, etc., applied to throat or chest. His work begins with looking to the cows before daylight; his wages 2s a day with a small cottage; his bill-hook he calls a 'ookut'.[11]

These expeditions were Thomas's first taste of adult freedom, and for a long time he could envisage nothing finer than rambling in the country and writing it up afterwards. His father did not approve at all. He knew enough of the world to know that writing in any form offered an uncertain income and was adamant that Edward seek security and advancement. Edward, on the other hand, was earning quite impressive amounts of money—for a boy of eighteen—from his published essays; moreover, thanks again to Noble, he was about to have his first book, a collection of nature essays together with his year's Diary in Fields and Woods, published by Blackwoods. He was thus ready to stand up to his father's dogmatism even though it meant painful scenes.

The fiction that he was working for the Civil Service exam was eventually abandoned, and it was agreed that he should apply instead for Oxford University, through a year spent in Oxford as a non-collegiate student. In many ways this was a satisfactory solution, and would have been a better had English been available as a degree subject instead of the history Edward was obliged to take. Philip Thomas provided the necessary funds for fees and board, on the understanding that Edward worked for a scholarship, but the struggle between father and son had done lasting damage to their relationship; for the rest of Edward's life there was open conflict and animosity between the two men.

His father was plainly disappointed and angry with Edward's choice of career and for years continued to remark, openly and obliquely, on his son's impecuniousness.[12] For his part, Edward had clearly found it psychologically necessary to establish his own identity against a too-dominant parent, but it proved equally difficult to free himself from notions of success and failure or anxiety and guilt concerning money matters. Having made his choice, he was to be emotionally compelled to stick to it through many lean years of reviewing and commissions, for to have taken a steady office job would have proved his father right after all. Yet the lack of success even within his own terms exacerbated the sense of worthlessness his father aroused in him and he soon came to refer to himself as 'an obvious failure'.[13] Like other ambitious parents, Philip Thomas left his mark on his child.

As the years went on, it became clear that no reconciliation was possible. In 1916, father and son were still quarrelling and Edward, aged 37, wrote the poem 'P.H.T.' as a plain statement of fact, with intimations of tragedy:

> I may come near loving you
> When you are dead
> And there is nothing to do
> And much to be said.
>
> To repent that day will be
> Impossible
> For you and vain for me
> The truth to tell
>
> I shall be sorry for
> Your impotence:
> You can do and undo no more
> When you go hence,

> Cannot even forgive
> The funeral.
> But not so long as you live
> Can I love you at all.

In most biographical accounts Edward's mother appears as a shadowy figure, her husband clearly the dominant force in the family. Yet Edward's wife Helen wrote of his adoration for his mother—'if such a word can be used of so reserved, so undemonstrative an affection.'[14] Thomas himself, in his autobiography, recalled his mother from his infancy, when she was the most important person in his world, as the personification of tenderness and beauty. 'I liked the scent of her fresh warm skin and supposed it unique,' he wrote. 'Her straight nose and chin made a profile that for years formed my standard. No hair was so beautiful to me as hers was, light golden brown hair, long and rippling. Her singing at fall of night, especially if we were alone together, soothed and fascinated me, as though it had been divine, at once the mightiest and the softest sound in the world.'[15] She cared for her children lovingly and well, always ready to comfort them when they were hurt or disappointed. She herself had no ambitions, and would love them whatever they did, regarding herself as not clever enough to follow their interests. With six sons and a somewhat demanding husband, she can have had little leisure, but appears to have created a stable centre from which they went out into the world.[16] She remained devoted to them, and was often on hand to help out in times of illness. During the last years of his life, Edward's visits home to see her became not only more frequent but also more loving; he was conscious of the deep but unspoken affection between them.

This is expressed in a poem written to his mother three days after that to his father, in the same short-lined quatrains. It is very different in feeling. Several critics have claimed that the poem is 'more satisfactory read as addressed' to Helen, although Helen herself is on record as having said that it was to his mother.[17] The date of the poem, its form, and above all its sentiments confirm this. 'No One So Much as You' takes its title from the first line, and leaves little to be said:

> No one so much as you
> Loves this my clay,
> Or would lament as you
> Its dying day.
>
> You know me through and through
> Though I have not told,
> And though with what you know
> You are not bold.

None ever was so fair
As I thought you:
Not a word can I bear
Spoken against you.

All that I ever did
For you seemed coarse
Compared with what I hid
Nor put in force.

My eyes scarce dare meet you
Lest they should prove
I but respond to you
And do not love.

We look and understand,
We cannot speak
Except in trifles and
Words the most weak.

For I at most accept
Your love, regretting
That is all: I have kept
Only a fretting

That I could not return
All that you gave
And could not ever burn
With the love you have,

Till sometimes it did seem
Better it were
Never to see you more
Than linger here

With only gratitude
Instead of love—
A pine in solitude
Cradling a dove.

It would have been sometime after he first went to school that Edward's
father's influence began to displace his mother's, and from then on
nostalgia characterised his memory of early childhood, the key element of
which was a sense of something lost and irrecoverable. For some reason,

perhaps directly connected with his mother, this sense first attached itself to two of his earliest books. One was a child's reader, in which a fairy introduced objects in everyday use, and it belonged to Edward himself. Then it was lent to someone else and never returned. At the age of ten, though he had long outgrown the book and indeed could hardly remember it, Edward began pestering his parents to retrieve it, in vain. The second book was his first school prize, called 'The Key of Knowledge', with coloured illustrations. It too disappeared, he recalled:

> I never had any idea how, before I had read far into it, and I never saw it again. From time to time down to the present day I have recalled the loss, and tried to recover first of all the book, later on the thread of its story, something that would dissipate from its charm the utter darkness of mystery. For example, fifteen years ago in Wiltshire two strangers passed me and I heard one of them, a big public schoolboy, say to the other, a gamekeeper, 'What do you think is the key of knowledge?' and back came the old loss, the old regret and yearning, faint indeed, but real.[18]

It is as if the book stood as a symbol of another sort of loss, for 'there were times when I fancied that the book held the key to an otherwise inaccessible wisdom and happiness'.[19]

Throughout his life indeed Thomas continued to search for some source of inaccessible wisdom and happiness, perhaps never quite understanding the large element of nostalgia for vanished infancy which was contained in this. At first, he tended to locate the source of happiness in Wales, where he had spent some very early holidays alone with his mother, visiting her relatives. This was recalled, many years later, in his poem 'The Child on the Cliffs', where a child is sitting with his mother hearing a bell ringing on a buoy out in the bay. It ends:

> Sweeter I never heard, mother, no, not in all Wales.
> I should like to be lying under that foam,
> Dead, but able to hear the sound of the bell,
> And certain that you would often come
> And rest, listening happily.
> I should be happy if that could be.

He thought of himself as Welsh, unhappily displaced; then, as he grew older, nature and the countryside took the place of Wales; the days he had spent out of doors gathering material for his youthful essays and nature diary gave him a taste of long-lost bliss. Yet there is a sense of something inaccessible at the heart of nature which often gives Thomas's poems a sad haunting quality. The sense of loss is never far away. In his most

direct poem about childhood, 'Old Man', Thomas writes of the feathery
plant known as Old Man or Lad's Love:

> As for myself,
> Where first I met the bitter scent is lost.
> I, too, often shrivel the grey shreds,
> Sniff them and think and sniff again and try
> Once more to think what it is I am remembering,
> Always in vain. I cannot like the scent,
> Yet I would rather give up others more sweet,
> With no meaning, than this bitter one.
>
> I have mislaid the key. I sniff the spray
> And think of nothing; I see and I hear nothing;
> Yet seem, too, to be listening, lying in wait
> For what I should, yet never can, remember:
> No garden appears, no path, no hoar-green bush
> Of Lad's-love, or Old Man, no child beside,
> Neither father nor mother, nor any playmate;
> Only an avenue, dark, nameless, without end.

This sense of searching, of having mislaid the key, is one of the central
themes of Thomas's life and work. It was, perhaps, the most enduring
legacy from his childhood.

2

Love and Marriage

I read the sign. Which way shall I go?
A voice says: You would not have doubted so
At twenty. Another voice gentle with scorn
Says: At twenty you wished you had never been born.
'The Sign-Post'

James Ashcroft Noble did more than simply encourage Thomas's literary efforts, though his help had been crucial. He also introduced him to his daughter.

Helen Noble was the middle one of three sisters, with a much younger brother. Both her sisters were brighter and, she believed, prettier than herself. She was solidly built and somewhat short-sighted, essentially a home-loving girl, devoted to her father, whose health had never been good. She also had a fund of affection which was lavished, at least in part, on dreams and fantasies of motherhood. On her own admission, she adored babies, and pregnant women hardly less.[1]

The first meetings between Helen and Edward at the Noble house were shy and conventional, but Mr Noble was neither, and he soon encouraged his daughter to accompany Edward on some of his nature walks. As they visited Wimbledon Common and Richmond Park they got to know each other and shed their shyness. In her books, *As It Was* and *World Without End*, written after Edward's death, Helen described their first walk, scrambling about looking for birds' nests in a roadside copse in still rural Merton. It was a new experience for her, both being out in the open, and being with the only boy she had ever known as a friend.[2]

Edward taught Helen all he knew about the natural world—a lot of which he was still learning himself—and the names of all the common birds, trees and flowers. To Helen, it was magical knowledge; Edward was awakening in her not only a love of nature to equal his own but also love for himself, and simultaneously, his own love for her. Henceforth, nature and love were virtually inseparable. Literature was a close third, for they talked about books, mainly the Romantic poets, and Edward introduced Helen to the work of Richard Jefferies. Thanks to Mr Noble's liberal views, his daughter already shared many of Jefferies' ideas even if she knew nothing of the outdoor life. She disliked clothes and was proud of her body, in an age when to do so was synonymous with vice. She disliked contemporary dress fashions, and chose for herself what were called 'Liberty dresses', plain in line, with coloured embroidery. Her sisters laughed, but Helen felt superior: 'I wanted less furniture in my bedroom, and more air', she recalled, 'and I read Ruskin and Morris and became their disciple.'[3]

Helen's mother did not approve of these tendencies, nor of her daughter's friendship with Edward. During the year spanned by Edward's nature diary, this had developed and strengthened until its direction was unmistakeable. Mrs Noble, who knew her husband was dying of tuberculosis, used this circumstance to try to make Helen promise to break off with Edward, but Helen was too much in love to keep such a promise, and after Mr Noble's death the conflict with her mother made living at home unbearable. Defiantly, she found herself a job as nursery governess to four young children with a family named Webb living in Broadstairs. It was independence and a job Helen loved, but far from Edward. Yet they were so young and so much in love that this seems to have hardly mattered; the rare occasions they did meet were heightened by the long absences. One such day was spent inland in Kent, when they walked and ran and laughed with happiness, and kissed in the privacy of a little copse. For lunch they had sandwiches and fruit wrapped up in leaves to keep cool, and a bottle of lemonade let down into a mill pond to chill; for tea they made a fire and boiled a kettle.

After some months Helen returned home at her mother's request, getting work as a daily nanny and paying her mother for her keep. Their relationship did not improve. Edward by this time had finally persuaded his father to drop the idea of his entering the Civil Service and agree to the idea of Oxford. Mrs Noble did not allow him in her house, and the two young people met in the evenings, usually on Wandsworth Common. The Thomas family welcomed Helen, however, and she visited their house frequently, getting on well with Philip, though she could never like him, and gradually winning his wife's confidence.[4]

By this time Edward and Helen were bound together not only by love but by a romantic and passionate idealism centring on nature and poetry. They were fervent believers in freedom and in the natural expression of emotion. They held hands as they walked and kissed and caressed in a manner quite remarkable when one considers the age and its conventions. Many young women of Helen's age were not allowed unchaperoned meetings with men. She and Edward went much further. On Helen's twentieth birthday in 1896, as she described in *As It Was*, they became lovers in a hidden sunlit mossy glade of a copse on Wimbledon Common and later pledged themselves to each other, Edward giving Helen a 'wedding' ring that had belonged to his great-grandfather.[5]

Well brought up young people rarely did such things. A decade later

Rupert Brooke was part of a group of young men and women at Cambridge who considered themselves 'progressive', free from many of the restrictions governing social life. Explaining their sexual code, Brooke wrote: 'We meet in cafés, talk on buses, go unchaperoned walks, stay with each other, give each other books, without marriage.'[6] 'But', he added, 'we don't copulate without marriage.'

Helen and Edward were ahead of their time. They discussed how to bring up their children in accordance with Jefferies' ideas of the open air life and did not contemplate marriage, for as Helen said: 'We hated the thought of a legal contract. We felt our love was all the bond there ought to be, and that if that failed it was immoral to be bound together. We wanted our union to be free and spontaneous'.[7]

Following the secret consummation of their love, they had a brief, secret honeymoon at the home of an old couple called Mr and Mrs Uzell, whom Edward had got to know while staying with his Swindon relatives. The Uzell house was just what the young country-lovers would have chosen, a cottage standing almost inside a wood and some way from the road. 'It had a deep thatched roof almost hiding the little windows of the bedrooms with its deep eaves', wrote Helen, 'and a porch with a little bench on each side, covered with traveller's joy and briar roses that filled the air with their musky scent.'[8]

Mr Uzell, or Dad as he was called, was an old countryman, sometime militiaman, with a wild youth behind him and a fund of country knowledge he delighted in sharing with Edward. He fished, poached, skinned animals, kept bees and made herb remedies. Both he and his wife, Granny, were lively and welcoming, quite free from any ideas about 'correct' behaviour; their closeness to nature and remoteness from all that could be called society and modern civilisation made them appear, to their young guests, as innocent 'children of the earth', to be loved and admired. Men like Uzell appear in Thomas's poetry, most notably in 'Lob', which opens:

> At hawthorn-time in Wiltshire travelling
> In search of something chance would never bring,
> An old man's face, by life and weather cut
> And coloured,—rough, brown, sweet as any nut,—
> A land face, sea-blue-eyed—hung in my mind . . .

By now, Wiltshire had all but replaced Wales as Thomas's adopted country, the place he claimed as his own by virtue of family connection and sheer affection. Wales still remained his ancestral home, but he had been there only rarely and as a child; Wiltshire was more real. When he was with Dad, he felt himself very close to the spirit of his hero Richard Jefferies, also a Wiltshireman.

In the autumn of 1897 Thomas went up to Oxford, to work for a

scholarship while living in lodgings. He was lonely and miserable, and
sought consolation in long solitary walks in the countryside around the
city, as a rare fragment of youthful verse from this period shows:

> O Nature! let me love thee more:
> For friendships fail
> And life is frail:
> I love: I hate; but as of yore
> I love thee—let me love thee more.[9]

He studied diligently, however, winning a history scholarship to Lincoln
College, where he took up residence in the autumn of 1898, and incidentally proving to his father that all was not lost. He was highly regarded by
his tutors and fellow students, and expected to get a first class degree. He
also continued to write and from pieces published in various magazines he
earned £80 in one year, with which to supplement his allowance. His first
book, *The Woodland Life*, had been published the previous year, and he
thus had a reputation as something of a literary figure already: the future
seemed relatively rosy. In college, too, he was able to find greater social
and intellectual companionship: he made friends, among them E. S. P.
Haynes, later a well-known lawyer and writer who edited the *New Witness*
newspaper and Ian MacAlister, later secretary of the Royal Institute of
British Architects. He learned how to drink, to adopt the decadent attitudes
then in fashion, to smoke opium and to write in imitation of Walter Pater,
then at the height of his influence. More surprisingly, he also rowed for
his college. Altogether, his undergraduate days appear to have been
enjoyable and successful.

Helen, meanwhile, had found herself a new home with a well-to-do
Bohemian household in Hammersmith belonging to a woman named
Beatrice Potbury. The house was furnished in William Morris style and
run on the principles then advocated by 'progressive' people—simplicity,
good taste, egalitarianism and easy manners. The house was a social centre
for artists of all kinds, poets, actors, painters and craftsmen. Helen was a
humble admirer of all, and an eager helper around the house; although the
household kept no servants on principle, Helen was a willing one in
practice. Beatrice Potbury knew of her relationship with Edward and
welcomed his occasional overnight visits to the house, when he slept with
Helen. But when in the spring of 1899 Helen discovered she was pregnant,
Beatrice strongly advised marriage. Helen was horrified: in her view
marriage belonged to the world of convention, not of the free life, and she
was upset when Edward agreed with Beatrice. Where Helen was blithely
confident of the future, secure in her love and advanced ideas, he was
worried and nervous, knowing only too well what both their families
would say.[10]

They were married secretly in June, but it was not possible to keep the secret for long, and as feared 'the jangle and confusion of family discussion'[11] was brought into what Helen persisted in regarding as a wholly healthy and natural event—two lovers and their child. Mrs Noble refused to have anything to do with her daughter, but the Thomases proved kinder, taking Helen to live with them and allowing Edward to finish his degree. Philip Mervyn Ashcroft Thomas, known as Mervyn, was born in January 1900, and in the summer Edward left Oxford, to his disappointment gaining only a second-class degree. He was now a husband and father, with responsibilities to be faced and no clear means of doing so. He had thought no further than a return to the kind of life he had led before Oxford—living in the country as much as possible, reading and writing essays.

However, the need to earn a regular income was pressing. Edward did not wish to go on living with his wife and child in his parents' home, particularly as his father's advice as to a career had been resumed, with greater force and reason. Conflicts between father and son were now bitter, the more so because of Edward's continuing financial dependence. He acknowledged his responsibility to provide for his wife and child—throughout his life he was to reproach himself with the poverty he inflicted on them, though Helen never complained—but he did not want to give up being a writer, to admit defeat and take a regular job, either in the Civil Service or elsewhere. It was then fashionable, in artistic circles, to be against employment requiring daily attendance: as we shall see, several young writers of the time dated their liberation to the day they 'escaped' from the purgatory of office work. Thomas determined never to succumb.

He believed he had beautiful and unique things to say in his essays (and the ease with which he had so far sold his pieces confirmed that there was an audience), and that there was little else he was fit for. He was, as he later described himself in the third person, 'ready to do anything so long as he can escape comfortable and conventional persons, and quite unable to be anything conspicuous, but a man who has been to the garden of the Hesperides and brought back apples that he alone can make appear to be golden in his rare moments of health.'[12]

On their own, however, his golden apples—his essays—would not pay the rent and so in the autumn of 1900 Thomas began looking for other literary work. He approached several editors, and was both diffident and proud: Henry Nevinson, then on the *Daily Chronicle*, described his manner:

When he first came to me, I said to myself 'Yet another poet!' . . . He was tall, absurdly thin, and a face of attractive distinction and ultra refinement was sicklied over with nervous melancholy and the ill condition of bad food or hunger. Almost too shy to speak, he sat down proudly and asked if I could give him work. I enquired what work he

could do and he said 'None' . . . I asked whether he would like some
reviewing on any subject, and on what. He replied that he knew nothing
of any subject, and was quite sure he could not write, but certainly he
did want work of some sort . . .[13]

Despite this inauspicious opening, Nevinson did give him work, and soon
realised that he had found a careful, conscientious and occasionally
original reviewer, in fact, one of his best. Thomas was given similar work
by other papers, but it was poorly paid: between August 1900 and June
1901 his earnings totalled £52.[14] More work was necessary, for he had
quarrelled openly with his father and moved his young family to cheap
rented rooms in another suburb of south London. Sorrowfully, he sold
some of his precious books—fine modern editions of poetry and prose that
he had bought with his earnings while at Oxford. And he trudged round
literary offices asking for more work.

He was often disappointed, and thrust into gloom by lack of success.
Now for the first time Helen came to know the moods of black despond-
ency that afflicted Edward at times of failure, when he was both depressed
and aggressive, taking things out on himself and her. When he came home
from seeking work, Helen wrote later,

> with the first glance at his face I knew what the day had been. If it had
> been a bad one there was no need of words, and none were uttered. I
> did nothing, for if I said one word which would betray that I knew what
> he had endured and was enduring, his anger and despair and weariness
> would break out in angry bitter words which would freeze my heart and
> afterwards freeze his for having uttered them.[15]

If only Edward could have been happy, Helen would have been radiant
in her longed-for role as mother. She took her small son out to the Common
as often as possible, letting him lie in the sun and picking flowers for him
to hold. She fervently believed that contact with earth and nature were
essential to growing things, and that her baby should feel natural beauty
around him, even though he was forced to live in a hideous suburb.
Perhaps the squalid rented rooms were an added cause of Edward's ill-
temper: neither he nor Helen had ever envisaged living anywhere but the
country with their child. Not to be able to do so was a negation of all they
believed in.

Gradually the reviewing increased and on the strength of a small but
steady income the young couple decided on the country at any price, and
rented a home called Rose Acre Cottage near the village of Bearsted in
Kent. It was an ugly brick house, belying its name and very different from
the image of the country cottage they had in their minds. But the rent was
within their reach, at £32 per year, and the village of Bearsted, with a

green, a pond, a manor house and a half-timbered inn, helped to compensate for the house's deficiencies. Here, in September 1901, Edward,
Helen and Mervyn moved. They sold some more books to help with
expenses.

Despite Edward's warning, Helen had refused to believe that a cottage
with such a lovely name did not indicate a dwelling as perfect as the
Uzells'. She was disappointed with its appearance, but drew consolation
from the fact that their home was now truly in the country. She recalled
leaning against the back door the first evening, taking a deep breath of
country air and sensing sweetness and elation:

> I stooped and took up a handful of earth and crumbling it let it fall
> through my fingers. Its harsh touch and its pungent clean smell thrilled
> me with a new awareness. My eyes were opened to the beauty of the
> night. . . . A white owl flew past me silently like a ghost and like the cry
> of a ghost sounded its quavering note from the elm tree at the end of
> the garden. The cherry trees thick with pendulous buds breathed—as
> it were—softly in sleep. The slender moon rising timidly above the
> trees laid her spell on the earth, and all was silence and darkness and
> sleep. On me too she laid her spell. I turned to go to [Edward] and met
> him coming towards me.
> 'There's a new moon', he said; 'you must wish.'
> 'There's nothing left to wish for', I said; 'we are in the country and it
> is spring.'[16]

(It was not spring, as it happened, when they moved to Bearsted; Helen's
recollections were often literally inaccurate as to facts although they were
true in spirit to her experiences and feelings.)

They had good times in Kent, often taking their lunch out on a walk
to the top of the Downs or along the nearby Pilgrim's Way, letting Mervyn
sleep on the grass as they rested and read. Living in the country enabled
Edward to understand more at first-hand of the rhythms of nature and
country life, and gave him subjects and ideas for his essays. Once a week
he would go up to London to collect more books for review and sell those
that he did not wish to keep. He still regarded reviewing as merely a
means to an end, and his own essays were his truly creative work. His
second collection, of fifteen pieces, was published by Duckworth under the
title *Horae Solitariae* in 1902. Most had been written and published, in a
variety of magazines, during his time at Oxford and show signs of the
decadence and classicism he had absorbed there. But there were also more
recent pieces, such as one about country lanes and footpaths, which 'are
footprints, perhaps, of the immortals' or 'vestiges of that older day when
this land also "was in Arcady." ' The essay continues:

One of these paths entered a lane which suddenly ceased, and round
the corner was the kingdom of heaven at my feet—the Kentish weald,
just grass and corn and trees, and like jewels on that delicate cloth, a
white hamlet or an auburn farmhouse with oast-houses around.[17]

Under the trees of a neighbouring park, a 'pale glorious face' is seen fading
into the dusk, an image or personification of the countryside's perfection.
Such a figure—real or imagined—is a recurring item in Thomas's essays,
as he sought to express what the countryside meant to him, and here as
elsewhere she is tinged with sadness, like Malory's Isoud of the White
Hands (the ostensible subject of the essay), despite the beauty and joy
surrounding her. Dryad or angel, she represents that lost and inaccessible
happiness which Thomas hoped to recapture in the 'unique geniality' and
divinity of the Kentish landscape.

Several of Thomas's Oxford friends came down to visit the young
couple in Rose Acre Cottage, and it was at this date that Thomas began
his life-long correspondence with the poet Gordon Bottomley. Bottomley
lived on the edge of the Lake District and suffered from a lung condition
making it difficult for him to work or travel. He spent most of his days
reclining on a sofa, writing.

Bottomley was four years older than Thomas and had corresponded
with James Ashcroft Noble, who had shown some of his verses to Thomas.
It was nearly seven years later that the two young men began writing to
each other. They wrote about books and authors, about their own writing,
fears and ambitions. They made suggestions on each other's manuscripts,
and corrected each other's proofs. They met for the first time in London
in 1903, when Bottomley's lung was enjoying a remission, again on a
couple of occasions when Edward travelled north to see Bottomley and
his wife Emily, and more frequently in the winters immediately preceding
the war, when the Bottomleys came to Surrey.[18]

From the beginning Thomas and Bottomley were kindred spirits, with
the same dreams of life and literature, the same liking for Celtic stories and
songs, and the same belief in the regenerative power of nature. Both
rejected the urban industrial world around them. In his last letter to
Thomas (the only one to survive) Bottomley wrote in reference to a
mutual friend: 'I know I would rather die than work in an office again as
my Father does . . .'[19] Almost all Thomas's letters to Bottomley survive,
showing that despite the geographical distance between them, Bottomley
was one of his closest friends. From the first Thomas confided in him with
his literary fears and hopes:

I look forward to writing & look back on it joyfully as if it were an
achievement & not an attempt—very often. But while I write, it is a
dull blindfold journey through a strange lovely land . . . Correction is

pleasanter, for then I have glimpses of what I was passing through as I wrote. This very morning the sun was shining, wide & pale gold & warm as it has done for two weeks, & the church bells suddenly beginning to ring were at one with it a part of Spring, & they set me to writing . . .[20]

The move to the Weald of Kent had not brought them into the kingdom of heaven, though it was a vast improvement on their former home. There were still money worries; Thomas sought desperately for new work, swallowing his pride to do so, and taking himself off for long solitary walks when anger and disappointment were too much to bear. Helen remained touchingly loyal and optimistic but bore the brunt of his anger. 'Your sympathy and your love are both hateful to me,' he would snarl as he came in. 'Hate me, but for god's sake don't stand there, pale and suffering.'[21]

Things got worse when Helen became pregnant again at the beginning of 1902, and even she gave way to anguish and despair. To her old friend and confidant Janet Hooton she poured out her pained bewilderment:

As I expect you know I am to give the world another baby in October. This alone is terrible for no-one wants the poor wee thing; no-one looks forward to its coming, and I least of anyone . . . You ask why I do not want it? Because we are very poor; because it means more anxiety for Edward, and more work for him. Home will become unbearable for him. Even now, poverty, anxiety, physical weakness, disappointments and discouragements are making him bitter, hard and impatient, quick to violent anger and subject to long fits of depression . . . He is selling some of his dearest books to pay for baby clothes and doctor etc., and as he packs them up I know he is rebelling at fate, how hard life seems to him, how he regrets it all . . . I have prayed that I and my babe may die, but we shall not, tho this would free Edward. I am as strong as ever. I pile work on work till my body can scarce move for weariness, but nothing lifts the darkness from my soul . . .[22]

The idyllic days of love and courtship were over, destroyed on the harsh rocks of marriage and parenthood. Only three years previously, Helen's ambition had been to live with Edward in the country and be the mother of his children. And his, to live with Helen in the country and write. Why had everything gone wrong?

In the early years of this century, children were a greater financial liability to middle class parents than is the case today, necessitating expenses which are now covered by the state, notably medical care and school fees. There were no social security benefits to alleviate poverty and if the Thomases failed to earn enough to care for their children, send for the doctor when necessary, and provide an education above Board school level, they would have to rely on the charity of relatives and friends. The choice between relying on low and uncertain earnings from writing or seeking a steady job with security and an income large enough to provide for a family was thus a hard one, though neither Edward nor Helen had difficulty in choosing the first course,[23] and they came to see that Helen's dearest wish, a large family, was incompatible with the poverty attendant on writing.

This was a problem that faced others besides Thomas. The poet and critic Lascelles Abercrombie, who followed Thomas in 'escaping' to the country, found the arrival of his third child a serious drain on his finances, while across the Atlantic Robert Frost and his wife had their own problems trying to reconcile the poetic temperament with the demands of a family.[24]

After their second child, Bronwen, was born in October 1902, (and by her happy disposition made up for all the anxiety that preceded her birth) the Thomases had no more children for eight years, when a second daughter, Myfanwy, was born. The decision was no doubt a sensible one in the circumstances. Yet it was not simply prudence that dictated it. Although his letters show Thomas to have been a devoted and loving father, he was not yet mature enough to cope with the demands of parenthood. His choice of career meant that he worked at home, in a room specially reserved as a study, yet within sound of all domestic happenings. The proximity tended to aggravate his ill-temper and some of his anger against the world and himself would be displaced onto his family. Although he knew they were not to blame, he could and did resent them. Thus in 1904 we find him writing to Gordon Bottomley that he is about to leave home and find lodgings in London because his work—even his reviewing —is suffering 'more and more from a silly but unavoidable nervous interest in the children's movements in and out of the house & equally silly but unavoidable interference in little household things & a continual wearing irritation . . .'[25] But London was worse, only intensifying his depression. Six weeks later he reported that he could not afford to live in town but the domestic irritation continued: 'Merfyn fidgeting is worse than a brass band practising at Chelsea: truly, tho' I am not sure why.'[26]

Perhaps the children's presence acted as a tacit reproach to Thomas for his failure (as he saw it) to provide adequately for them; perhaps their childish unselfconsciousness exacerbated his own introspectiveness, which could at times be morbid. For some reason he found Mervyn particularly annoying. By a sad irony Thomas's relationship with his son was destined to be almost as difficult as his own with his father, though in a different way, and it may have been that the latter had some indefinable influence on the former, making it difficult for Thomas to show his affection. From an early age he tried to give Mervyn lessons, as a means of delaying the decision and expense of a school, but the attempt was disastrous, for he had no patience to teach a child, and preferred reading Shelley aloud to teaching Mervyn how to read. As if in defiance of his father, Mervyn early showed an interest in things mechanical, and towards the end of Edward's life some harmony was restored between them through this unlikely subject. For most of Mervyn's childhood, Thomas was needlessly critical of his son's personality and behaviour, to the extent that visitors were sometimes moved to remark on his harshness.[27]

But it was not so always. For much of the time Thomas enjoyed his children's company, and made a delightful, inventive father, exploring fields and woods, suggesting an impromptu picnic or a rambling walk. Bronwen was imperturbably cheerful, and shared with her father a delight in nature, especially wild flowers. At school she became a keen swimmer. Mervyn and Edward went cycling together when Mervyn was in his teens, and generally all three children adopted the family love of an open air life.

They shared too their father's delight in the curious and expressive place-names of England, which were the inspiration for the group of poems Thomas wrote to his children on three consecutive days in 1916, not long after the poems to his parents. The first, to Bronwen, begins with an ironic glance at the family's poverty, in the conventional sense:

> If I should ever by chance grow rich
> I'll buy Codham, Cockridden, and Childerditch,
> Roses, Pyrgo, and Lapwater,
> And let them all to my elder daughter.
> The rent I shall ask of her will be only
> Each year's first violets, white and lonely,
> The first primroses and orchises—
> She must find them before I do, that is.
> But if she finds a blossom on furze
> Without rent they shall all for ever be hers,
> Codham, Cockridden, and Childerditch,
> Roses, Pyrgo and Lapwater,—
> I shall give them all to my elder daughter.

It has been said that the style of these poems to the children is impersonal in a way that 'belies the gaiety of their actual life together',[28] but to me they are full of tender affection and humour. Nonsense, in the names and the absurd conditions (how could Bronwen fail to find a blossom on furze when gorse is the one flower that blooms all year round?) plays across the surface of the poem, almost masking the serious, loving content.

The second poem, to Myfanwy, not yet six when it was written, expresses a sober respect for a small child's identity and shows in its lack of sentimentality or possessiveness a maturity of affection that matches the confident handling of the verse:

What shall I give my daughter the younger
More than will keep her from cold and hunger?
I shall not give her anything.
If she shared South Weald and Havering,
Their acres, the two brooks running between,
Paine's Brook and Weald Brook,
With pewit, woodpecker, swan, and rook,
She would be no richer than the queen
Who once on a time sat in Havering Bower
Alone, with the shadows, pleasure and power.
She could do no more with Samarcand,
Or the mountains of a mountain land
And its far white houses above cottages
Like Venus above the Pleiades.
Her small hands I would not cumber
With so many acres and their lumber,
But leave her Steep and her own world
And her spectacled self with hair uncurled,
Wanting a thousand little things
That time without contentment brings.

These poems were in a very real sense Edward Thomas's legacies to his
children. They are remarkable for being so finely balanced between the
childlike and the adult—poems that the children no doubt loved when they
first heard them, but only later came to appreciate fully.

In the third poem to Mervyn there is no more than a hint of the troubles
in their relationship. Outwardly the poem is a celebration of shared
country pleasures:

If I were to own this countryside
As far as a man in a day could ride,
And the Tyes were mine for giving or letting,—
Wingle Tye and Margaretting
Tye,—and Skreens, Gooshays, and Cockerells,
Shellow, Rochetts, Bandish, and Pickerells,
Martins, Lambkins, and Lillyputs,
Their copses, ponds, roads, and ruts,
Fields where plough-horses steam and plovers
Fling and whimper, hedges that lovers
Love, and orchards, shrubberies, walls
Where the sun untroubled by north wind falls,
And single trees where the thrush sings well
His proverbs untranslatable,
I would give them all to my son

If he would let me any one
For a song, a blackbird's song, at dawn.
He should have no more, till on my lawn
Never a one was left, because I
Had shot them to put them into a pie,—
His Essex blackbirds, every one,
And I was left old and alone.

Then unless I could pay, for rent, a song
As sweet as a blackbird's, and as long—
No more—he should have the house, not I
Margaretting or Wingle Tye,
Or it might be Skreens, Gooshays, or Cockerells,
Shellow, Rochetts, Bandish, or Pickerells,
Martins, Lambkins, or Lillyputs,
Should be his till the cart tracks had no ruts.

Elsewhere in Thomas's verse confusions of thought are often marked by
rather rough grammar or doubtful sense, as in the hectic sentences of this
poem. Is it clear exactly what bargains are being struck? And there is
something disturbing about the reference to the nursery rhyme Four and
Twenty Blackbirds; why should a father threaten to shoot his son's
favourite birds to put them in a pie? The childish mode has a slight edge,
too, when we remember that Mervyn was over sixteen when the poem
was written.

If there were difficulties with Mervyn, a poetic rendering of the relationship with Helen was even more problematical. Towards the end of his
life, when Thomas was deliberately casting up his accounts, in verse, with
those close to him, he was as clear and honest as he knew how to be in his
poems to Helen. Perhaps the high pitch of idealism on which their love
had been founded had made it difficult for him to resolve the difficulties
and setbacks that inevitably accompanied marriage, or fully to believe in
the strengths of love's maturity. In one sense, he always regretted the
passing of the simple ecstasies of the early days, and blamed himself for
what he came to see as a loss of love.[29]

Helen never lost her faith in him and his ability to be a great writer (the
Noble household had early on nicknamed him 'The Genius'). She sought
fulfilment only through him and her children, yet without demanding it;
when Edward suffered, she suffered, both for and through him. In World
Without End she wrote:

I used to wish and pray to be different. If only I could be angry at his
unkindness instead of hurt, I thought it might be better for him. If only
I could really take no notice, instead of pretending not to do so! How I

longed to be able to change my nature. In these times I used to wish
I was beautiful, or that he would find another woman who would keep
him always happy . . .[30]

It was not Helen who needed to change her nature. Thomas often hurt
his wife deliberately, particularly by his long absences from home in later
years, and by a brusque, sarcastic manner when he did return. His behaviour sometimes shocked friends who happened to witness it.[31] Once,
after being needlessly angry with one of the children, he took an ancient
revolver out into the woods, intending Helen to think he was going to
shoot himself.[32] Perhaps he was—his suicidal feelings will be considered
in a later chapter—but the chief effect was to make his wife suffer, though
he knew she was not to blame.

It is clear that whatever was or was not wrong in their relationship,
Thomas came to blame his marriage for a good deal else in his life. In 1908
he told Bottomley that he thought fornication less evil than marriage
because 'its evil does not continually encrust the soul.'[33] When Bottomley
demurred, he replied: 'I didn't say fornication was good and marriage bad.
Only . . . there is something worse, more steadily deadening in marriage . . .'[34] This was ironic in view of the fact that it was he who had
persuaded Helen into marriage, but it was a conviction that grew in his
mind. By the spring of 1913, according to Robert Frost, he had become
obsessed with the idea that divorce was the only solution to his problems.[35]
He believed that he had failed Helen, and denied her happiness.[36]

Eventually, as we shall see, Thomas came to understand that marriage
was not the root of his problems, and although he never regained the joy
or gladness of the early days with Helen, he came to terms with the
present. It was against this background that he wrote the two poems to his
wife in the spring of 1916. The first was composed after the poems to his
parents, and takes its inspiration from the early spring flower of its title,
'Celandine':

> Thinking of her had saddened me at first,
> Until I saw the sun on the celandines lie
> Redoubled, and she stood up like a flame,
> A living thing, not what before I nursed,
> The shadow I was growing to love almost,
> The phantom, not the creature with bright eye
> That I had thought never to see, once lost.
>
> She found the celandines of February
> Always before us all. Her nature and name
> Were like those flowers, and now immediately
> For a short swift eternity back she came,

Beautiful, happy, simply as when she wore
Her brightest bloom among the winter hues
Of all the world; and I was happy too,
Seeing the blossoms and the maiden who
Had seen them with me Februarys before,
Bending to them as in and out she trod
And laughed, with locks sweeping the mossy sod.

But this was a dream: the flowers were not true,
Until I stooped to pluck from the grass there
One of five petals and I smelt the juice
Which made me sigh, remembering she was no more,
Gone like a never perfectly recalled air.

This poem has nowhere been identified as being written about Helen, and in one sense, it appears to be addressed to a person now dead, certainly lost. But the date of its writing (4 March 1916), between the poems to Thomas's parents and those to his children, and the internal evidence of 'Her nature and name Were like those flowers'—*Helen: celan*dine—point to this conclusion. And its sense would confirm this: Edward reproached himself for having destroyed with his sulks and sarcasm the bright cheerful girl he had fallen in love with all those years ago. Compared with that Helen, the woman of 1916 could indeed be likened to a shadow or a phantom, existing no more or lost 'like a never perfectly recalled air'.

A month later, immediately after the poems to his children, Edward returned to Helen again in verse. This time he was able to address her directly, acknowledge all the injury he had done her in the years of marriage, and face up to things as they were, not as they had or might have been. The result is a poem of such compelling maturity and honesty, with verse and rhyme so perfectly complementing the sense that one can almost not regret the experiences that gave rise to it. It stands as Thomas's final statement on his marriage:

And you, Helen, what should I give you?
So many things I would give you
Had I an infinite great store
Offered me and I stood before
To choose. I would give you youth,
All kinds of loveliness and truth,
A clear eye as good as mine,
Lands, water, flowers, wine,
As many children as your heart
Might wish for, a far better art
Than mine can be, all you have lost

Upon the travelling waters tossed,
Or given to me. If I could choose
Freely in that great treasure-house
Anything from any shelf,
I would give you back yourself,
And power to discriminate
What you want and want it not too late,
Many fair days free from care
And heart to enjoy both foul and fair,
And myself, too, if I could find
Where it lay hidden and it proved kind.

3

Back to the Land

Thrushes and blackbirds sing in the gardens of the town
In vain: the noise of man, beast, and machine prevails.
'Good-Night'

'There is nothing left to wish for', Helen Thomas had said on moving to Kent. 'We are in the country and it is spring.' To understand the full force of that remark, and the important part the countryside played in Edward Thomas's life, we must look briefly at contemporary attitudes towards the country in the last years of the nineteenth century.

The pastoral impulse—the desire to quit the city for the country—is as old as, if not older than, Theocritus (c.310–250 BC) and has been most powerfully felt in times of acute social change such as the Renaissance. Thus Ben Jonson's translation of Horace's *beatus ille* is a representative poem of its time:

> Happie is he, that from all Businesse cleere,
>   As the old race of mankind were,
> With his own Oxen tills his Sire's left lands,
>   And is not in the Usurer's bands.

This opinion was normally not shared by those living in the country, who tended to look enviously at the town. Whatever the objective virtues of town and country life, however, the long and honourable pastoral tradition in Western literature was, until fairly recently, composed when the countryside formed the undeniable economic base of society, for only by the food and raw material produced there could the commerce and culture of the city be sustained. By the mid-nineteenth century in Britain, this was changing. Food and raw materials still sustained civilisation, but they came increasingly from elsewhere, particularly from far-away places like the colonies. City and country became less interdependent, and the former grew in both economic importance and population, until Britain had become what it is today, an urban nation.

The Romantic movement may be seen in part as a response to the initial stages of modern industrial development, especially through the work of

Wordsworth and Shelley. Strictly speaking, however, the pastoral is concerned not with the wild and sublime in nature but with the cultivated and tame, preferably in the past, and it was later in the century that a truly pastoral poetic re-emerged, concerned classically with shepherds and by extension with country life in an idealised form. Matthew Arnold was one who revived the pastoral mode; in 'Thyrsis' he lamented his involvement in the world of men and affairs:

> Too rare, too rare, grow now my visits here!
> But once I knew each field, each flower, each stick,
>   And with the country-folk acquaintance made
> By barn in threshing-time, by new-built rick.
>   Here too our shepherd pipes we first assayed.
>   Ah, me! this many a year
> My pipe is lost, my shepherd's holiday. . . .

By this time, however, the impact of industrialism had become unassailable, and the new technology of steam power and mass production had created a wholly new way of life based on manufacturing, mining and trade. Factory, pit and office were now the common work-places. Agriculture was declining and with it the political power of the landed interest. It was, however, the collapse of farming in the 1870s and the accelerated depopulation of the rural areas which followed that had most impact on the countryside. For a whole generation, while the total population of Britain was growing, the farming areas recorded a net human loss.

The people were driven off the land not only by the agricultural depression and the competition of cheap food from overseas, but also by industrial development which offered employment and undercut the village craftsmen and women who had hitherto produced tools, clothing and domestic utensils. Those who remained on the land suffered from both the loss of material prosperity and the social impoverishment that went with a declining community. Developments in transport, education and entertainment added to the attractions of town life. London was a particular magnet, with its vast expansion of commercial and clerical employment in the docks, railways, banks, businesses and public services.

By 1900, then, the majority of English people no longer belonged to the village. They or their parents had come to the cities in search of work or advancement, leaving behind their rural roots. Although the British class system proved strong and enduring, the latter part of the last century was a period of great social (and geographical) mobility. One upwardly mobile citizen was, as we have seen, Philip Henry Thomas, who came from a family of miners and tin platers. In his sermons Mr Thomas compared himself with Lloyd George, who had risen from a relatively lowly background, also in Wales, to become Chancellor of the Exchequer—and, later, Prime Minister.[1]

But even as the virtues of industrial progress were being acclaimed, flaws were being discovered in its structure. The expanding cities spawned slum areas where poverty, squalor, ill-health and crime were concentrated on an unprecedented scale and traditional systems of welfare, based on the parish and the squire, proved inadequate forms of relief. The new economic order produced a mass urban proletariat and altered the relationship between the producers and consumers of wealth. At the same time, mass production and consumption led to a vast increase of machine-made goods and the decline of individual craft work. And after the middle of the century there was a perceptible turning away from industrialism and modern civilisation as a source of evil and ugliness. Thus it was that, while agriculture and the land declined in economic importance, the countryside began to acquire an enhanced emotional significance as a reservoir of purity and peace, which it still retains.

Ruskin was perhaps the first major figure of influence in this anti-industrial movement. By connecting aesthetic, moral and economic matters he encouraged his contemporaries to reject the prevailing economic system and the machine-made article. In his political writings, Ruskin was mainly concerned to demonstrate the logic and scientific basis of his arguments that the modern system produced 'illth' rather than wealth, but every so often a proselytising streak breaks through, as at the end of *Unto This Last* (1862), where a discussion of the meanings of value and price is suddenly interrupted by a vision of What Might Be which is essentially pastoral in its outlook:

> The presence of a wise population implies the search for felicity as well as for food; nor can any population reach its maximum but through that wisdom which 'rejoices' in the habitable parts of the earth. No scene is continually and untiringly loved but one rich by joyful human labour; smooth in field; fair in garden; full in orchard; trim, sweet and frequent in homestead; ringing with voices of vivid existence . . . As the art of life is learned, it will be found at last that all lovely things are also necessary: the wild flower by the wayside, as well as the tended corn; and the wild birds and creatures of the forest, as well as the tended cattle. . . .[2]

New aims in life were urged:

> We need examples of people who, leaving Heaven to decide whether they are to rise in the world, decide for themselves that they will be happy in it, and have resolved to seek—not greater wealth, but simpler pleasures; not higher fortune but deeper felicity . . .[3]

Ruskin demonstrated his belief in the possibility of an alternative economic order through his support of an agrarian settlement called the Guild of St George, located outside Leeds, where a community of manual workers, some of whom came from industry, lived and worked together growing their own food, making their own shoes, clothes, tools and furniture, and generally escaping from the soul-destroying wage slavery of mechanical labour in factory or mill.

It was this last feature that distinguished St George's Guild from the many agrarian communities that preceded it, and whose history is given in W. H. G. Armytage's *Heavens Below: Utopian Experiments in England 1560–1960* (1964). Before 1850 such communities were almost always religious and millenarian in character, signifying a withdrawal of the elect from the world, to await the Day of Judgment. From 1850 onwards, there was a slow but steady increase in the secular variety of agrarian community, which flourished—if that is the right word for what were mainly short-lived idealistic enterprises—between 1880 and 1920. Most were based on Ruskinian ideals, with a belief in the nobility of labour and the importance of being close to the land. Later Tolstoy was to be a major influence.

The loss of religious faith had other consequences too, notably in a general sense of uncertainty, of a void at the centre of life, which was variously filled by devotion to good works, nature worship, utopian socialism, mysticism, vegetarianism and a number of other enthusiasms which were felt to give purpose to existence. Several of these strands came together in the founding of the Fellowship of the New Life in 1883. This was an association of individuals including Havelock Ellis and Edward Carpenter who believed that social progress could be achieved only through personal progress towards moral improvement—socialism with a spiritual rather than material basis. The New Life was based on the ideals of discussion, simple living, manual labour and brotherhood; it was genuinely democratic, though without the structures needed to put democracy into practice. Within months, some founder members of the Fellowship, including Bernard Shaw, had rejected the cultivation of one's soul as self-indulgent avoidance of the real problems, and had departed to establish the Fabian Society, dedicated to a more rigorous analysis of social ills and the means to combat them—a difference of emphasis described epigramatically at the time as 'one to sit among the dandelions, the other to organise the docks.'[4]

Because the dandelion-sitters were eventually less influential than the dock-organisers, their contemporary importance has been largely forgotten, and their idealism dismissed as mere wishful thinking. At the time, how-ever, they were regarded as the more truly radical group, and the zeal of the Fabians was dismissed as essentially reformist. As *The Open Road*, a magazine dedicated to the cause of freedom and the outdoor life, com-mented: 'Fabianism provides merely for the limitation of the hours of actual slavery to eight, for crèches and labour exchanges and insurance schemes ... It deals with results, not with their cause.'[5] In similar vein, *Seed Time*, journal of the agrarian community movement in Surrey and Kent, claimed that the cities could not be improved by 'rosewatering their leprousness with model buildings and lighting their darkness through the dungeon windows of public parks. Do we not all know that the modern city is unnatural? No child can be healthy that from the first breath does not breathe the pure air of the fields. ... Socialism or no socialism, reform or no reform, the city must go.'[6]

Edward Carpenter was perhaps the foremost exponent of the New Life, which included an altogether un-Victorian belief in sexual freedom and homosexual love. Originally an ordained Cambridge Fellow who, experiencing the familiar crisis of faith, renounced a promising career, he espoused Socialism and went to work with the University Extension Movement in Sheffield. Within a short while he had moved to a smallholding at Millthorpe above the city which a young working couple and later a male companion ran for him while Carpenter continued with his teaching and writing. His aim, as he described it, was

> just to try and keep at least one little spot of earth clean: actually to try and produce clean and unadulterated food, to encourage honest work, to cultivate decent and healthful conditions for the workers, and useful products for the public, and to maintain this state of affairs as long as I was able, taking the pecuniary result to myself ...[7]

The smallholding was never self-sufficient and all that was produced for the public were some Indian-style sandals which Carpenter made. But through his writings and example, his influence on the age was far wider, through such books as *The Simplification of Life* (1886) and *Civilization: Its Cause and Cure* (1889) in which he expounded his ideas, and particularly through his long Whitmanic poem *Towards Democracy* (1883).

Carpenter was a vegetarian and a believer in the importance of the body's contact with air and earth. He advocated simple meals and the reduction of clothing to a comfortable minimum, i.e. a shirt, underpants, loose-fitting woollen jacket and trousers, and sandals. He also believed that contact with nature was essential for any sustained creative work and accordingly built himself a small hut by the side of a stream at Millthorpe where he did his writing. 'It seems almost necessary', he wrote, 'that one should have the quietude and strength of nature at hand, like a great reservoir from which to draw.'[8]

Richard Jefferies, whose work was the first and most lasting influence on Edward Thomas, held the same beliefs in regard to the importance of nature. 'If you wish your children to think deep things, to know the holiest emotions', he wrote, 'take them to the woods and hills and give them the freedom of the meadows. Do it at any cost to yourself if you wish them to become great men and noble women.'[9] This was the advice Edward and Helen Thomas followed when they took their baby son to play on the grass of Wimbledon Common and when they moved, despite financial insecurity, to their first country cottage in Kent.

Jefferies was a countryman himself, the son of a small farmer near Swindon, who began his career as an agricultural correspondent on local newspapers. His books on country life were widely read and admired, and his popularity came not only from the detail with which he could describe the countryside to a readership no longer personally familiar with it, but also from the range and variety of his writings. He was the author of several novels, notably *Bevis* (1882) and *Amaryllis at the Fair* (1887), which created positive and enduring images of country life, and of one, *After London* (1887), which takes the destruction of the city as its starting point, postulating a return to a more primitive, adventurous way of life. Most importantly, however, in an age of religious doubt, he proclaimed a new faith: nature as a source of spiritual strength and regeneration. Lacking religious belief himself, Jefferies moved towards a mysticism of the earth which answered his need to worship an immanent, immaterial godhead. In his confessional *The Story of My Heart* (1883)—a book whose influence was far greater than we would now suppose from reading it—he described how contact with the earth and solitary communion with nature led him to feel, almost to touch, 'the unutterable existence infinitely higher than deity'. The strained superlatives indicate the often wishful nature of Jefferies' mysticism: in his writings he often seems to be reaching for rather than attaining the tranquillity he describes. But many of his generation shared his need and took his precepts to heart:

> It is enough to lie on the sward in the shadow of green boughs, to listen to the songs of summer, to drink in the sunlight, the air, the flowers, the sky, the beauty of all. Or upon the hilltops to watch the white clouds rising over the curved hill-lines, their shadows descending the slope. Or on the beach to listen to the sweet sigh as the smooth sea runs up and recedes. It is lying beside the immortals, in-drawing the life of the ocean, the earth, and the sun.
>
> I want always to be in company with these, with earth and sun and sea and stars by night. The pettiness of house-life—chairs and tables—and the pettiness of observances, the petty necessity of useless labour, useless because productive of nothing, chafe me the year through. I want to be always in company with the sun and sea and earth . . .[10]

William Morris was another influential figure. Beginning as a painter and poet with the Pre-Raphaelite Brotherhood, Morris at first turned his back on the modern world, seeking instead to return to the values of an imagined medieval world such as existed, if anywhere, in the pages of Malory and Chaucer. His long poem *The Earthly Paradise* (1868) was deliberately escapist, with its opening lines 'Forget six counties overhung with smoke ...' But through his daily work, particularly in household design, Morris came to perceive that the attainment of paradise on earth was dependent on action rather than dream, and he thereupon turned to Socialism and lent his considerable energies to its cause. His writings are still quoted and analysed in political circles today, and his utopian romances, *The Dream of John Ball* (1888) and *News From Nowhere* (1891) (which describes a pastoral, post-industrial society), were among the most widely-read and admired books of his age. In design Morris was scarcely less influential, creating wall-papers and fabrics still in production today; Helen Thomas, as we have seen, was among their original admirers.

Morris composed a prodigious amount of verse,[11] among which were his translations of *Beowulf* and the Icelandic Sagas. This reflected the contemporary revival of interest in the mythology of Northern and Western Europe which became widespread towards the end of the century. Scriptural and classical legend were put aside in favour of rediscovered Germanic and Celtic tales, which evoked a long-lost world of violence and simplicity. In Ireland, the recovery of myth was part of the emergent nationalist political movement. In London, Edward Thomas read the eleventh-century Welsh poem *Mabinogion* to feel himself closer to the land of his ancestors.

At the same time the foundations of anthropology were being laid with the publication of *The Golden Bough* (1890–1915), Frazer's mammoth work on legends in different parts of the world. Suddenly there was a rise of interest in 'primitive' peoples and a revival of the Rousseauean idea of the noble savage. In comparison with the natives of industrial civilisation, those who lived in the most 'backward' regions of the globe were seen to possess far greater qualities of courtesy, compassion to the less fortunate, generosity and contentment. Gauguin and Robert Louis Stevenson were among the Europeans who travelled in search of a simpler, better world. Among the representative writers in this field was W. H. Hudson, who later became a close friend of Edward Thomas. Hudson was born in Argentina and had a naturalist's interest in wild life. In 1885 he published *The Purple Land*, an account of his adventures in Uruguay as a young man, where he encountered many remote settlements whose inhabitants, though wild and 'uncivilised', showed far finer hospitality and sensitivity to others than citizens of more 'advanced' regions. The book appears to have become something of a cult; forgotten by most, it was revered and passed on by a few until the publisher was persuaded to reissue it twenty years later. By this time Hudson was living in Britain where he wrote other books, among them *Green Mansions* (1904) and *A Shepherd's Life* (1910).

The pastoral impulse implicit in the passion for distant, simple ways of
life took another form in the rediscovery and collection of rural folksong,
then thought to be vanishing under the impact of urbanisation. Country
music was rescued, rearranged and presented to schoolchildren in an
attempt to preserve the national heritage. In Ireland W. B. Yeats, J. M.
Synge, Augusta Gregory and others were attracted by the songs and speech
of Irish peasants and brought them into art through their dramas at the
Abbey Theatre in Dublin. In his *Autobiographies* (first published 1926)
Yeats recounted how strong and pervasive the anti-industrial feeling was
among his contemporaries, and the various alternatives adopted. He
himself dreamed 'of living in imitation of Thoreau on Innisfree, a little
island in Lough Gill',[12] and thus was his best-known poem born. At other
times he immersed himself in occult and mystical practices, hoping to
reach through to a world of magic; in later years he was to disconcert
young admirers by asking them in all seriousness if they had ever seen a
fairy.[13]

Anti-industrialism and its offshoots were visible in many fields besides
literature, and the full account of its content and course is yet to be
written; in many respects it has been more totally forgotten than any other
social and cultural phenomenon in recent history. Evidence is, however,
visible wherever one looks in the record of the years between 1880 and
1914, in the names of publications like *The Open Road*, *The Tramp* and
The Simple Life Limited,[14] in the founding of societies for the preservation
of footpaths, for the provision of allotments, and in some quite serious
schemes to alleviate poverty by resettling people on the land, such as the
farm set up for the unemployed in Laindon, Essex by the Poor Law
Guardians of Poplar in East London.[15]

There is architectural evidence, too, in the buildings of Letchworth
Garden City, Hampstead Garden Suburb, Cadbury's Bourneville Estate
and Lever Brothers' Port Sunlight, where the aim was to return, as far as
possible, to a village mode of design and community. In education there
was a similar movement, with the founding of the first 'progressive'
schools. The New School movement actually began in the 1880s with the
establishment of Abbotsholme and Bedales. According to the founder of
Bedales, J. H. Badley, the New School movement stood for the following
ideals (which were indeed remote from those operating in either existing
state elementary schools or private public schools):

Physical Education: Life in the country. Water, air and light in abundance. Manual work obligatory for all: agriculture, carpentry, gardening,
forge. The balance and health of the body regarded as the primary
condition for the health of the mind.

Intellectual Education: Not learning or memory work imposed on the child from without but reflection and reasoning acting from within. Beginning with facts and proceeding to ideas. Following the scientific method: observation, hypothesis, verification, law.

Moral Education: Not authority exercised from without but moral liberty creating a personal and social law from within. Gradual freedom from authority won by personal service. Training in initiative, responsibility and self-government.[16]

With such a prevailing intellectual atmosphere, it is easy to understand how and why idealistic young people like Edward and Helen Thomas looked to the country with such desire. They were not alone. For the most part the keenest adherents of the movement 'back to nature', or 'back to the land', were like themselves from the middle classes, reared in the anonymous suburbs which had grown up around the great cities of London, Birmingham, Manchester, Leeds and so on. For the most part the working people were too preoccupied with earning a living to dream of returning to village life, although the vision of a green and pleasant utopia formed a large part of the appeal of popular socialism, as is evident in Robert Blatchford's *Merrie England* (1893), first printed as a series of articles in the working men's paper *The Clarion*. Essentially the movements must be seen as a nostalgic impulse on the part of those who had lost their rural roots and as yet failed to find themselves a modern, urban identity. Again and again in this period one finds individuals 'adopting' some part of the country with which they profess an ancestral or affectionate affinity.

Rupert Brooke, for instance, who was born and brought up within the confines of Rugby School, adopted the village of Grantchester after moving there from Cambridge. In 1913 he visited Canada and found himself countering boasts about the rapid growth of Calgary by laying claim to an older tradition. 'My village', he said, 'is also growing. At the time of Julius Caesar it was a bare 300. Domesday Book gives it 347 and it is now close on 390.'[17] 'My village'—on the basis of a few months' residence!

James Guthrie, printer and craftsman, looked back at his early years recalling his determination to be an artist rather than something in the City as his family wished. He had another ambition, too: 'It sounds ridiculous now, but to live in the country all the year round was an idea which attracted me enormously. It was equivalent to being in Heaven.'[18] The hero of Virginia Woolf's first novel, *Night and Day* (1911), shared a similar dream: 'The idea of a cottage where one grew one's own vegetables and lived on fifteen shillings a week filled Ralph with an extraordinary sense of rest and satisfaction.'[19]

Lascelles Abercrombie, one of the new generation of Georgian poets,

recalled in later years how he had 'escaped' from Merseyside to the depths
of Gloucestershire. 'What great things I meant to do', he reminisced,
'now that I was my own man and living at last in the country!'[20] Harold
Monro, owner of the Poetry Bookshop and editor of the Georgian
magazine *Poetry and Drama*, was remembered by his assistant as having
frequently spoken 'of the necessity, if one would save one's soul, to leave
the city and revert to the simple life in the country.' He had more extensive
aims as well—a Morris-like 'self-supporting colony of writers and craftsmen living in common and devoting part of each day to manual labour.'[21]

These writers and artists were Edward Thomas's contemporaries and
often his friends as well, and in their work as well as their lives one can see
expressed their deep and abiding love of nature and the countryside. The
whole of Georgian poetry, which flourished between 1910 and 1930, is
informed by such feeling. It may be argued, of course, that love of nature
is an enduring English characteristic, illustrated in poetry from the earliest
times up to the present. But in the years around the turn of the century it
was something more than that. It was, for one thing, virtually a religion-
substitute. Darwinism and the advance of science had destroyed the belief
in a personal deity, but did not satisfy the need for worship, for belief in
something larger and more lasting than mankind.

Richard Jefferies claimed to have found this through communion with
nature. In *The Story of My Heart* he wrote:

From earth and sea and sun, from night, the stars, the trees, the hills,
from my own soul—from these I think. I stand this moment at the
mouth of the ancient cave, face to face with nature, face to face with the
supernatural, with myself. My naked mind confronts the unknown. I
see as clearly as the noonday that this is not all; see other and higher
conditions of existence; I see not only the existence of the soul, immortality, but, in addition, I realise a soul-life illimitable; I realise the
existence of a cosmos of thought; I realise the existence of an inexpressible entity infinitely higher than deity . . . Prone in heart today I pray,
Give me the deepest soul-life.[22]

Edward Thomas, though himself an agnostic, lamented the loss of
religious feeling. 'Myths have been destroyed', he wrote, 'which helped
us to maintain a true and vivid acknowledgement of the mystery of the
past. Apollo, Woden, Jehovah have been put away for the sake of an
unsectarian education. No wonder we are languid, fretful, aimless.' The
country yet remained a source of serenity and reverence: 'There is nothing
left for us to rest on, nothing great, venerable or mysterious, which can
take us out of ourselves and give us that more than human tranquillity now
to be seen only in a few old faces of a disappearing generation . . .'[23]

Not everyone was converted to the new creed. There were those who looked on the enthusiasm for all things rustic and old with some scepticism, wondering when the fashion for sandals, or gardening, or no corsets, or vegetarianism, or walking sticks, or open windows, or ancient music, or camping out, or hand-weaving, or natural fertilisation of the soil, or any one of the myriad elements that went with the Return to Nature or the Escape from Industrialism would work itself out and the world would return to normality. In fact it must be said that despite its popularity, the desire for the Simple Life remained at all times a minority interest. Upper class society in the late Victorian and Edwardian periods was marked by extravagant expenditure and conspicuous consumption on a large scale while at the other end of the ladder working people endured poor housing, ill-health, hard work and a constant struggle against poverty and the workhouse.

The middle class sceptics included Leslie Stephen, who remarked sardonically in an essay:

a love of the country is taken, I know not why, to indicate the presence of all the cardinal virtues. It is one of those outlying qualities which are not exactly meritorious but which, for that very reason, are the more provocative of a pleasing self-complacency. People pride themselves upon it as upon early rising, or upon answering letters by return of post ... I too love the country—if such a statement can be received after such an exordium; but I confess—to be duly modest—that I love it best in books. In real life I have remarked that it is frequently damp and rheumatic and most hated by those who know it best.[24]

Thomas Hardy, who knew the material condition of rural England in the years of the depression better than most of the suburban country-lovers, pointed out the contradictions involved. The attractions of the country were in direct relation to the poverty and backwardness of its inhabitants: 'That seclusion and immutability, which was so bad for their pockets, was an unrivalled fosterer of their personal charm in the eyes of those whose experiences had been less limited.'[25]

It is undeniably true that many of those who turned so wholeheartedly towards the country were often blind to the poverty and narrowness of village life; they reacted against the horrors of the city slums but failed to perceive the equal squalor and misery that existed in the country. Coming from the more egalitarian America, Robert Frost was shocked by the condition of English farm-workers, whom he called 'the genuinely submerged classes', in particular by the virtually feudal subservience demanded of them. He was shocked, too, by the way his English friends—poets and country-lovers—accepted this situation without protest or indignation.[26]

Most country-lovers, however, were not concerned with such political and economic matters, and to condemn them for their blindness is to mistake the sources of their feeling for the country. It was, essentially, founded on nostalgia and personal or general regret for a lost world of contentment and simplicity. It is easy enough to prove that the Golden Age, whenever it is supposed to have existed, was not as it is claimed to be, and that every age tends to look back with longing towards better days remembered or imagined in the past. But nostalgia, and particularly the pastoral nostalgia which yearns for the peace and security of country life, appears to be a perennial impulse, stretching from the distant past to the present. The popularity of *Akenfield*, Ronald Blythe's book about a Suffolk community published in 1970, may show us that it is not dead yet.

It is arguable that the pastoral impulse, which is not infrequently compounded with personal regret for the lost world of childhood, is at its strongest in periods of rapid social and technological change which bring with material benefits a sense of insecurity and maladjustment, and that it may be an inevitable response to such change, on both an individual and communal level. Certainly it does not represent an engagement with the problems of the present. Thus, while the countryside is frequently the focus for such feelings, it is not often the country as it is which inspires the emotion but rather a remembered or wishful vision of it—an escape from reality. As the editors of the *Penguin Book of English Pastoral Verse* (1974) point out, the pastoral mode has always been 'a way of *not* looking at the country at least as much as a way of looking at it.'[27]

To the displaced, dispossessed and disbelieving middle class intelligentsia of the late nineteenth century, the revival of the pastoral mode offered an escape from the political, economic and personal problems of the contemporary world, which they could neither ignore nor solve. The country was another place, another world. Perhaps, unconsciously, they were fleeing from the tensions inherent in their class position, turning their backs on the drawing rooms whose comforts were sustained by toil and poverty in mine and mill.

Edward Thomas was initially drawn to the country by some such impulse, as we shall see in the next chapter; in this he was more clearly a product of his age than has generally been recognised. He himself was aware of the escapist elements in the movement to the country, when he wrote:

> we go to it as would-be poets, or as solitaries, vagabonds, lovers, to escape foul air, noise, hard hats, black uniforms, multitudes, confusion, incompleteness, elaborate means without clear ends—to escape ourselves . . . and thus we may truly find ourselves.[28]

His years of living in the country taught him to distinguish the reality from the dream and that what he sought was not to be found in nature but in himself. Yet although his relationship with it was to change, the country remained the central passion of his life, as his poetry testifies, and though the idealistic vision of youth gave way to the realism of maturity, Thomas never regretted or rescinded his decision to live in the country.

4

A Country Writer

Then the hills of the horizon—
That is how I should make hills had I to show
One who would never see them what hills were like.
'Wind and Mist'

In moving to the country, Edward Thomas had fulfilled the first of his ambitions. His second was to write about it. 'Even as a young child', Helen Thomas wrote later,

> he found his way out of the streets which were his playground to the lanes and fields ... There, in the country, hunting for birds' nests, fishing in the Wandle, noting the ways of wild creatures, his spirit found satisfaction and pleasure. This was, as he grew older, further heightened by writing of what he had seen and heard ... As time went on, the two experiences—that of observing and enjoying all the country had to offer him and of transmuting it into words—became the consummation of the day's spiritual pleasure.[1]

The inspiration was nature and the countryside, the chosen form the essay. But it was not easy to make a living from essays alone, and so Thomas was grateful for the book reviewing which, after a slowish start, became a major source of income and one which was never entirely relinquished. But he often referred to it disparagingly, as a lower form of writing. This contempt may have been partly affectation, for Thomas did not entirely despise his reviews, always remembering to read them in print, to cut them out and paste them into a scrapbook, and to correct any deletions or emendations made by his editors—a habit which suggests a very deliberate pride in his own work. There were six scrapbooks in all, showing that in thirteen years Thomas completed some twelve hundred reviews.[2]

Thomas's essays met with a reasonable degree of success, for there was a market for such pieces. In 1902, as we have seen, he published *Horae Solitariae* with Duckworth, and in 1904 a further collection was published with Brown Langham, *Rose Acre Papers*. Essays of the kind contained in these two slim volumes are seldom encountered today, but in the early 1900s it was a fashionable literary form, and essayists such as 'Alpha of the Plough' and Robert Lynd were widely read and admired. The standard for the genre was set by Hazlitt, and aspiring young writers sought to model themselves on the master. In his autobiography, Arthur Ransome described how he came to London with Hazlitt's *Table Talk* in his pocket, composing his own essays at night while working as an office boy by day.[3]

Ransome's position and hopes were in fact very similar to Thomas's own and it was not long before the two met, in the St George's coffee house in St Martin's Lane, where on the third floor there were cheap coffee and chess boards. Here, Ransome recalled,

> One day, while we were playing chess, a man with a fine-cut, sad face, looking very unlike a townsman, stopped beside our table. This was Edward Thomas, come up from Kent with a bag full of books he had reviewed. I went with him to Thorp's across the way, where he emptied his bag and sold the books, and then walked along the Strand to Fleet Street and so to the office of the *Daily Chronicle* where he refilled his bag with new books to take home with him and review in the country.[4]

Thomas was five years older than Ransome, but they became immediate friends and, after a fashion, also competitors, although the rivalry was always friendly.

As an essayist, Thomas aimed to encompass both Hazlitt and Pater in his reflective, ironic and limpid style. First encouraged by Ashcroft Noble, he had acquired more of the Paterian manner while at Oxford, for at this period the author of *The Renaissance* and *Appreciations* was the dominant influence on prose writing. Pater's early essays had inspired and fuelled the Aesthetic Movement, with its idea of art for art's sake and its vision of the artist as a figure of exquisite sensibility. Good prose, according to Pater's essay 'On Style' which was both precept and example,

> should be an instrument of many stops, meditative, observant, eloquent, analytic, plaintive, fervid . . . It will exert in due measure all the varied charms of poetry down to the rhythm which . . . gives its musical value to every syllable.[5]

It should also be correct and well-mannered, full of propriety and a 'general air of sensibility':

> The literary artist, I suppose, goes on considerately, setting joint to joint, sustained but yet restraining the productive ardour, retracing the negligences of his first sketch, repeating his steps only that he may give the reader a sense of secure and restful progress, readjusting mere

assonances even that they may soothe the reader, or at least not interrupt him on his way; and then somewhere before the end comes is burdened, inspired with his conclusion and betimes delivered of it, leaving off not in weariness and because he finds himself at an end, but in all the freshness of volition.[6]

Under this instruction, prose became an art as consciously and carefully wrought as that of poetry (if indeed not more so, given the late-Victorian tendency to looseness in verse) and was treated as a form of fine art made not for use but for aesthetic pleasure. Young men who in another age would have turned naturally to poetry to express their emergent feelings took to prose in the Paterian manner instead.

As far as content was concerned, Pater felt art had little to do with actuality. The artist was enjoined to be faithful to the 'vision within' rather than the facts without, for this was 'preferable, pleasanter, more beautiful'.[7] The unpleasant and the ugly, if they entered into art at all, were distanced and softened into types and images until they lacked all power to disturb.

A strong strand of escapism, akin to that expressed in some versions of Back-to-the-Landism, is evident in the Aesthetic Movement but the immediate source of Pater's ideas was of course Platonism. Like so many classically-educated Englishmen of his day he was heavily influenced by Greek civilisation and only less slightly so by the Italian Renaissance. Idealism offered an alternative to the squalor and cynicism of modern civilisation, and also a substitute for religion. In this scheme Art, in Pater's famous words, became 'a refuge, a sort of cloistered refuge from a certain vulgarity in the actual world', and a perfect poem, in his view, had something of the uses of a religious retreat.[8]

Pater's influence on writing in the 1890s was enormous. Prose began to aim for the condition of lyric—musical, timeless, full of imagery. The term 'prose-poem' came into use from the French, describing the result, a kind of poetry without metre, rhyme or line. And one of those to adopt it most enthusiastically was Edward Thomas:

> . . . so grand the silence, the nightingale dares not sing; only now and then its voice leaps forth—like a sigh from the breast of silence; the vasty night heaves through and through; the birch sprays rise and fall once, and are still.

and

> . . . a dead, bleak day in February, when the trees moan as if they covered a tomb—and they do cover a tomb, the tomb of the voices, the 'thrones and dominations' of summer past. The rabbits are housed. Dead as soon as born, the first lesser celandine puts forth one flower.

he wrote in *Rose Acre Papers*. The words have come to dominate and obscure the things described; the writer appears more interested in what he is saying than what he is seeing. As the reviews remarked, these are 'essays like embroidered altarcloths,' delicately penned 'surely with a gold nib upon vellum, in condescending recognition of nature's beauty'.[9] Fortunately the influence of Pater did not entirely eclipse the earlier influence of Jefferies, with its solid detail and direct address, but the elevated manner soon came to predominate. Thus a lament for the destruction of open countryside, such as Thomas himself knew in south London as he grew up, begins in fact but soon moves into fancy and rhetoric:

> A railway bisects the common we cross. Everything is haggard and stale; the horizon is gone; and the spirit chafes and suffocates for lack of it (but the gorse is in flower still). Then the feet weary on gravel paths downhill. On either side are fields, edged by flaccid suburban grass, with an odour as of tombs—as though nothing fair could blossom in a soil that must be the sepulchre of many divinities. ... Who shall measure the sorrow of him that hath set his heart upon that which the world hath power to destroy, and hath destroyed? Even today the circuit of a cemetery is cutting into the field where we gathered buttercups.

It was with pieces of this kind that Thomas hoped to make a name for himself. At the same time, he had to make a living by other, lesser forms of literature. Not long after moving to Kent, he was offered his first commission, an introduction to the poems of John Dyer. A full-length book on Oxford was to follow. In the next thirteen years Thomas undertook thirty-eight such tasks. He edited Dyer, Herbert, Marlowe, Jefferies, Cobbett and Borrow; he wrote critical and biographical studies of Jefferies, Maeterlinck, Swinburne, Borrow, Lafcadio Hearn, Pater, Keats and the Duke of Marlborough; he prepared collections of Celtic tales, Norse tales, popular natural history on birds, butterflies and flowers, and anthologies of folk songs and English verse.

In addition he wrote a number of works which he described as 'colour books' as they consisted of description and illustration. There were nine such books, including ones on Windsor Castle and the Isle of Wight produced for tourists and visitors, but more significantly, several simply describing the countryside, aimed at the growing reading public with 'Back to Nature' ideas. We shall look more closely at these books shortly.

On the strength of the £100 promised by Black for *Oxford* in 1903 the Thomases moved from the disappointing Rose Acre to Ivy Cottage, not far away on Bearstead Green. The children were now aged three years and five months respectively. This was the first of several family moves

and with each, Helen recorded, she 'had the feeling that [Edward] would
be the better for the change.'[10] Thomas too felt strongly that a new house
meant a new beginning.

Ivy Cottage was ivy-covered, and half-timbered, and had a picturesque
attic room where Thomas arranged his books and sat down to pursue his
calling as a writer. Thirteen years later he was to remember this attic in
his poem 'The Long Small Room', with its oblique comment on his
youthful aspirations and the long years of writing which followed:

> The long small room that showed willows in the west
> Narrowed up to the end the fireplace filled,
> Although not wide. I liked it. No one guessed
> What need or accident made them so build.
>
> Only the moon, the mouse and the sparrow peeped
> In from the ivy round the casement thick.
> Of all they saw and heard there they shall keep
> The tale for the old ivy and older brick.
>
> When I look back I am like moon, sparrow, and mouse
> That witnessed what they could never understand
> Or alter or prevent in the dark house.
> One thing remains the same—this my right hand
>
> Crawling crab-like over the clean white page,
> Resting awhile each morning on the pillow,
> Then once more starting to crawl on towards age.
> The hundred last leaves stream upon the willow.

At Ivy Cottage Thomas finished *Oxford*, but he had to write sixty
thousand words in a little more than four months, and for one whose talent
lay in essays, the effort to sustain interest was a tough one and he felt
exhausted. There was a conflict too between his desire to write a master-
piece and his publisher's desire for a superior guidebook. Moreover,
although picturesque, Ivy Cottage was old and insanitary, and was
therefore held responsible when first Bronwen and then Helen fell seriously
ill. This was doubly worrying, for as well as the very real possibility of
Bronwen dying (in an age when child mortality was common) there was
no money with which to pay doctors' fees or domestic help. To escape
from such troubles, the family moved again, in May 1904, to a charming
old farmhouse at Weald near Sevenoaks. Here at last was a near-perfect
country home.

Elses Farm stood in the midst of a group of Kentish farm buildings—
oast houses, cowsheds, stables, hayricks and a huge barn. The farmer who

worked the land lived nearby and the Thomases, as well as being encircled by agricultural activities, had the run of a large garden and orchard. They were delighted with their proximity to the daily business of farming, and from this date the human and agricultural features of rural life became as important and integral to Thomas's view of the country as any aspect of nature. Here he was able to observe and share the processes of farming in a way that was to give his writing an increasingly solid basis. Helen wrote:

The bush harrow, plough, sickle and the team of horses became familiar objects to us all and we saw and took part in many of the operations of the farm. We came to know the whole process of the cultivation of hops from the ploughing between the 'hills' and the stringing and 'twiddling' to the picking and the drying and the feasting on pay day.[11]

It was at Elses Farm that Thomas had the first of his study cottages, where he went to work daily, like Edward Carpenter at Millthorpe, amidst the beauty and quiet of nature. The study was a tiny cottage, built for a farm labourer, about a mile from the farm, rented at half a crown a week. 'We wore a footpath to this cottage', Helen recalled, 'first through a copse, then past a pond and then over a fence into a rough meadow. It has now been obliterated and no-one would know that the cottage and the big farm house had ever had any connection with each other.'[12]

In this study cottage Thomas wrote the second of his commissions, *Beautiful Wales*. The subject was very congenial, a welcome opportunity to express his feeling for the land (which he had visited in childhood) and its literature (which he had read in translation). To gather material he and Helen went on a short visit to Ammanford and then Thomas set out alone on a long solitary tramp across mid-Wales during October 1904. He took a notebook with him, as he had on his first long walk from London to Wiltshire and when he returned home he began to turn his notes into a book.

Beautiful Wales was the first of Thomas's country books, as his 'colour books' are more properly described. He was conscious of his publishers' guidebook expectations, and began with overtly topographical material, almost in the manner of Baedeker, with plenty of place names. However, he did not intend to write a guidebook, although he described his itinerary in detail:

The night had almost come, and the rain had not ceased, among the hills of an unknown country. Behind me, twelve desolate miles of hill and sky away, was a village; and on the way to it, half-a-dozen farms; and before me were three or four houses scattered over two or three miles of winding lanes, with an inn and a church. The parson had just come away from his poultry, and as his wife crossed the road with her apron over her head, I asked where the inn was, and whether it had a room ready in the winter. Two minutes after she had seen me—if she could see me in the dark lane—she told me that if the inn had no room I was not to go further, but to stay at the vicarage. But the inn had a bed to spare, and there was good beer to be had by a great fire in a room shining with brass and pewter, and overhead guns and hams and hanks of wool . . .

He was, however, more concerned to express his feeling for the landscape, and the sense of holiness he received from it:

more than once, as I was pausing to count the first white clusters of nuts or to remind myself that here was the first pale-blue flower of succory, I knew that I took up eternity with both hands, and though I laid it down again, the lane was a most potent, magic thing, when I could thus make time as nothing, while I meandered over many centuries, consulting many memories that are as amulets.

The landscape had not only power to 'make time as nothing'; it could almost undo the modern world:

This mountain and this sky, for that first hour, shut out, and not only shut out but destroyed, and not only destroyed but made as if it had never been, the world of the old woman, the coal-pits, the schools and the grown-up persons . . .

We can see here the influence both of Back to the Land ideas and of Paterian thought and style.

Perhaps it was partly the strength of Thomas's feeling for Wales that led him into his friendship with the Welsh-born poet W. H. Davies. Davies had been brought up by grandparents in Newport, Monmouthshire, and apprenticed to a picture-framer, a trade he disliked. When his grandmother died leaving him a small legacy of ten shillings a week, Davies crossed the Atlantic to try his luck in the United States. He intended to work but found it possible to survive by begging, 'beating' his way on freight trains and alternating casual jobs with short jail sentences in small towns. He travelled in this fashion for six years, enjoying the freedom and adventure, as he was later to chronicle in his *Autobiography of a Super-Tramp*, until he fell jumping a train at Renfew, Canada, and as a result had his leg amputated below the knee. This effectively brought his days as a hobo to an end, and he returned to Britain, bought an artificial leg costing £12.10s, and calculated how he was to live.

As a boy he had liked reading and a newspaper article on Robert Burns reawakened his interest in poetry, making him feel that he might make his name through literary composition. With a tiny income, he moved to a succession of cheap lodging houses in London where he pursued this ambition with naïve determination. He wrote a blank verse tragedy, a long poem-fable, a string of a hundred sonnets, a neo-Elizabethan drama, a comedy, even a series of humorous essays. None was accepted for publication. Doing without food, he spent thirty-five shillings on having a selection of his best poems printed in broadsheet form, which he then tried to sell as a hawker from door to door. He sold none and burnt his two thousand sheets 'with the fury of a madman . . . taking care not to save one copy that would at any time in the future remind me of my folly.'[13] But he continued to write, choosing now short lyrics, which were perhaps the only form lending themselves to composition under the conditions in which Davies was living, in a crowded lodging house kitchen, with men quarrelling over their cooking or washing, often drunk and often fighting. 'To protect myself against some of these little inconveniences', Davies later wrote, 'I used to sit quietly in a corner of the kitchen, fold my arms, bow my head and pretend to be asleep. By these means I often managed to compose a poem, which I would commit to paper before I went to bed.'[14]

Davies persisted. By early 1904 he had found a publisher willing to bring out a modest selection of his verses at the author's expense and by the following year he had amassed sufficient cash to do this. Two hundred and fifty copies of *The Soul's Destroyer and Other Poems* were duly printed and review copies sent to all the papers. Apart from two provincial notices, not one mentioned the book, and there were no orders. In desperation Davies drew up a list of prominent people and sent them each a copy, asking them to buy it 'as I am at present without means of support.'[15]

Thanks to the recipients' kindness or curiosity, the strategy eventually succeeded in attracting some attention. An article appeared in the *Daily Mail*, and visitors began to arrive at Davies's lodging house in Southwark. His story was undoubtedly romantic—a tramp, even a sturdy beggar, who was also a poet. Here was living proof that it was good to live simply and out of doors, and that out of simplicity and poverty came forth finer art than all the elaborate products of high culture.

Bernard Shaw was one of the first to respond favourably to Davies's begging letters, and it was through him that copies were sent out to a number of critics and literary men, including Edward Garnett and Edward Thomas. On 12 October 1904 Thomas called at the lodging house to meet Davies, and his review of *The Soul's Destroyer* appeared in the *Daily Chronicle* of 21 October, in which an account of Davies's life is mixed with praise of his verses:

He has travelled: he knows Wales, London, America and Hell. These things and many more his poems tell us; and to see him is to see a man from whom unskilled labour in America, work in Atlantic cattle boats, and a dire London life, have not taken away the earnestness, the tenderness, or the accent of a typical Monmouthshire man. . . . He can write commonplace and inaccurate English; but it is also natural for him to write, much as Wordsworth wrote, with the clearness, compactness and felicity which makes a man think with shame how unworthily, through natural stupidity or uncertainty, he manages his native tongue . . .[16]

Unlike many of Davies's other admirers, Thomas set out to render him practical help as well as praise. The Welshman's financial position was poor and as he was anxious to bring out a second volume and also to begin work on a prose book he was looking for a cheap home. Thomas invited him to live in the study cottage. This plan was delayed by Thomas being given notice to quit his study, but within a few weeks he had found another to rent, in Egg Pie Lane nearby, and Davies was soon installed. He was allocated the main room downstairs and the bedroom, while Thomas came to work every day in the other downstairs room. Davies set to work revising his autobiography, looking, Thomas told Bottomley in a letter, 'most solemnly happy whenever I pass through his room to mine & he says he is happy. But I leave him mostly to himself; we are not born for one another.'[17] As an honorary member of the Thomas family, however, Davies was always welcome at Elses Farm, where he felt at ease with Helen and the children. It proved an anxious time financially for Thomas, for he was at this period only earning about £5 a week, by dint of multiple reviewing and some editing, and he could barely afford extra expenses. In July 1905 a financial crisis occurred, when Davies's artificial leg collapsed beyond repair. Thomas wrote round to friends collecting funds for a new one and in the meantime asked the local wheelwright to fashion a substitute peg-leg to enable Davies to walk. To spare Davies's feelings, as he was sensitive about his disability, the wheelwright was given the specifications only. Back came the leg, with the bill made out 'Item: one Curiosity Cricket Bat'.[18]

While thus engaged in helping Davies, Thomas was also undertaking his most important commission to date, and one upon which he pinned great hopes. His own reputation had grown sufficiently for the publisher J. M. Dent to approach him with the idea that he write a book about the country. This, even more than Oxford or Wales, he felt to be his own subject. The contract for sixty thousand words under the title *The Heart of England* was signed in February 1906.

This was Thomas's first opportunity to express at full length all his thoughts and feelings for the countryside—feelings which, in the absence of other convictions, had become the deepest emotions he knew, and ones he believed he could communicate to others. In the course of the book he was able to draw on his past four years' experience of Kentish farming country, and there are many descriptions of rural life, which are often imbued with a pastoral nostalgia for a vanishing way of life, as in this account of a retired farmer:

The old man's tools in the kitchen are noble—the heavy wrought-iron, two-toothed hoe, that falls pleasantly upon the hard clay and splits it without effort and without jarring the hand, its ash handle worn thin where his hand has glided at work, a hand that nothing will wear smooth; the glittering yellow-handled spades and forks; the disused shovel with which he boasts regretfully that he could dig his garden when he lived on deep loam in a richer county than this; and still the useless 'hop-idgit' of six tynes—the Sussex 'shim'—which he retains to remind others, and perhaps himself, that he was a farmer once.

More frequently, however, such figures provoke a pastoral effusion. Here a farmer's daughter walking in the fields is transformed into a classical nymph living not in Kent or Surrey but in an untarnished Arcadia:

To look at her is to take deep breaths of the savour of warm bread, of honeysuckle, of cows when they come from the meadows into a dusty road. A speech that should be all sapphires and pearls would not be worthy of her—today. She is at the altar of Aphrodite 'full of pity'— today. She has been carried far in the goddess' dove-drawn chariot over mountains and seas, and has bathed in the same fountain as Aphrodite, nor yet been seen of men—today. Delay, sun, above the sea; wait, moon, below the hills; sing, birds; rustle, new-leaved beeches; for tomorrow and the day after and for ever until the end this will be but a memory and may be all she has. She walks hardly faster than the shadows over the fair grass; and you, Time, O Woodman! set not your axe at the foot of this tree, lean not upon it with your strong hands. See! the crest nods and the air trembles; let it not fall today.

Although it is possible to guess at what Thomas is trying to express here, his language and style are hardly appropriate and the final effect is pretentious and rather silly. Elsewhere, however, he was able to convey his feeling for the countryside in a less extravagant manner, as here:

The hills rejoice with long shadows and yellow light; the tall hares stretch themselves and gallop. The little pools hum pleasantly as the rain drips from their overhanging brier and bramble into the leaden water with bright splash. And in our own muscles and heart the evening strives to form an aspiration that shall suit the joy of the hills, the meadows, the copses, and their people. We will go on, they say; we will go on and on, through the beeches on the hill and up over the ridge and down again through the grey wet meadows and to the old road between hawthorn and guelder rose at the foot of the downs; and still on, not as before, but out of time and space until we come—home—to some refuge of beauty and serenity in the heart of the immense evening.

Although the thought here is somewhat strained and the manner over-rhetorical, we can recognise a central aspect of Thomas's love for the country. To him, the country was not just pleasant and pretty; it was a source of ultimate tranquillity, a 'refuge out of time and space'. The interjection of the word 'home' is not accidental—all his life Thomas was searching for a place, or a state of mind, where he felt at home, where he belonged, where he was not anxious and unsatisfied. Later this theme was to play a dominant role in his verse.

Thomas wanted *The Heart of England* to be good. He wanted to be recognised as a writer with original things to say about the country and an elegant style. He had much material, notebooks full of detailed observation, half-finished essays and ideas for prose-poems. If only he could weld them into a full and complete statement about the countryside! But the actual writing of the book was painful; perhaps because it was so important to him, he felt its inadequacies keenly. To Bottomley he wrote:

I work continuously at the cottage from 9.30 to 4.30 every day & squeeze from 1,000 to 1,500 words out of myself, & the result is to be my worst book. There are plenty of landscapes & 'spurred lyric'—in fact ¾ of the book will be of this kind and far inferior to *Wales* because I have less impulse and less material. The rest is pseudo-genial, or purely rustic—Borrow and Jefferies sans testicles and guts—except one short love story told just before a fox hunt which I think pretty good . . .[19]

By dint of scraping together all his topics, from a page of old country customs to lavish quotations from newly-discovered folk songs, and avoiding well-worn 'country' themes, he arrived at half the length required and declared:

Even now I would give up if I dared and lose the £100 cheerfully. Henceforth I cease to write 'about the country' & become a reviewer with a wife & family tout court and no deception.[20]

Of course, he did not, and continued to the end, hoping that it would turn out all right.

Unfortunately, the result was indeed 'a string of subjects', as he had perceived, without overall shape or structure. Multiple pictorial images move in and out of each other, like film dissolving from scene to scene. Landscapes are separated by small character studies, short stories, bursts of pastoral philosophy. The defects arise clearly from the attempt to marry the short essay style to the full-length book, creating only a series of essays and articles strung together along a theme. There is no disputing that *The Heart of England* is a tedious work to read, although it has many fine passages.

It was these that Thomas was most anxious about. On publication in 1906 he wrote to Bottomley: 'Oh, will some really good man praise my "Ship, Chariot and Plough", my "Earth Children", "Metamorphosis" etc? I feel perhaps they are really good & I am almost sure they are new. But who knows?'[21] These three passages are given the full essay treatment. 'Earth Children' is a romanticised account of Dad and Granny Uzell in Wiltshire, while 'Ship, Chariot and Plough' is a paean to enduring values:

The ship, the chariot and the plough, these three are, I suppose, the most sovereign beautiful things which man has made in his time, and such that were his race to pass away from the earth, would bring him most worship among his successors.

All are without parallel in nature, wrought out of his own brain by unaided man; and yet, during their life, worthy by their beauty, their purpose, and their motion to challenge anything made by the gods on the earth or in the sea; and after their life is done, sublime and full of awe, so that when we come upon them neglected and see their fair heroic curves, the dirge at their downfall passes inevitably into a paean to their majesty. And they are very old. Probably the beasts and birds, the winds and waves and hills know us as the creatures who make the ship, chariot and plough. These things, as they go about their work, must have become universal symbols, so that when a man comes in sight, the other inhabitants of the earth say: Here is he who sails in ships and drives the chariot and guides the plough. And the greatest of all is the plough. It is without pride and also without vanity. The ship and the chariot have sometimes tried to conceal their ancient simplicity, though they have never done without it. But the plough is the sema— in shape like a running hound, with tail uplifted and muzzle bowed to the scent.

It is not just that this is over-effusive and out of place in a nature book, with such grandiose assertions and rhetorical poses. It is surely remarkable that such a passage could be seriously meant at all in the age of steamships, omnibuses, even aeroplanes. But of course its purpose is to deny the significance of modern inventions and assert instead that the ancient simplicity and security are not lost—at least not as long as the plough remained, as it still did in Thomas's day, a single share drawn by a team of horses. Of such was pastoral nostalgia made.

On publication, Thomas's fears were realised; *The Heart of England* was received without enthusiasm. He reported to Bottomley, 'So far my only intelligent review is from the *Athenaeum* and that is not favourable. . . . So far no-one has discovered "The Ship, the chariot and the plough". . . .'[22] Arthur Ransome, who also supplemented his writing with reviewing, was covering the book for the *Bookman*—but Thomas had to draw his attention to the ship, chariot and plough section before he would quote it.[23] Perhaps it was neither good nor new. And if friends failed to appreciate what he was trying to say, the general public would hardly be more receptive.

Thomas's disappointment was not outweighed by the praise of certain friends, chief among them Edward Garnett, who had become an important literary friend and adviser. Garnett lived at Limpsfield, about twenty miles from Sevenoaks on the edge of Surrey, and worked as publisher's reader for Duckworth's, spending part of the week in London. He was a kindly, unaffected and generous man, with a genius for encouraging writers—Joseph Conrad is perhaps the most famous of those he aided— and every Tuesday he presided over a literary lunch at the Mont Blanc restaurant in Soho, to cultivate his friendships with a wide variety of writers. All Garnett's own attempts at composition ended in failure: in his youth he wrote two novels and some prose-poems in fin-de-siècle style, and he afterwards took to writing for the stage, with no greater success. He was ten years older than Edward Thomas.

'Thomas was brought to our Surrey cottage by a mutual friend, I think, at the close of 1905', Garnett wrote later, and the visit was shortly returned when Garnett met the Thomases fresh from an expedition in the fields. 'That scene lingers in my memory as an idyll of gracious youth', he recalled. 'The charm of Thomas in the freshness of his strength, of his beautiful eyes and hair which shone in the sunlight, brown bleached to fair gold, appeared at its best in the open air.'[24] Garnett was introduced to Davies in the study cottage, and later, when both Thomas and Garnett were supervising the Supertramp's autobiography, Garnett's son David, then aged about fourteen, came to stay with the Thomases. He and his host shared a passion for fishing.

It was not long before Thomas came to regard Garnett with something of the same admiration he had once felt for James Noble and to value his opinion highly. Garnett liked and encouraged the younger man's work, and a friendship of mutual trust, criticism and praise was quickly established. Thomas privately compared himself with Garnett, telling Bottomley that he was pleased to find that Garnett's prose-poems were not much better than his own, and for several years he aimed, in his essays and country books, to write something that would please Garnett. Garnett made detailed comments on all the work Thomas sent him, and his suggestions were generally adopted. In general their opinions coincided to a remarkable degree, leading Thomas to say of his book on Richard Jefferies that 'very little but the expression is mine ... they are your [Garnett's] ideas, or the ramifications of them.'[25]

Above all Garnett liked the essays Thomas was writing, which were later to be collected and published by Duckworth, presumably on Garnett's recommendation, as *Rest and Unrest* (1910) and *Light and Twilight* (1911). Writing Thomas's entry for the Dictionary of National Biography (1912–21) Garnett mentioned several of these essays by name, saying 'they excel by their clear beauty of imagery, grace of contour and delicate limpid English.' Elsewhere, he repeated this praise, stating that 'for me, the strength of Thomas's genius, its essence, lies in his imaginative pieces', and leaving the clear implication that he thought the prose reveries better than the poems.[26] Indeed, Garnett's admiration was such that he complained that, despite 'a long enthusiastic review in the Times Literary Supplement' (presumably by himself), Thomas's essays had not sold more than a hundred copies, and that 'the pathos of Thomas's lack of success lay in the almost total lack of response on the part of the public and the editors to such imaginative masterpieces.'[27] Garnett deserves praise for the constancy of his critical judgement and the moral support he gave Thomas, but at the same time one wonders if on the whole his encouragement did Thomas more harm than good. Later Thomas came to perceive the deficiencies of his essay writing, and to move towards other modes, a shift that might have happened earlier if Garnett has not liked the essays so much. But it is also true that Garnett's praise did not entirely compensate for others' silence, nor help pay the rent.

Partly to mask his disappointment over the reception of *The Heart of England*, Thomas agreed to a heap of other commissions which left him little time for anything else—except, as always, long rambling walks in the surrounding countryside, long circular walks which brought him home in the end. Home was now in Hampshire. The Thomases had been given notice to quit Elses Farm and for several months they searched for an alternative. They had in any case been considering a move, for Mervyn (whose name was now usually spelt in the Welsh way, Merfyn) was over six and in need of schooling.

The decision was left to Helen, who was already interested in the type of education being practised at Bedales. She went to visit, liked what she saw, and set about finding a home near enough to the school at Petersfield, Hampshire, for Mervyn to attend as a day pupil, since they could not afford boarding fees and in any case did not approve of children leaving home at such a young age, usual though it was at the time.

They moved into Berryfield Cottage, Ashford, near Petersfield in Hampshire in November 1906. It was, Edward wrote, 'the most beautiful

place we ever lived in. We are now become people of whom passers-by
stop to think: how fortunate are they within its walls. I know it. I have
thought the same as I came to the house and forgot it was my own.'[28]
Helen described it in more detail:

> The house was originally a small farmhouse. It was about a hundred
> years old and built of the warm grey local stone. It stood on a little rise
> of a winding lane which ran at the foot of the steep sides of a vast raised
> plateau. The irregular sloping edge was in some parts bare like the
> downs; in other parts covered in a thick growth of tree—beech and yew
> for the most part—called hangars ... A large old-fashioned garden
> stretched in front of the house running parallel to the lane—and above
> it, for you entered the garden up half a dozen steps from the lane. . . . On
> the other side of the house the land sloped down to the stream which
> flowed through a wild water meadow full of forget-me-nots, meadow-
> sweet, mares' tails and loosestrife. At night all we could hear was the
> wind in the hangar, the barking of foxes who lived there and the hooting
> of owls. It was a romantic and beautiful spot, and the house belonged
> to it and we loved it from the first.[29]

She liked the school too, for its 'love of the open air, its unscholastic
freedom from discipline, its freedom from moneyed snobbishness and its
social life, simple and free and happy.' The staff were 'kind, serious,
intellectual people believing in co-education, temperance, votes for
women and hygiene and liberalism. I liked them very much.'[30] Helen was
a sociable person who enjoyed the company and the social and cultural
activities which centred on Bedales. Moreover her experience with
children enabled her to take a part-time job in the school kindergarten,
defraying some of the cost of the fees and making her own contribution
to the family finances.

Edward did not like the Bedales staff in general. They were too sensible,
too confident for him. Helen wrote:

> Their houses were in faultless taste outside and in. Their simple oak
> furniture was made by skilful craftsmen and their curtains were hand
> woven. Their meals were lavish and good, inclining to brown bread and
> vegetarianism . . .
> Their politics inclined to socialism and they were on more than usually
> friendly terms with the villagers though owing to their temperance they
> could not hob-nob with them at the inn.[31]

Just the sort of people and ideas (apart from the temperance) to whom
and which one would have expected Thomas to have responded. Yet he

was immediately antipathetic, except towards one or two individuals, and from the beginning left all matters to do with the school to Helen. The dislike was mutual, the Bedales staff regarding Thomas as 'a solitary wandering creature who worked irregularly, who drank and smoked in village inns, who had no political or social theories and who was not impressed by the school or its ideals.'[32] One suspects that something of the awkwardness was financial: though refusing to take a regular job, Thomas never became resigned to poverty, and hated other people to know of it, which was hardly possible in a small community; and perhaps defensively he cut himself off from the school's social life. At the same time, one senses a real conflict between two differing versions of Back to the Land ideas, as interpreted by Thomas and Bedales. The school's was practical and social, expressing itself through co-education and progressive teaching, and tending towards Fabianism and social planning for a responsible future in a garden city utopia. Thomas's was individualistic, idealistic, felt rather than thought, concerned more with personal than social benefit and aiming at freedom, pleasure and a life of rural hedonism, with a touch of mystical elation thrown in.

Despite Thomas's reservations, the family settled near the school and remained there for nearly ten years. The literary career continued. The next commission was a collection of folk songs and country lyrics, with tunes attached, called *Songs for the Open Air*. Thomas liked the idea of doing an anthology: 'at least', he said, 'I should like to possess such a book.'[33] For his own pleasure he had sought out and learnt country songs and some of his best moments were spent with friends who shared this enthusiasm, swapping words and airs. With his children, he often sang old songs when out on a walk or getting ready for bed by the fire, and he determined to make his anthology a very good one. It appeared in July 1907, an eclectic and lively mixture of songs ranging from medieval lyrics and well-known pastoral airs to the English folk verses recently collected by Baring-Gould and Sharp. Thomas's book encompassed these and more, including some previously unpublished sea shanties. The result is a tribute both to his diligence and love, for the book is neither antiquarian nor easily popular, and fully illustrates his pleasure in the sweet and robust songs of old England.

Later, he was to express something of this in two of his own poems, both entitled '*An Old Song*'. The first, consisting of six stanzas, is based on 'The Lincolnshire Poacher', and is indeed a song for the open air. It begins:

I was not apprenticed nor ever dwelt in famous Lincolnshire;
I've served one master ill and well much more than seven year;
And never took up to poaching as you shall quickly find;
But 'tis my delight of a shiny night in the season of the year.

I roamed where nobody had a right but keepers and squires, and there
I sought for nests, wild flowers, oak sticks, and moles, both far and
    near.
And had to run from farmers, and learnt the Lincolnshire song:
    'Oh, 'tis my delight of a shiny night in the season of the year.'

The next commission was a subject very dear to Thomas's heart: a
biography of Richard Jefferies. This would be his most substantial undertaking to date and on any basis. No full biography of Jefferies, who had
died twenty years previously in 1887, had been written, and the publishers,
Hutchinsons, asked for eighty thousand words of life and criticism. The
scale asked for made completeness necessary.

Thomas was well qualified to write on Jefferies, knowing the books
thoroughly and having explored Jefferies' native county Wiltshire for
himself. We have seen how Thomas modelled his earliest writing on that
of Jefferies, whom he read and re-read constantly, and in many respects
his style remained close to that of Jefferies, particularly in his descriptions
of country scenes. Significantly, Jefferies had begun his career as a journ-
alist, and his full-length books exhibit some of the same problems of
shape and movement as are evident in Thomas's country books, suggesting
that both men were more suited to short pieces and essays.

For the biography, Thomas researched Jefferies' background and life as
fully as was possible given the paucity of information. He went to Wiltshire to look for ancestors on gravestones and in parish records, and con-
tacted Jefferies' widow. But there was little to uncover about the life, for
Jefferies had been an invalid for much of his thirty-eight years, and in any
case Thomas preferred to approach his subject through his work. By far
the larger part of the book is devoted to Jefferies' writing.

The result, as Mrs Leavis said in *Scrutiny*,[34] is a model biography which
has not yet been superseded and which exists to present the work as fully
as possible and as far as possible in Jefferies' own words, without overmuch
critical comment. The lengthy quotations enable the reader to check the
critical claims being made, although Thomas himself was not entirely
happy with this approach, realising that so many quotations would end up
like a 'load of good things' in 'an untidy anthology'.[35]

To Thomas, Jefferies' importance and specialness lay in two aspects of
his work. First, his genuine rural background and 'wide knowledge of
labourers, farmers, gamekeepers, poachers, of fields and woods and waters
and the sky above them by day and night; of their inhabitants that run
and fly and creep, that are still and fragrant and many coloured'[36]—in
other words, his authentic country background, not shared by many of
those who professed to love the country. Secondly, Jefferies' passionate
belief in the wholeness and healthiness of life lived freely amidst the
regenerative spiritual power of nature. Jefferies, says Thomas, 'has re-

discovered the sources of joy in nature and foresees that what has fed his lonely ecstasy in the Downs will distribute the same force and balm among the cities of men below.' And he concludes:

He is on the side of health, of beauty, of strength, of truth, of improvement in life to be wrought by increasing honesty, subtlety, tenderness, courage and foresight. His own character and the characters of his men and women fortify us in our intent to live. Nature, as he thought of it and as his books present it, is a great flood of physical and spiritual sanity, 'of pure ablution round Earth's human shores' to which he bids us resort. Turning to England in particular he makes us feel what a heritage are its hills and waters; he even went so far as to hint that some of it should be national. It is he who above all other writers has produced the largest, the most abundant and most truthful pictures of Southern English country both wild and cultivated.[37]

We shall remember this praise of Jefferies' Englishness when we come to look at Thomas's own response to his native land.

Richard Jefferies took a full year to write, and was the occasion of a brief interlude in Thomas's life. To write it, he went to stay at a cottage at Minsmere near Dunwich in Suffolk, close to the sea and in an area of heathland. When he was not writing, he walked along the wintry beach, collecting flotsam and exquisite pebbles—and falling in love with a girl of seventeen. Her name was Hope and she was one of a family for whom Helen had worked many years ago.[38] She had long brown plaits, grey eyes and a timid wildness that greatly attracted Edward. Together they walked on the beach and talked of poetry, saying nothing of their walks to Hope's parents, who would not have approved. She herself had doubts about the correctness of accepting a present (a volume of his own essays) from Thomas, until she was reassured by a letter from Helen. Then she began to write back, expressing to Helen some of what she could not say directly to Edward. At the phrase 'how wonderful it must be to be his wife', Helen realised what was happening and advised Edward not to encourage the affair. Shortly afterwards Hope went away to school, where Thomas wrote to her. Eventually, overburdened with emotions she could not control, Hope confessed to her family and like a naughty boy Thomas was told off by her father and ordered not to write to her again.[39]

He was angry and humiliated, and that was the end of the affair. Thomas was perhaps more smitten than he would admit, except to Bottomley, to whom he had written:

I liked her for her perfect wild youthfulness & remoteness from myself & now I think of her every day in vain acquiescent dissatisfaction & shall

perhaps never see her again & shall be sad to hear she ever likes anyone
else even tho she will never like me.[40]

Bottomley, perhaps perceiving more acutely than Thomas the reason
for this flirtation, suggested that despite the abrupt break, Thomas would
be able to find consolation in an 'unassailable vision' of the girl.[41] Many
such visions are to be found in Thomas's books, essays and poems—
visions of perfection which arise unbidden from the landscape and offer
brief bliss before being lost to sight. They are unreal, imaginary girls, the
sort a man might day-dream of without ever attempting to find in real
life. One such figure is 'Olwen' in the essay of that name:

> The curlew, the hare, the sheep upon the mountain, were not wilder, or
> swifter, or more gentle than she. Her face and stature were those of a
> queen in the old time, whose father was a shepherd on the solitary
> mountains.[42]

In verse, she has no name. The poem 'The Unknown' ends:

> She is not here, but there
> She might have been.
>
> She is to be kissed
> Only perhaps by me;
> She may be seeking
> Me and no other; she
> May not exist.

The girl at Minsmere certainly existed, but perhaps she meant more as a
symbol than as a person.

As soon as *Jefferies* was finished, Thomas plunged into more commitments—a book on Borrow and another on the country. 'Can I do both in
six months', Thomas wrote in mock despair to Bottomley, 'and review
also and take medicine and walk and dig in the garden and abstain from
beating my children?'[43]

Again, he wanted the country book to be good, to establish his reputation
as an original writer on the subject. It was to be called *The South Country*,
and in it he hoped to avoid some of his earlier defects. Yet he confessed to
Bottomley that he still could find no scheme or framework on which to
hang his various landscapes and characters. He was basing the new book,
he said, on his '15 closely written notebooks' into which he dipped 'for
solid details to support my soarings and flutterings about the South
Country!'[44] His publishers appeared to believe that the trouble lay in
Thomas's refusal to identify his country places and scenes; rather sur-

prisingly, he agreed to remedy this and accordingly re-explored Sussex, Kent and Surrey 'collecting place names', and spent five days in Cornwall on a similar errand.[45]

There is little evidence of this activity in the finished book. As if in defiance of his critics, there are long stretches of nature description without a single locating detail, of which this is a typical example:

> Newly dressed in the crystal of the rain the landscape recalls the earlier spring; the flowers of white wood-sorrel, the pink and white anemone and cuckoo flower, the thick-clustered, long-stalked primroses and darker cowslips with their scentless sweetness pure as an infant's breath; the solitary wild cherry trees flowering among still leafless beech; the blackbirds of twilight and the flower-faced owls; the pewits wheeling after dusk; the jonquil and daffodil and arabis and leopard's bane of cottage gardens; the white clouds plunged in blue floating over the brown woods of the hills; the delicate thrushes with speckled breasts paler than their backs, motionless on dewy turf; and all the joys of life that come through the nostrils from the dark, not understood world which is unbolted for us by the delicate and savage fragrances of leaf and flower and grass and clod, of the plumage of birds and fur of animals and breath and hair of women and children.

Though still too full of words, Thomas's writing here is fresh and vivid, at least in small doses. Perhaps the best passages are about people rather than nature. One such 'character sketch' is about a farm labourer:

> He is short and immensely broad, black-haired, with shaved but never clean-shaven face creased by a wide mouth and long narrow black eyes— black with a blackness as of cold, deep water that has never known the sun but only the candle light of discoverers. His once grey corduroys and once white slop are stained and patched to something like the colour of the moist, channelled thatch and crumbling 'clunch' of the stone walls ... He is half cowman, half odd-job man—at eight shillings a week—in his last days, mending hedges, cleaning ditches, and carrying a sack of wheat down the steep hill on a back that cannot be bent any further. Up to his knees in the February ditch, or cutting ash-poles in the copse, he is clearly half-converted into the element to which he must return.

Years of living in the country had shown Thomas something of its reality as experienced by those who work on the land as opposed to merely enjoying its beauty, but even so the picture of the old man is idealised—a man to whom ordinary aches and pains scarcely apply, who is rather a part of the landscape, a part of the land, 'half-converted' into the clay he works. As such he is but the obverse of the nymphs and dryads that rise, like Olwen and 'The Unknown', to personify the beauty and joy of the English countryside. A mixture of idealism and wordiness still obscures the things described.

In *The South Country* Thomas sets out, for the first and only time, a rationale for the Back to the Land impulse, in the following words:

> Literature sends us to Nature principally for joy, joy of the senses, of the whole frame, of the contemplative mind, and of the soul, joy which if it is found complete in these several ways might be called religious. Science sends us to Nature for knowledge. Industrialism and the great towns send us to Nature for health, that we may go on manufacturing efficiently, or, if we think right and have the power, that we may escape from it.

But it is not, he says, such reasons that inform his love of the country; rather a vague nostalgia, with intimations of childhood:

> I recall many scenes: a church and churchyard and black pigs running down from them towards me in a rocky lane—ladslove and tall, crimson, bitter dahlias in a garden—the sweetness of large, moist yellow apples eaten out of doors—children: . . . the moment that I return to them in fancy I am happy.

Such images can still be caught. Country life is full of such scenes—a boy driving cows out to pasture down a lane bordered with wild flowers—which suggest that a 'roving, unhistoric Eden' can still be found.

Beyond nostalgia, there is a further question. What does the countryside mean to us? What is its deeper significance?

> Some of these scenes, whether repeated or not, come to have a rich, symbolical significance; they return persistently and, as it were, ceremoniously—on festal days—but meaning I know not what. For instance, I never see the flowers and scarlet-stained foliage of herb-robert growing out of old stone-heaps by the wayside without a feeling of satisfaction not explained by a long memory of the contrast between the plant and the raw flint; so also with the drenched lilac bloom leaning out over high walls of unknown gardens; and inland cliffs, covered with beech, jutting out westward into a bottomless valley in the midst of winter twilights, in silence and frost . . .
> Something in me belongs to these things, but I hardly think that the mere naming of them will mean anything to other people.

It is clear that Thomas is searching for something more than pleasure, knowledge or health to be had from nature; he is looking for something deeper, though he does not know what it is. The search for the meaning of 'nature's secret', and the quest for 'whatever it is I seek' were to stay with him throughout his life; they were to be major themes in his poetry.

With the completion of *The South Country* in the autumn of 1908, Thomas temporarily stopped writing. He had put a great deal of himself into the book, yet he sensed that it would be no better than its predecessor. And perhaps to forestall the feelings of failure he feared would follow its publication, he moved in an entirely new and unexpected direction, applying for and securing a salaried job in the Civil Service, as assistant secretary to the Royal Commission on Ancient Monuments in Wales and Monmouthshire. It was, in one sense, a victory for his father; in another it was nothing of the kind, for Thomas proved, with five full-length books to his credit, that he could support himself by writing, and anyway the post was not that of an ordinary deskbound civil servant, for it involved historical research, travelling in Wales, visiting castles and prehistoric sites, taking notes and photographs. It was thus one of the few regular jobs which could have suited Thomas's temperament and disposition.

Whatever his motive for taking it, however, his enthusiasm was very brief. Within a month he had decided to resign. In true Civil Service fashion, leaving the Commission took longer than joining, and before Thomas left, the first of his trips to Wales, the delay of which had been one of his reasons for resigning, came on schedule, and he visited Swansea, Penard and Careg Cenen castles. Nevertheless he was not at all sorry when the end came, shortly before Christmas. His main reason for resigning had been his dislike of London, for finding commuting daily from Petersfield too tiring, he had tried living weekly in town, and had felt himself become oppressed and ill as a result. 'How I hate London', he wrote to Bottomley; 'no exercise, no air, & continual bellyache & head ache & discomfort all over.'[46] Poverty in Petersfield could scarcely be worse than this.

So it was that the New Year 1909 saw Thomas a freer man than he had been for some years, for while at the Commission he had not embarked on any new literary commitments, and he returned home with no promises or deadlines to keep, and with some months' wages in the bank. This was in fact the freedom he had sought when first contemplating a move to the country—the freedom to write only what and when he liked. And although he had worried that too much hack work would eventually kill off his creative talent, he found that a short period of leisure was enough to bring back all his old impulses. At the beginning of February he was able to write to Bottomley with only half-concealed delight:

My dear Gordon, when I tell you I have delayed writing to you because I have been writing not reviews, not commissioned books, not landscapes, but character sketches, stories, etc, I believe you will forgive me. Since the beginning of the year I have had an extraordinary energy in writing & have done nothing else.

'I have done with "country books" ', he added, 'though of course my sketches are full of landscape.'[47]

It was a bright start to what promised to be a good year. *Richard Jefferies*, published in February, received good notices from, amongst others, *The Times* and Edward Garnett, and as a result Thomas was asked to edit Jefferies' uncollected essays for Duckworths. And at the same time the Thomases were contemplating another move, which held its own excitement.

Notice to leave Berryfield Cottage had become a blessing in disguise when Geoffrey Lupton, a neighbour and old Bedalian who was also a craftsman with a private income, offered to build them a house at the top of the hill near to his own house and workshop. Being a disciple of Ruskin and Morris, Helen explained, had led Lupton to the determination to live a simple and useful life, making strong and beautiful things. He both designed and built the new house:

> In his workshop great oaks—which he himself years ago had chosen as they grew—and which he had seasoned and sawn and planed—were transformed into beams, doors and window frames. Everything for the house that could be made locally was so made: the bricks, the tiles, the hinges and the hasps were forged by our landlord, and he taught us how to make the oaken pegs which held the tiles in place . . .[48]

In addition to the house Lupton undertook to build Thomas a new study cottage—a little thatched room a hundred yards from the dwelling on the edge of the wood that filled the steep-sided coombe. Thomas had come to love the surrounding countryside as much as, if not more than, that of Wiltshire or Kent.

It was good walking country, with the edge of the South Downs not far away the other side of Petersfield, and Gilbert White's Selborne and Jane Austen's Chawton within reach to the north-west. Petersfield was easily accessible, and so too was the railway to London, when necessary. The landscape, like the best in England, was infinitely varied, ranging from Green Lane in Froxfield,

> the straight
> Broad lane where now September hides herself
> In bracken and blackberry, harebell and dwarf gorse.
>
> ('The Lane')

to the dark mysteriousness of the wooded coombe, whose

> mouth is stopped with bramble, thorn, and briar;
> And no one scrambles over the sliding chalk
> By beech and yew and perishing juniper
> Down the half precipices of its sides, with roots
> And rabbit holes for steps.
>
> ('The Combe')

From the top, the view was fine—'angled fields of grass and grain bounded by oak and thorn' and on the horizon 'sixty miles of South Downs at one glance.' Without doubt Hampshire was a pleasant place to live.

A new house, built entirely in the style preferred, every detail fashioned with care, and a new study must have promised a good future, if not rural bliss itself. There was a good deal of work to be done breaking new ground for the garden, and the months while the house took shape were filled with digging and expectation, bringing back memories of three years previously when the Thomases had first arrived in the neighbourhood:

> When first I came here I had hope,
> Hope for I knew not what. Fast beat
> My heart at sight of the tall slope
> Of grass and yews, as if my feet
>
> Only by scaling its steps of chalk
> Would see something no other hill
> Ever disclosed.

The study was completed before the house, and in April 1909 Thomas moved into it with his books. He was just thirty-one and, on the face of things, had much to look back on and forward to. He had shown that even with a family to support, he could survive as a writer, even if he had not made his fortune. Although he had been obliged to do more commissioned work than he would have chosen, yet he had had several congenial subjects, and he was not short of work. He had made a name for himself as a nature writer and as the author of delicate, subtle essays. He had also established himself as a conscientious and reliable reviewer. Above all, for eight years he had succeeded in living in the country in several pleasant places and was about to move into the best yet. There were many who would have envied him.

Far from flourishing in his new study, however, Thomas sank almost at once into deep lassitude and despair, turning the hopeful spring into a bleak summer. He took Mervyn to Wales for a brief Easter holiday, and on his return he wrote to Bottomley from the study:

I felt suddenly very weak & sad & could do nothing but turn out the
work asked for and then stare in the fire & wonder why I should be
like this, physically weak, purposeless, hopeless . . .

And I read mechanically at dullish review books & got up here & lit
a fire & sat down & looked at the Downs & read & got home tired, day
after day . . .[49]

His melancholy had returned.

5

The Dark Woods

Since I could not boast of strength
Great as I wished, weakness was all my boast.
I sought yet hated pity till at length
I earned it. Oh, too heavy was the cost!
'There Was a Time'

Thomas's attacks of melancholy or, as we should now call it, depression, were never far off. In time, he became more renowned for his moods than for his writing. There were indeed many occasions when the acuteness of his misery threatened to overwhelm him. To Helen, the affliction was inexplicable, coming to blight their lives unbidden, and 'having its roots in no material circumstance.'[1] But it was aggravated, she felt, by poverty and by the necessity for so much reviewing and so many commissions 'which though he did them well did not at all satisfy his own creative impulse, the damning up of which contributed largely to his melancholy.'[2]

Thomas himself only sporadically blamed his commissioned work, though he complained often enough of the labour involved. He saw the cause of his unhappiness as lying within himself. He blamed his intense self-consciousness, his proneness to introspection, his tendency to self-criticism. He longed to be a different person. Often his depression took the form of gloomy, listless brooding, when he would sit staring into the fire or go long solitary walks. At other times misery turned in on itself and became anger, an unbearable sense of dissatisfaction that was displaced in nervous irritation and sheer bad temper. In such moods he would snap and snarl at Helen and the children, it seemed deliberately trying to make them as miserable as himself.

Although by temperament Thomas was shy and reserved, not easily able to confide in others, he found it possible to express himself in letters to Gordon Bottomley. A typical instance is contained in a letter written in July 1905. Thomas had two books to his credit and other commissions were in view. Helen and the children were away, and he had taken opium to dull his feelings. He wrote:

I am sure I get worse & worse & no week,—hardly a day—passes without my thinking that I must soon cease to try to work and live. But I am so irritable & restless that even if I go so far as to resolve not to work, in a few hours out of sheer ennui I get down a review book & a little later perhaps write a review. If I have now & then ten oblivious minutes at sunset or midnight, I am very lucky; for at all other times, whether I am reading or writing or talking or trying to sleep, I am plagued by such little thoughts as how much shall I earn this week or what train shall I catch tomorrow or whether I shall have my letters by the next post & such big thoughts as whether any thing is worth while, whether I shall ever again have hope or joy or enthusiasm or love, whether I could for any length of time be quite sensible in taking food, sleep, drink & whether if I could be, I should be any better. You see— I must have some motive & to be honest my responsibility to Helen & Merfyn & the dear & joyful Bronwen is not a motive. I must believe in myself or forget myself and I cannot. I get more & more self-conscious every day—of the little good in myself & work—of the much bad—of the futility of reviewing—of my insolence in reviewing any book—of my way of doing things—my way of speaking—my very attitudes, dress, expression—Shall I ever have the relief of true and thorough insanity? Oh, for someone to help . . .[3]

Thomas had first taken opium at Oxford, where it was a fashionably Decadent thing to do. Now he was using it seriously, as an escape from his troubles. But it was an occasional habit only, a resort of despair and, one would imagine, indulged in only if Helen was not present. In any case it was no help: under its influence, Thomas noted to Bottomley, neither his work nor his opinion of it improved[4]—and he soon had no difficulty in giving the drug up altogether.

Other forms of self-denial followed. The depression manifested itself in physical symptoms, notably indigestion and lassitude. Thomas consulted a series of doctors who prescribed various remedies such as abstinence from alcohol and tobacco, and special diets. Medical understanding of psychosomatic disorders was limited at this period; psychology itself was only in its very early stages and few doctors had any knowledge of it. Thomas followed various of the regimens prescribed, without visible improvement. In 1912 he became a vegetarian. In certain circles meat-eating was held to be an unnatural habit, responsible for many of the ailments and agonies of modern civilisation; simplified meals were also advocated in place of the multi-coursed Edwardian institutions, and emphasis laid on brown bread and plenty of vegetables.

There is much to be said for such a diet, but it was hardly likely to help Edward Thomas, whose ailments were not physical. When black moods threatened, the best solution, he believed, was to immerse himself in nature: to take himself off for long solitary tramps, often for days at a time, trying to recapture some of the joy and freedom from care that had characterised his first long walk from London to Wiltshire. Away from home and deep in the woods and meadows of the countryside, he could hope to regain some tranquillity of spirit. As he told Bottomley:

Really I am never so well as when I am rid of the postman & all company walking 20 or 30 miles a day. I was as well as ever I hope to be in my week's walk, & its effect has lasted over another week. I get as depressed and irritable as ever but seem to recover faster. Five months purgation of course has something to do with it. . . . a feeling of extreme virtue after 5 months teetotalism & almost abstinence from tobacco is hard to avoid. But seriously I wonder whether for a person like myself whose most intense moments were those of depression a cure that destroys the depression may not destroy the intensity—a *desperate* remedy?[5]

Friends were some help, but not if, like Ransome, they were too successful. Thomas got on better with those like Garnett, whose work did not command the acclaim its author deserved. Or with James Guthrie, who had set out to be a printer in despite of his family, and who continued to struggle against both poverty and compromise with commercialism. Guthrie had started his Pear Tree Press in Essex and then moved to South Harting, a few miles from Petersfield in Hampshire and within walking distance of the Thomases when they moved to Berryfield Cottage. Guthrie and Thomas became immediate friends, and continued to see each other frequently even after the Guthries had moved to the coast at Flansham. Despite his cares, Guthrie maintained his integrity as an artist and, as a later visitor put it, his house 'hummed with the activities of brain and spirit, and the intention to make a perfect thing of the job in hand, even if buying handmade paper to do it meant going short of bread.'[6] To Guthrie, Thomas was a man after his own heart, determined to resist the world and survive without succumbing to its demands. He was also a restless, wandering figure:

He [Thomas] went everywhere in the fields and the house, with his thick walking shoes. A house was, indeed, a continuation of the road to him; a fire—a few kindled sticks served well enough—no more than a slight courtesy to the common custom, indulged in from no weak desire to make it do instead of the natural warmth of health and exercise. Home to him was by way of being a temporary shelter from cold night or inclement weather and Thomas went home much as he might enter a wood or stand behind a stack, being all the while a traveller, at any moment ready to engage with the wind and the rain.[7]

This was an acute observation, though Thomas himself might have added that his restlessness was due to a chronic sense of dissatisfaction. 'I am not well, worried, hard at work, discontented with myself and every one I see', he wrote to Bottomley in 1907. 'I begin to think this kind of life can't go on for ever . . .' He continued:

Why have I no energies like other men? I long for some hatred or even sharp despair, since love is impossible, to send me out on the road that leads over the hills & among the stars sometimes. Till then I must grind everything out, conscious at every moment of what the result is & so always dissatisfied . . . think of the pain of going on living & not being able to do anything but eat & drink & earn a living for 5 [sic] people. Would anyone do it that was aware of what he did?[8]

The causes of Thomas's melancholia cannot be determined precisely at this distance in time. According to medical opinion depressive illnesses are neuroses with external causes connected with experiences of loss and failure, although the exact origins may be concealed. Loss and failure are felt in childhood through separation or rejection, and in adulthood through bereavement, rejection or failure. Feelings of worthlessness, unloveableness, unlovingness, and consequent anger inwardly or outwardly directed are common.

It is not difficult to see that in Thomas a sense of failure had been nurtured from an early age by his father's high expectations and unconcealed contempt; rejection would not be too harsh a term for this. The difficulty of living up to his father's ambitions made adolescence a painful time for Thomas and led him to opt out of the academic race at St Paul's, turning instead to nature, country walks, and essay writing. Here for the first time he tasted success and paternal encouragement from James Ashcroft Noble. To have a book published before going to Oxford was no mean achievement; it was indeed a visible sign of ability and success, and, as we have seen, it fired Thomas with the ambition to be a writer, for here was a field in which he could excel.

Yet perhaps this first success was too easy, too early. Certainly Thomas lacked the underlying self-confidence to face the practical difficulties and inevitable reverses which came when he tried to earn his living by writing. Though he knew he had nothing much to offer editors except promise, he nevertheless reacted very badly—very blackly—to initial rebuffs when seeking work; his letters testify how anxious he was for recognition, how deeply he feared failure. Most, if not all, writers will be familiar with these anxieties, for however much the public or the critics may be despised it is hard to carry on writing without external recognition or praise. Possibly Thomas's plunges into despair at his failure to achieve fame were more than usually acute because his belief in himself was only fragile: he had only his ambition and Helen's love to sustain him.

Ambition was certainly closely related to his moods of depression. He told Bottomley:

I was told the other day that I seemed a calm dispassionate observer with no opinions. I hope I am more. I have no opinions, I know. But cannot the passive temperament do something, a little? For I have impressions of men & places & books. They often overawe me as a tree or a crowd does the sensitized paper; & is that nothing or as good as nothing?[9]

and again:

I feel as if I would never try to write again. There is no form that suits me & I doubt if I can make a new form. At any rate, I must avoid long things. Perhaps the 'man & landscape' plan has a future for me . . .[10]

With each published book there was hope that his fortune and fame would improve, yet as the years went by this looked less and less likely. The special pieces in his country books went unrecognised. He was told that *Richard Jefferies* would make his name and bring in new and better offers of work. It did neither. His essays and sketches, though they were still published in magazines, were praised by few and they, he suspected, were mainly personal friends. Others might see a modest success in his published work and reputation, but to Thomas as he reached and passed thirty this was not enough. He had not made the name or the income he had hoped to make as a country writer and subtle essayist; he had found neither financial nor psychological security. He described his professional position in 1909 thus:

A difficulty will soon arise unless *Jefferies* brings me offers of work—which it has failed to do except from the editor of a new magazine who asked me for a short 'semi-poetical' article on 'why I love an out-of-door life'! I don't lead an out of door life & can't be semi-poetical to order so I asked a prohibitive price & so got out of it. Meantime I get articles returned on every hand. The *New Age* printed a thing last week. Did you see it? But it was written a year ago nearly . . .[11]

Things were not always gloomy. The new house built for them by Lupton, with its study cottage, held much promise for the future. The Thomases' third child, Myfanwy, was born in the new house at Wick Green in August 1910. The same year most of the essays written during the creative burst early in 1909 were published by Duckworth under the title *Rest and Unrest*. They had been encouraged by Edward Garnett, who commented on each essay and was responsible for much recasting and alteration, as Thomas's letters make clear.[12]

But *Rest and Unrest* attracted little attention. It was, Thomas told Bottomley, the only book he had written that would bring in no money at all. He continued with sketches, however, and the following year Duckworth brought out another collection, *Light and Twilight*. One of the essays included, entitled 'July', was a recreation of Helen's twentieth birthday, the day they had become lovers. The tale is couched in the form of a lament, for the girl is dead and the lover looks sadly back at the idyllic day and at his past self:

> Was that not one of the dead walking with her? He was equally distant and out of reach and recall, and in the sunlight of that land his eyes could not distinguish the ghost of the living from the ghost of the dead.

Of this essay Thomas remarked: 'It is one of those crude mixtures of experience and invention which prove me no artist. Damn it. I am only just beginning to discover it.'[13]

He was later to become even more dissatisfied with his creative work, but for the time being most of his contempt was heaped on his commissioned books, which had never been more numerous or more banal. A book on Maurice Maeterlinck was followed by ones on Windsor Castle and the Isle of Wight, and then by *Feminine Influence on the Poets*, a half-biographical, half-critical account of selected poets and the women in their lives and work. It was literary popularising of the worst kind, written for readers more interested in private lives than great poetry, and Thomas hated it. 'I feel as if I ought to walk day & night for weeks if I am ever to get rid of the effects', he said. To have done the book at all was bad enough, he added, but worse still was the damage it might do his reputation: 'I don't want to be always the man that wrote Women & Poets.'[14]

Early in 1911 he had no less than four books in hand: one on Lafcadio Hearn, a long forgotten exotic travel writer who lived in the West Indies and Japan; one a collection of Celtic tales for use in schools; one a country book on the Icknield Way, the old drove-road running from Norfolk to Wiltshire, and his latest collection of essays. The proliferation of work did not indicate an improved state of mind for indeed the opposite was true—Thomas was piling work on work in order to stave off depression. In February he wrote to Bottomley:

> I am at the end of a second week of extraordinary weakness, unable to work in the garden or to walk & considerably dejected therefore, but not quite so frantic as I should have been a few years ago . . . I creep and slink about the earth doing small immediate things . . .[15]

Two months later he reflected:

> I only hope that I am still suffering from the transition out of youth and
> that someday I shall laugh at having taken myself so tragically . . . It
> is connected with my work, too, the unpleasant tendency of producing
> many books . . .[16]

In August he wrote:

> I am more and more oppressed by necessity & *the consciousness of it* &
> unless I meet some good fortune things are likely to get even worse.
> Apparently I shall have to increase my income yet submit to a decrease
> in the price of my work . . .[17]

and later:

> It is being discussed whether I shall do books on Pater *and* Swinburne
> *and* Borrow *and* De Quincey. Laugh and then pity me . . .[18]

He was heading for a breakdown. His mood was becoming seriously
suicidal, as if reflecting his need to escape from the tensions and conflicts
within. He told people that he had now virtually given up creative writing,
and was concentrating only on paid commissions, in order to feed his
family. But he admitted too that he still had 'enough ambition left to find
utterly uncongenial work very humiliating.'[19] His sense of mental stress
was acute: 'My head is almost always wrong now—a sort of conspiracy
going on in it which leaves me only a joint tenancy & a perpetual scare of
the other tenant and wonder what he will do.'[20]

Life at home became more and more unpleasant, with the children
learning to avoid their father in his black moods. Thomas criticised them
and Helen for small faults, displacing his self-hatred onto his dependants.
Helen remained solicitous and sympathetic, and even her sympathy
provoked attack, as she recorded in *World Without End*, when a typical
outburst from Edward would be full of resentment and anger:

> Tired! Tired is not what I am. I'm sick of the whole of life—of myself
> chiefly, of you and the children. You must hate and despise me but you
> can't hate me as much as I hate the whole business, and as I despise
> myself for not putting an end to it . . . I don't want you fussing about
> me. I know what I am. I know what I've done to you. Don't stand there
> looking grey and worn till I could hate you for it . . .[21]

He had, on one occasion at least, taken a step towards putting an end to everything. One day he had actually taken an ancient rusty revolver out into the woods, apparently intending to shoot himself. He describes such an incident in an essay entitled 'The Attempt', written in the third person, where the would-be suicide is named Morgan Treharon, and is mocked from the start for being vain and foolish and full of 'luxurious self-contempt'. His intention is romantic:

> Death was an idea tinged with poetry in his mind—a kingly thing which was once only at any man's call. After it came annihilation. To escape from the difficulty of life, from the hopeless search for something that would make it possible for him to go on living like anybody else without questioning, he was eager to hide himself away in annihilation ... There was also an element of vanity in his project; he was going to punish himself and in a manner so extreme that he was inclined to be exalted by the feeling that he was now about to convince the world that he had suffered exceedingly . . .[22]

There was never much chance that the suicide attempt would succeed, though the feelings were real enough. And one may suspect that Thomas's real-life attempt was in part a melodramatic gesture directed towards others as well as himself It was surely intended to hurt Helen, for the gun had been taken out and pocketed for her to see and she had reason to fear his black moods. In *World Without End* she described the terrible day she passed with the children, not knowing if she would see her husband alive again.[23] He left her to suffer as long as he could, returning home late at night, having been for a long walk after he had realised the impossibility of actually shooting himself. What he sought was rather oblivion than death. Oblivion features frequently in the essays written in 1909–10, for example in 'The Flower Gatherer' from *Light and Twilight*, where a child drowns in a stream: 'She sighed as she seemed to float higher and lighter into soft darkness, into utter darkness, into nothing at all, where there was never anything or will be anything . . .'

A full nervous breakdown in the autumn of 1911 was averted when Helen appealed to an old friend, who forwarded enough money to allow Edward to be sent on holiday to Llaugharne, Carmarthenshire, where it was hoped he could recuperate. He insisted on taking his next commission, a book on George Borrow. Pater and Swinburne were to follow. Although the writing of these was later to prove useful to him, he was clearly driving himself too hard and in directions he did not want to follow. He had renounced essay writing, but he could not come to terms with himself as simply a professionally paid author, without creative talent.

Characteristically, he blamed the new house as a contributing factor to his depression. As he wrote later in 'Wind and Mist':

the eye watching from those windows saw,
Many a day, day after day, mist—mist
Like chaos surging back—and felt itself
Alone in all the world, marooned alone.

He seemed powerless to change things, as he told Bottomley in 1912:
'Now & then I remember that I am 34 & ought to stand alone, help
myself & keep silent, but really I still feel as I did 12 years ago that people
ought to help or might help me to solve my difficulties although I have no
claims . . .'[24] Even a new home, which was found down in the village of
Steep, a small workman's house called Yewtree Cottage into which the
family moved in July 1913, could not help him. He began to spend more
and more time away from home, returning full of remorse at his neglect,
yet unable to tolerate being there for more than short periods, convincing
himself that separation was better for all concerned. But it was not his
family he wished to escape from, it was himself.

This he partly knew already, and during 1912 he was helped towards a
more mature understanding of his condition by Godwin Baynes, a young
doctor specialising in nervous diseases, who had been introduced to him
by Edward Garnett's son David.[25] Baynes was interested in Freud's ideas
about the workings of the mind; himself a man of remarkable physical and
mental energy, with a wide circle of friends and interests in music, politics
and literature as well as medicine, he had the capacity to see into and
understand depression. Although not trained in psychoanalysis as it is
known today, he appears to have offered Thomas a form of treatment
based on conversation and friendship. His help was useful, although his
ultimate diagnosis was that Thomas had not yet abandoned the childhood
tendency to rely on others to solve his problems. He would have to start
helping himself. Thomas agreed; as he wrote: 'I have got to help myself
and have been steadily spoiling myself for the job for I don't know how
long . . . The central evil is self-consciousness carried as far beyond
selfishness as selfishness is beyond self-denial [and] now amounting to a
disease . . .'[26]

Looking at Thomas's life as a whole it is easy to see the years 1912–13
as the darkest hours before dawn, but this was not at all evident at the
time. There was no indication that things were going to change. Apart
from a few close friends, whose affection was not diminished by Thomas's
gloomy looks or self-pitying remarks, people generally regarded him as a
writer of minor talent who was being suffocated under the years of commissioned work and reviews. Some thought he would be wiser to give up
writing altogether, seeing that it brought nothing but anxiety and ill-
temper. Others were more or less openly unsympathetic, made so perhaps
by Thomas's apparent quest for pity, when, in company, he played, all

too sincerely, the part of the failed writer. With a character in a later book, Thomas was describing himself:

> he wrote what he was both reluctant and incompetent to write, at the request of a firm of publishers whose ambition was to have a bad, but nice-looking, book on everything and everybody . . . His books are not the man. They are known only to students at the British Museum who get them out once and no more, for they discover hasty compilations, ill-arranged, inaccurate and incomplete, and swollen to a ridiculous size for the sake of gain. They contain not one mention of the house under the hill where he was born.[27]

Others were likely to be aware of his unhappiness only through his brusqueness or grumpy silence, in an age when social life was more formal than today. Many were rebuffed by the barriers he erected, as he himself noted later:

> I built myself a house of glass:
> It took me years to make it:
> And I was proud. But now alas!
> Would God someone would break it.

Leaving the fine house on the hill top was one more admission of failure, for it was such a house as a successful writer on the country would be envied for inhabiting, but one which Thomas felt he could not afford. It appears in two of his poems. The first, 'The New House', opens with the poet alone in the house for the first time hearing the wind moaning, foretelling

> Nights of storm, days of mist, without end;
>   Bad days when the sun
> Shone in vain: old griefs and griefs
>   Not yet begun.
>
> All was foretold me: naught
>   Could I foresee;
> But I learned how the wind would sound
>   After these things should be.

The second poem, 'Wind and Mist', also emphasises the sound of the wind and the house's isolation. It is in the form of a dialogue between a visiting stranger and the man who once lived in the house, who answers the stranger's questions:

'I have seen that house
Through mist look lovely as a castle in Spain,
And airier. I have thought: " 'Twere happy there
To live." And I have laughed at that
Because I lived there then.' 'Extraordinary.'
'Yes, with my furniture and family
Still in it, I, knowing every nook of it
And loving none, and in fact hating it.'

A house, the man continues, is not a castle in Spain, a palace of dream, and
must not be treated as such:

'I did not know it was the earth I loved
Until I tried to live there in the clouds
And the earth turned to cloud.' 'You had a garden
Of flint and clay, too.' 'True; that was real enough.
The flint was the one crop that never failed.
The clay first broke my heart, and then my back;
And the back heals not. There were other things
Real, too. In that room at the gable a child
Was born while the wind chilled a summer dawn:
Never looked grey mind on a greyer one
Than when the child's cry broke above the groans.'
'I hope they were both spared.' 'They were, Oh yes!
But flint and clay and childbirth were too real
For this cloud-castle . . .

In the past Thomas had usually been able to overcome his worst bouts
of melancholy by immersing himself in nature. Consolation of this kind
is expressed in one of the essays from *Light and Twilight* entitled 'The
Stile', which describes the end of a country walk:

I took one or two steps to the stile and, instead of crossing it I leaned
upon the gate at one side. The confidence and ease deepened and
darkened as if I also were like that still sombre cloud that had been a
copse under a pale sky . . . Somewhere—close at hand in that rosy
thicket or far off beyond the ribs of sunset—I was gathered up with an
immortal company . . . And in that company I learned that I am something which no fortune can touch, whether I be soon to die or long
years away. Things will happen that will trample and pierce, but I shall
go on, something that is here and there like the wind, something
unconquerable, something not to be separated from the dark earth and
the light sky, a strong citizen of infinity and eternity. The confidence

and ease had become a deep joy; I knew that I could not do without the Infinite, nor the Infinite without me.

But such moments were now rare, or experienced only with an effort of will, assertions rather than expressions of spontaneous feeling. As often as not, the country made Thomas feel weary and oppressed. There was a change in his country writing, best seen in the book *The Icknield Way*, an account of his journey along this ancient road undertaken in the summer of 1911, notebook to hand. He was under instructions to produce a literal account, with accurate descriptions of places, but this was no more than partly responsible for the heaviness with which the book drags itself along. Rather it is the interludes, when Thomas allows himself to expand on a mood or a fancy in the style of his essays, which are lengthiest to read— and it is they that convey the depths of his despair. One such passage is a three-page monologue of misery, as the narrator lies in bed in an inn, listening to the rain:

> I am not a part of nature. I am alone . . . Once there was summer, and a great heat and splendour over the earth terrified me and asked me what I could show that was worthy of such an earth. It smote and humiliated me, yet I had eyes to behold it, and I prostrated myself, and by adoration made myself worthy of the splendour. Was I not once blind to the splendour because there was something within me equal to itself?

In his moods of self-disgust rather than despair, Thomas could look sourly on what had, up till now, been the chief purpose of his life—to live in the country and write about it. In *Light and Twilight* the essay entitled 'Hawthornden' describes a man with this rustic name who moves to the country and does nothing but read books. He is an admirer of Borrow and all things simple and antique. 'When he moved into the country he was prepared for adventures.' Hawthornden is the type of country-lover who poses as a real countryman. Because of his long solitary walks, he is believed by others to be full of country knowledge, and also to be a liberated unconventional spirit freed by the country from the constraints of modern life. Neither is true: he is a solitary figure knowing country people less well than his wife, while his walks involve much equipment— maps, haversacks, walking sticks—the marks of a townsman in pursuit of the country. Moreover his life is as regulated by routine as that of any city-dweller; Hawthornden is not free but a man who always returns home in time for tea.

Thus Thomas mocked his own situation. And in a little book he wrote for Batsford called *The Country* (1913) we may see still more clearly the change in attitude. He still has hope that nature will provide the tranquillity and contentment he seeks: 'Calming us all with its space and patience, the country relates us all to Eternity', he wrote, continuing (in the passage already quoted in Chapter 3):

We go to it as would-be poets, or as solitaries, vagabonds, lovers, to escape foul air, noise, hard hats, black uniforms, elaborate means without clear ends—to escape ourselves . . .

He is thus harsh on the whole country impulse of the Back to the Land movement, and particularly so on those like himself who write books about the country. They, he says, regard the country as

a source of rest, relief, stimulation, a kind of religion, poetry, cash; or as a refuge for thinkers, poets, lovers, children, tired workers, or players. For some the country is hardly more than an alternative to theatres, exhibitions, clubs and pills.

Thomas was a man whose faith had not suddenly but gradually left him. He had believed in the country as a source of peace and happiness; now he saw it only as an escape. Slowly he had realised that to idealise the country—as he had done—was to follow a false trail. The countryside of itself could not solve the problems he was unable or unwilling to solve for himself.

Later, when he came to write poetry, Thomas recreated some of his melancholic moods in verse. One such occasion is the poem 'Beauty':

What does it mean? Tired, angry, and ill at ease,
No man, woman, or child alive could please
Me now. And yet I almost dare to laugh
Because I sit and frame an epitaph—
'Here lies all that no one loved of him
And that loved no one.' Then in a trice that whim
Has wearied. But, though I am like a river
At fall of evening while it seems that never
Has the sun lighted it or warmed it, while
Cross breezes cut the surface to a file,
This heart, some fraction of me, happily
Floats through the window even now to a tree
Down in the misting, dim-lit, quiet vale,
Not like a pewit that returns to wail
For something it has lost, but like a dove
That slants unswerving to its home and love.
There I find my rest, and through the dusk air
Flies what yet lives in me. Beauty is there.

This is a curious poem, which although all of a piece is made up of two distinct parts, each of which uses a different kind of language. The first is that of life—the everyday realism of 'Tired, angry, and ill at ease'—with images and verbal hints supporting the theme, as in 'Cross breezes cut the surface to a file.' The second sort of language (from the twelfth line on) is that of 'poesy'—a place where vales are misting, dim-lit and quiet, where doves slant unswerving to their homes and loves. We shall look more closely at these different kinds of poetic language in a later chapter; here it is only necessary to point out that the final statement that 'Beauty is there' comes in the second part of the poem. The real world is full of coldness and discord, and the solutions of happiness and beauty sought by the poet exist only in a dream-world. Beauty is *there*, floating somewhere in the dusk air; it is not here, where it is needed.

The poem 'Beauty' is usually read as a vindication of what nature and the countryside could do for Thomas in his melancholy moods. The language used, however, makes it plain that the consolation is wished for rather than attained. And in several other poems it is clear that far from bringing happiness and peace of mind, the countryside often increased the despair he felt. One such poem is 'The Glory', quoted in the Introduction to this book:

> And shall I ask at the day's end once more
> What beauty is, and what I can have meant
> By happiness?

Another is 'October', where the poet watches leaves slip to the ground from a great elm tree, and reflects on his own state of mind:

> now I might
> As happy be as earth is beautiful,
> Were I some other or with earth could turn
> In alternation of violet and rose,
> Harebell and snowdrop, at their season due,
> And gorse that has no time not to be gay.
> But if this be not happiness,—who knows?
> Some day I shall think this a happy day,
> And this mood by the name of melancholy
> Shall no more blackened and obscured be.

Thomas's depression never entirely left him, but it was much abated in subsequent years, as the rest of this book will show. Partly this was due to new friends and greater self-confidence, but it arose chiefly from his discovery of new modes of expression. To anticipate: I believe Thomas began his working life under a dual illusion or handicap. He idealised the countryside both in his life and in his writing, and expressed his feelings for it through a correspondingly idealised or poeticised language such as was fashionable among the aesthetes of the time. Neither the attitude nor the language was intended for dealing with real life, and when confronted with the actualities and emotions of real life they could not withstand the strain. For a long time Thomas continued to pursue both the way of life and the kind of writing that belonged to this pastoral-aesthetic manner, but the rewards steadily diminished, and by the years 1911–12 he had virtually abandoned his original ambitions in despair. Before he could emerge again as a creative writer and a poet he had to adjust himself, slowly and painfully, to a new kind of writing and also a new kind of thinking.

6

New Friends, New Forms

You please yourself. I should prefer the truth
Or nothing.

'The Chalk-Pit'

Outwardly, there were few indications of change. Thomas continued to feel an acute sense of frustration, and be unable to do anything about it. He gave vent to this mood in *The Icknield Way*, with

> Oh, for a horse to ride furiously, for a ship to sail, for the wings of an eagle, for the lance of a warrior or a standard streaming to conquest, for a man's strength to dare and endure, for a woman's beauty to surrender, for a singer's fountain of precious tones, for a poet's pen!

little realising that before long he would indeed achieve the last in this list of rhetorical flourishes. His attacks of depression were as bad as ever and in the autumn of 1912 he had left home to lodge with Dorothy and Vivien Locke-Ellis near East Grinstead. Vivien Locke-Ellis was a minor poet and publisher of a magazine called *The Open Window*; he admired Thomas's essays.

The books on Borrow, Pater and Swinburne were completed, as was his little book *The Country* for Batsford and a last nature book, *In Pursuit of Spring*, for Thomas Nelson. Financially things were reasonably cheerful, for a bulk order of two thousand copies of his *Celtic Tales* had been placed by the Australian education authorities,[1] and Thomas did not appear anxious for new commissions. He was asked for another book by Batsford, on his own choice of subject and 'in a fit of curiosity & daring'[2] he volunteered 'Ecstasy'. A strange choice, perhaps, yet Thomas's melancholy was closely linked to his search for bliss and he may have hoped to discover more by writing about it. However, having written about a third, he 'soberly and finally decided it was mostly muck'[3] and abandoned it.

This was the first time he had actually relinquished a commission, forfeiting the advance. There were other developments too. After long years of concentrating on the jewelled and often elegiac essay, written as it were late at night by the sensitive, imaginative observer of men and nature, he now began to try out new modes of writing. 'I am only just learning how ill my notes have been making me write', he told Bottomley, 'by all but destroying such natural rhythm as I have in me.'[4] At first the direction of his endeavour was uncertain. In October 1912 he told Bottomley with some surprise that he was now busy on 'a fiction!'[5] This was *The Happy-Go-Lucky Morgans*, a loosely-strung collection of sketches and reveries on the theme of an old suburban house and family, incorporating many of Thomas's own memories.

As so often in Thomas's prose work, fact and fancy are ill distinguished in the story, with stretches of narrative tending to wander off into airy imaginings. Thus a detailed description of two lads being chased by a farmer moves without warning into describing the Palace of the Mountain of the Clouds, 'separated by great distances and great enchantment from the rest of the world ... surrounded by running water sweeter than honey.' A page later and we are back with the boys 'fishing, birds-nesting and trying to shoot birds with cross-bow, pistol, or home-made gun.'

The book was published by Duckworth in 1913 and although it cannot be regarded as a very successful attempt at fiction, since it lacks narrative structure and contains too many of the discursive mannerisms of essay-writing, yet it was a move in a new direction and was received as such by many of Thomas's friends. W. H. Hudson wrote to Edward Garnett:

> The *Happy* etc., *Morgans* interested me greatly, but I don't think it will interest the reading public one bit. It interested me because of my esteem and affection for him (and my admiration too) also because I believe he has taken the wrong path and is wandering lost in the vast wilderness ... He is essentially a poet ... and this book shows it, I think, more than any of the others ... But I should say that in his nature books and fiction he leaves all there's best and greatest in him unexpressed ... I believe that if Thomas had the courage or the opportunity to follow his own genius he could do better things than these.[6]

Was it courage or opportunity that was wanting? Thomas was still searching for an adequate means of expression, by trying out new forms. The second of these was in the shape of Proverbs—short pieces purporting to explain the origin of several common proverbs, an idea which had come from the tales Thomas had made up to amuse his children, and which were presented in a faux-naïf manner as children's stories intended for adults. Typical titles are Birds of a Feather Flock Together, A Cat May Look at a King, and People in Glass Houses Shouldn't Throw Stones—which, much abbreviated, reappeared as the poem 'I Built Myself a House of Glass'. The Proverbs were eventually published by Duckworth in 1915 under the title *Four and Twenty Blackbirds*.

This idea had been encouraged by a new circle of friends who had been introduced to Thomas through Godwin Baynes. Baynes had a wide circle of friends, or rather a number of overlapping circles which were collectively known, in jesting affection, as the Kingdom of Godwinia. One of the circles was located, geographically, in Hampstead and included a number of young people, relatively well-off though not rich, with artistic interests, humanitarian sentiments and a great capacity for enjoying themselves.

Among the members of this circle were the Bax brothers—Arnold the composer, later to become Master of the King's Musick, and Clifford, who variously pursued painting, poetry, theosophy and astrology but came into his own as captain and host to a famed literary cricket team on pre- and post-war village greens—and the Farjeon family, particularly Herbert (Bertie), the writer of musical comedy and revue, and Eleanor (Nellie to the family), then aspiring writer of 'exquisite' fantasies, later author of renowned children's books, regular poems in the *Daily Herald* and theatrical shows in collaboration with her brother.

Thomas first met the Baxes in 1911. Oddly enough, it was to Clifford, the shallowest and perhaps most selfish member of the group, that Thomas was most attracted; perhaps it was the very lack of seriousness, the witty, hedonistic attitude to life, that appealed to him. Clifford was recently married and the owner of a fine Jacobean manor house at Broughton Gifford in Wiltshire, where Thomas was invited for a short visit. Here Bax's conversation and Baynes's athletic energy temporarily suspended Thomas's melancholy; writing his thank-you letter he said his stay had been 'a long and happy dream'.[7]

The following year Thomas returned to Broughton Gifford for a longer visit, from April to June, to write his book on Swinburne, though for part of this time he stayed at nearby Dillybrook Farm. Bax invited him to join the cricket team for its second season of intensive country cricket in August. Thomas accepted, though not a cricketer, for the cultivated pleasures of his new friends had many attractions, and who could resist a week of country games with a congenial group of artists and professional men, travelling by bicycle and waggonette to cricket matches in neighbouring villages, with a chess championship in the evenings, a tennis tournament on Sunday, and sparkling conversation all the while?

Bertie Farjeon was one of the cricketing party, and Thomas found him pleasant company. Both men liked early morning angling, and got up before the rest of the party to enjoy the fish and the summer mornings. In the evenings those not playing chess amused themselves and others with games of literary skill such as bouts rimés. Bertie's wit was sharp and topical. At other times, particularly when Godwin was in charge, the games were more boisterous—hide-and-seek or hare-and-hounds. For one so reserved, Thomas found these house parties remarkably enjoyable, and was able to join in the fun and forget his worries. He began to arrange to meet Bertie when he came up to London to collect his review books.

Women had not been included in the cricketing week and so it was not until later in the year that Thomas met Eleanor Farjeon. Arranging to meet Godwin and Bertie for tea, he asked if Godwin's fiancée and Bertie's sister would join them at the Cottage Tea Rooms in the Strand.

As she described herself later, Eleanor Farjeon was, at the age of thirty-one, shy, ignorant and 'only just emerging from a fantasy life into one of a natural human relationships.'[8] As a child in a close, late-Victorian family, she had been particularly attached to her elder brother Harry, who had devised a strange fantasy game—a version of 'let's pretend' played while circling the kitchen table until a state of semi-hypnosis or trance prevailed—which continued long beyond the normal reach of childhood, until Eleanor was in her late twenties. In her writing Eleanor preserved a make-believe world, while in real life she and Bertie formed part of the circle that included Baynes and the Baxes and held advanced views on art, women's rights, religion and politics. They enjoyed music and drama, enthused about the Russian Ballet, Wagner's *Ring* and the Irish Players, and adopted new pastimes. Chief among these were the progressive out-of-door pursuits of tramping across the Downs, swimming in rivers, sleeping under the stars, and defying signs saying Trespassers will be Prosecuted.

On the face of it, Eleanor was the least likely to become Thomas's friend, for she was shy and timid, afraid of swimming and woefully ignorant of the natural world. A clump of trees was to her an abode of Pan, not oak, ash or sycamore.[9] When they met, Bronwen Thomas was appalled at Eleanor's ignorance of wild flowers. Nor was Eleanor the fair nymph of Thomas's dreams, for she was plain and spectacled and he was prejudiced on such matters. Friends, however, they did become and from Thomas's letters to Eleanor, collected in her autobiographical account of this period, *The Last Four Years* (1958), it is clear that it was a close and responsive relationship.

Most of the feeling was on Eleanor's side, for it was not long before she fell fully in love with Thomas. This remained always undisclosed between them but it would appear that Eleanor's silent, undemanding love, with its implicit faith in him, gave Thomas something of what he was looking for. To Eleanor he was able to express his doubts and hopes without fear of rejection; as his letters show, he valued her friendship and trusted her as he did few others, not least for her utter discretion. It would be a mistake to imagine that here was a passionate love affair curbed by Edwardian moral conventions against unmarried girls and married men. Neither the Thomases nor the Farjeons belonged to that part of society which subscribed to such a code and it was not the risk of scandal that kept the friendship platonic, but the disparity between their feelings. 'He counted on me for friendship', Eleanor wrote later; 'and I loved him with all my heart.' But he relied on her never to tell him of her feelings, for 'if I had, our friendship must have come to an end.'[10]

In a curious way, the relationship would seem to have satisfied both of them, incomplete though it was. For Eleanor, loving Edward satisfied her emotional needs without making the same demands as a full relationship, for which she was not yet ready. For Thomas, too, it was a relationship without risks, offering sustained support and confidence, both of which he needed.

So their friendship grew during 1913. Soon they were meeting for lunch or tea without others' company, and corresponding. Thomas began sending Eleanor samples of his new work, in particular the Proverbs. She herself wrote children's rhymes which appeared in various magazines, and she was able to suggest possible publishers for the Proverbs. In June she made a bolder gesture, inviting Edward to accompany her and two other friends, Gertrude and Stacy Aumonier, on their pre-planned August holiday week on the Norfolk Broads (Bertie had dropped out). As it happened, Helen was to be away with the girls at that time and Edward was to be in charge of Mervyn, who was thereupon included in the invitation. The plans for the week provide a glimpse into Edward's concern with his diet: he stipulated 'green vegetables, fruit, fat, grease, butter, etc.', no sugar, no alcohol and 'brown bread if it is to be had without revolution.' However, he added that he was inclined to be less than serious about these rules, as they were 'perfectly futile, because perfectly and exclusively physical.'[11]

Before leaving for the Broads, however, Edward arranged for Eleanor to come to his new house at Steep. No doubt it was necessary that Helen should meet the woman with whom he was about to spend a week aboard a small boat, albeit with several chaperones. Immediately before the allotted week, Edward went again to Broughton Gifford, to join in the annual cricket party. Helen was detailed to meet and welcome Eleanor. She was apprehensive, for she had met other members of this new circle of friends at Broughton Gifford, and had disliked them for their wealth and sophistication:

> They were rich and young and intellectual and I hated the atmosphere they created in that dignified house. I hated the cold luxury, the polished insincerity, the clever bloodless wit, and the exotic vegetarian food. Their poor wan baby whose nursery was like a princess's out of the Arabian Nights filled me with pity and horror.[12]

She felt out of her depth amid the sparkling conversation, and her reaction had annoyed Edward, perhaps because he too knew it was affected and insincere. Associating Eleanor with this set, no wonder Helen was worried.

When they met, however, misgivings faded away. Eleanor was shy and one suspects a little gauche—far from the sophisticated woman Helen had imagined. She had a real liking for children and, more important, the ability to win their friendship by joining in their pursuits and devising stories. In her book Eleanor recounts how on her first visit to Yewtree Cottage she overcame baby Myfanwy's prejudice against spectacles by means of a charming piece of make-believe involving 'Cocky Peacock' (Eleanor) and 'Polly Parrot' (Myfanwy). She was appreciative, too, of Helen's domestic genius, and delighted to be a guest in the homely family setting. Helen must soon have realised she had nothing to fear from her new friend.

Yet this was in its way remarkable. For Helen soon perceived Eleanor's love for Edward. In *World Without End* she described how this happened, as they stood at the gate watching Thomas go off on a midnight walk. He was at his most unloving and had spoilt the evening and astonished Eleanor by repeatedly snapping at Helen for her supposed deficiencies; he had gone to walk his ill-temper away. Somehow the feelings both women shared for this prickly, unresponsive man brought them together.[13] Helen remained one of the few who shared Eleanor's secret.

Thomas enjoyed his week on the Broads and at the end of September wrote to Eleanor with news of new work he was planning:

> I am trying to hit on a subject—an itinerary or a fiction—I can't yet do an autobiography—which will enable me to put my material in a continuous and united form instead of my usual patchwork. Can you help? If you can—Yours ever, Edward Thomas.[14]

The formality of the ending—used by him right up to the end—belies the intimacy hinted at in the 'can you help', and illustrates the delicate, unspoken nature of their relationship. Yet I think it is true that Eleanor could and did help Edward in his slow progress towards self-confidence and self-expression through poetry. She was not the only one to do so, nor is there anything startling to discover about their relationship. But after a long period of despair things were beginning to change.

When in October Edward sent Eleanor a copy of his last book of essays, *Light and Twilight*, commenting that they represented 'something which 3 years have shut a door on', he spoke of his sense of waiting for something to happen: 'during the last few weeks I have been like a misty wet dull flat shore, like that at Flansham when the sea seemed to have gone away for ever & I haven't believed in another tide.'[15] Was this empty state of mind a prelude to a major change of direction? Was it pure coincidence that it was just at this moment that Thomas happened to meet the man who was to prove the chief catalyst in his transformation into poet—Robert Frost? The meeting took place on 6 October 1913, but the reaction was not instantaneous, and otherwise Thomas's life continued as usual.

He took on two more poorly-paid commissions in the form of a small book on Keats (published in 1916) and one which began as 'Homes and Haunts of Writers' and was eventually published by Methuen as *A Literary Pilgrim in England* in 1917. The first was a simple and straightforward introduction to its subject, but the second proved as tiresome and detestable as the earlier book on 'Women & Poets' and for much the same reasons—the treatment demanded was essentially vulgarising. Thomas groaned over the book, called it 'Omes and Aunts' in disparagement and considered giving it up and forfeiting the £70 advance. Despite the pain of its creation, however, the book wears well, for the subject of a writer's relationship to the places where he has lived is not always trivial and was a theme Thomas was well fitted to tackle. Briefly but not hastily selecting the major places in the lives of thirty writers, it goes some way towards becoming a companion volume to *This England*, the anthology Thomas compiled two years later to express the idea of Englishness in verse. But Omes and Aunts took many months to complete, and in the meantime Thomas had embarked in a different direction—that of autobiography.

It was, he told Eleanor in December, 'an attempt to put on paper what he sees when he thinks of himself (E.T.) from 1878 to about 1895.'[16] The use of the third person indicates the task he had set himself: to write with objectivity and fidelity to fact. This was, for Thomas, a new form of literary self-discipline; hitherto his writing had always aimed at imaginative flights and higher significances. Now there were to be no dreams, no nymphs, nothing but undecorated actuality. 'I am trying to be true to the facts', he wrote. 'I extenuate nothing.' He was diffident: 'I don't trust myself to build up the self of which those things were true. I don't know what I was. I only know what I did.'[17] The structure was also a problem, for events tended to flow out of each other without cause and effect. Yet he did not wish to impose a structure on the material if to do so would mean faking.

One may appreciate how this meant a new way of writing for Thomas by comparing the treatment of the same theme in essay and autobiography. The subject is a child's romantic fantasies about his homeland. In a *Light and Twilight* essay called 'Home', a young soldier dying in the tropics recalls a childhood visit to 'the land of his fathers'. In his delirium, the real world of white-washed inns and stone-walled fields is mingled with the world of ancient battles and ruined castles. Everything is loaded with great sentiment; his brain is

> full of the mists, the mountains, the rivers, the fires in the fern, the castles, the knights, the kings and queens, the mountain boys at cricket, the old man with the foxes, the inn dogs lying in the sun . . . the mist . . . his country . . . the country he was going to, up and up and over the mountains, now that he was dying, now that he was dead . . .

The device of delirium is not illegitimate but interesting; why did Thomas choose it to convey this theme? Precisely because, surely, it permitted the mingling of fact and fancy, the bringing of knights and castles into the same world as old men and inn dogs. Wales had long represented this kind of ideal make-believe world in Thomas's imagination. In the auto-biography—published under the title of *The Childhood of Edward Thomas* in 1938—fact and fancy are clearly demarcated. As a child, he says, he visited Wales twice. The first time, at his aunt's house, he was told

> that a certain islet or peninsula or level meadow half-encircled by water was the site of King Arthur's Round Table. Either ideas suggested by 'King Arthur' and 'Round Table' even then vibrated in my brain or they remained there until, a very short time afterwards, they did so undoubtedly when united with the stories of love and battle in The Adventures of King Arthur and his Round Table. . . . Afterwards we had some days at Swansea with great-aunt Mary and I saw the sea and the Gower cliffs and rocks.[18]

The marked shift in style and tone indicates the new phase in Thomas's writing, and was, in effect, the reverse of the process he had set in motion when first beginning to write. Then he had endeavoured to adapt his own rather pedestrian manner to the more elevated style expected of essayists. Now he was beginning to throw off the over-literary manner and return to directness.

Fiction and autobiography were necessary stages in this progress. The latter, I believe, was written as a literary exercise rather than as an appraisal of Thomas's life, although it is incidentally an attractively straightforward account of childhood. It was meant to end at the year 1895, when Thomas was seventeen, and not proceed to adulthood in the usual autobiographical manner.[19] It was concerned above all with fidelity to memory, refusing to use imagination or interpretation to fill any gaps. Moreover, it was clearly not regarded as a priority but, as Thomas told his friend John Freeman, 'mainly an occupation for those days when I've no work and have nothing to be at but vain thought that comes against a Wall of China every 5 minutes & I can't fly nor have the patience to mine.'[20] What kind of blockage is represented by the 'Wall of China' cannot be known, but it is clear that Thomas hoped for some new purpose to his writing, some definitive change.

Robert Frost was not, as is often thought, the sole agent of this change, though without him it would never have happened. At the time of their meeting in 1913 Frost at thirty-eight was four years older than Thomas, also married and the father of four children, the two eldest of whom were about the same age as Mervyn and Bronwen and had been largely reared on a small farm in New England where the Frosts, assisted by an annuity, had attempted to run a poultry business. Since 1906–7 Frost had in fact abandoned the pretence of being a farmer and had become a teacher at the local school Pinkerton Academy until, in 1912, he had brought his family to Britain for a year to try if at last he could make his name as a poet. He had been writing, irregularly but seriously, since his schooldays but had made no more impact on the American literary scene than the occasional poem in magazines. In many ways the transatlantic market for verse at this time was greater than that in Britain, but still it looked to London and tended to neglect the home-grown poet.

On arrival in Britain Frost had assembled his poems into volume form and submitted them to the publishing firm of David Nutt; they were accepted and published early in 1913 as *A Boy's Will*. Unlike most first collections, the volume was arranged around a theme—that of growing from boyhood into manhood through fluctuating moods of withdrawal and return—and overall it was not badly received. It happened to be a good time to publish, for 1913 was the height of the pre-war revival of interest in poetry. The late-Victorian tradition was still popular, but the most admired poets—Tennyson, Swinburne, William Morris, Rossetti—were dead, while others such as Yeats appeared to have forsaken poetry for the theatre. Drama and fiction were the literary forms where most was happening. The major published poets of 1900–10 were the imperialists Newbolt, Noyes, Watson and Kipling, whose verse was admired, in the main, by non-literary readers. Hardy was writing some of his best poetry, but was still regarded as essentially a novelist, and thus paid little attention.

By 1913 a new generation of poets had begun to emerge, determined to make their voices heard and to reinvigorate the poetic scene. There were Walter de la Mare, John Masefield, James Stephens, Ralph Hodgson, W. H. Davies, Wilfrid Wilson Gibson, John Drinkwater, Rupert Brooke, Lascelles Abercrombie, Harold Monro and, not least, Ezra Pound, who arrived in London in 1909 and proceeded to make his very distinctive mark on literary society.

Things began to move in 1911 with the publication of Masefield's long poem 'The Everlasting Mercy'. With its vigorous narrative and daringly colloquial language, the poem made an immediate impact and its reception with the public acted as a stimulus to other writers, as they perceived that poetry could be popular, and that the public was ready for new things. In 1912 Harold Monro became for one glorious year editor of the Poetry Society journal *Poetry Review*. Under him its hitherto staid pages were devoted to publicising everything that was new and interesting in contemporary verse. The Poetry Society administrators were horrified, and took steps to relieve Monro of his post, but such was the enthusiasm generated by the *Review* that Monro immediately went on to found his own magazine, called *Poetry and Drama*, and to open a poetry centre in Bloomsbury, in a house and shop known as the Poetry Bookshop, where books were sold, poetry readings held, the magazine edited and needy poets accommodated (in attic bedsittingrooms).

At the same time another magazine was being edited by Middleton Murry and Katherine Mansfield. Called *Rhythm*, it was dedicated to all that was modern in literature and art; it contained poems, stories, criticism drawings and woodcuts. The visual side had strong connections with Paris, while the literary side shared contributors to some extent with *Poetry and Drama*, though *Rhythm* gave more space to fiction, and published many of Katherine Mansfield's short stories.

Despite these two magazines, the major event of 1912, rivalling the publication of 'The Everlasting Mercy' the year before, was the appearance of the anthology *Georgian Poetry* in December. This was a selection of seventeen new poets' work from the preceding two years, published by Monro. It was compiled by Edward Marsh—a famous figure in the literary history of this period, who combined the roles of career civil servant, as private secretary to Winston Churchill, then First Lord of the Admiralty, and patron of the arts, disbursing hospitality, encouragement and small amounts of cash to aspiring poets and painters. *Georgian Poetry*, which included contributions from most of the young poets listed above, was designed to present to a wider public evidence of the 'new beauty and strength' which were beginning to flower in contemporary verse. Rather than looking back to past success, it pointed forward to future achievements; thanks to a skilled blend of publicity (Marsh had literary-minded friends in high society and the volume became a fashionable Christmas present) and merit, the anthology was astonishingly successful. It not only brought in small amounts in the form of royalties to each contributor, many of whom had earned practically nothing from poetry, but it stimulated a wider readership for their work.[21]

It also provoked reaction and imitation. Ezra Pound, who had been asked to contribute and had refused on the grounds that the poem Marsh requested was unrepresentative of his current work, at once collected together a number of young poets not in *Georgian Poetry* and established a new vers libre mode which he called Imagisme, a direct rival to the 'Georgianism' which, thanks to the anthology, was now found on every hand. Within a few years Imagisme, Futurism, Vorticism and Modernism had all made their impact on English poetry. But in 1913 the Georgians were the vanguard of the new poetry.

At the height of the anthology's success, Monro opened his Poetry Bookshop in January 1913. A large crowd was present, including Thomas, invited in his capacity as reviewer, and Robert Frost, who had invited himself; but the two did not meet on this occasion. Through the Bookshop Frost met many of the Georgian poets, including Wilfrid Gibson and Ralph Hodgson.

Here we may pause a moment and look more closely at what was being written in this period. If we do so we shall see that the shift Thomas was laboriously making for himself in prose, from the high-flown work of the imagination and fancy to the plain and direct rendering of actuality, was also taking place in poetry as a whole. Over a decade, English poetry had been gradually loosening its dependence on the late-Romantic inheritance of dream, vision, and beauty.

This inheritance had restricted both the matter and manner of poetic composition. An anonymous critic was typical of many when he wrote: 'Things as they are are not beautiful . . . the first essence of poetry is beauty.'[22] Such an attitude was essentially Paterian in its view that art took one away from the everyday world into a world of beauty and perfection. As F. R. Leavis later pointed out (when the spirit was still not entirely laid to rest): 'Victorian poetry admits implicitly that the actual world is alien, recalcitrant and unpoetical and that no protest is worth making except the poetry of withdrawal'.[23] The idea was current that poetry was a magical kind of activity; in the words of A. C. Bradley, Oxford Professor of Poetry:

> Poetry is a spirit. It comes we know not whence. It will not speak at our bidding, nor answer in our language. It is not our servant; it is our master.[24]

The idea of the poetic world as one of dream and withdrawal is perhaps best exemplified by Swinburne, though it was pervasive in that generation. Dream permeates Swinburne's verse:

> Here, where the world is quiet;
>   Here, where all trouble seems
> Dead winds' and spent waves' riot
>   In doubtful dreams of dreams.

Though often hectic, the mood is always escapist:

> Let us take to us, now that the white skies thrill with a moon unarisen
> Swift horses of fear or of love, take flight and depart and not die.

A luxurious death-wish is perhaps his strongest theme:

> From too much love of living,
>   From hope and fear set free,
> We thank with brief thanksgiving
>   Whatever gods may be

>   That no life lives for ever;
>   That dead men rise up never;
>   That even the weariest river
>   Winds somewhere safe to sea.

Swinburne's verse had a wide appeal, despite the opinion that it was somewhat depraved and unfit for drawing rooms. The content probably was, but most of the appeal is to the ear and not the mind. If one looks closely at some of the lines, they are often 'extraordinary near nonsense', as Thomas was to put it in his own book on Swinburne. They are short on sense, but offer an aural flood of assonance and illusion, stimulating verbal intoxication through the use of rhythm and rhyme.

The entire poetic generation that came after Swinburne was marked with his influence; try as they might to escape, it was his manner that thrilled them most, and to an extent their comparative achievements can be measured by the distance they succeeded in putting between their own verse and his. Rupert Brooke was one such example. Poetically, he was weaned on Swinburne and never wholly lost his admiration, despite his mockery of the Victorian age and his determination to be different. His own verse varies from the cynically witty to the loosely sentimental, and when asked to give the first poetry reading at the new Poetry Bookshop he chose 'Selections from Donne and Swinburne'.[25]

In his own verse Brooke constantly echoed Swinburne and re-worked his images, particularly in his sonnets and love poems. Yet he poured scorn on the Victorian poetic mode, with its elevated language and predilection for ' "God, or Earth, or Eternity", or any of the Grand Old Endings'.[26] His two impulses came together in the taking of a Swinburne title, 'A Channel Passage', for a very 'modern' poem:

>   Do I forget you? Retchings twist and tie me,
>   Old meat, good meals, brown gobbets, up I throw.
>   Do I remember? Acrid return and slimy,
>   The slobs and slobber of a last year's woe.
>   And still the sick ship rolls. 'Tis hard, I tell ye,
>   To choose 'twixt love and nausea, heart and belly.

This is evidence of the radical change which was taking place in poetry. It was happening, most significantly, to W. B. Yeats.

As we saw in the chapter on pastoralism, Yeats's early work was heavily influenced by the anti-industrial impulse of the nineteenth century. He turned from the modern world towards that of mythology and the Irish peasantry. From 1904, when he was working at the Abbey Theatre, Dublin writing plays incorporating both heroes and peasants, he virtually gave up lyric poetry; when he returned, it was with a new approach. Hitherto, he said in *Responsibilities* (1914):

> I made my song a coat
> Covered with old embroideries

Now, he recognised:

> There's more enterprise
> In walking naked.

Yeats had been influenced by Synge. Looking back at his days at the Abbey in 'The Municipal Gallery Revisited', Yeats recalled how he, Synge and Lady Gregory had been inspired by a common vision of blending beauty with simplicity, 'Spenser with the common tongue', and of bringing everything to 'that sole test again, Dream of the noble and the beggar man'. Synge had his own version of the Abbey days. 'Yeats and I are running the show', he said. 'He looks after the stars and I do the rest.'[27] Synge also had firm opinions on the condition of poetry. He identified 'poetic material' as a limitation of the same kind as poetic diction and condemned the separation between the poetry of real life and that of 'a land of fancy', adding:

> What is highest in poetry is always reached when the dreamer is leaning out to reality, or where the man of real life is lifted out of it . . . When men lose their poetic feeling for ordinary life and cannot write poetry of ordinary things, their exalted poetry is likely to lose its strength of exaltation in the way men cease to build beautiful churches when they have lost happiness in building shops . . . it is the timber of poetry that wears most surely, and there is no timber that has not strong roots among the clay and worms. . . . It may almost be said that before verse can be made human again it must learn to be brutal.[28]

In his own short career as dramatist and poet, Synge's work blended both the beautiful and the brutal in plays such as *The Playboy of the Western World*, *Deirdre of the Sorrows*, *The Tinker's Wedding* and a number of poems that mix romance and realism.

Within a few years the young poets in England had followed Synge's lead. There was a great deal of opposition to the idea of everyday life in poetry, but Rupert Brooke was not alone in pointing out that this had led to poetry becoming too soft and pretty, and that there were other important things to write about:

> There are common or sordid things—situations or details—that may

suddenly bring all tragedy, or at least the brutality of actual emotions to you. I grasp rather relievedly at them after I've beaten vain hands in the rosy mists of poets' imaginings.[29]

He explained that by restricting itself to conventional 'beauties', poetry was denying itself large areas of life, for real beauty was to be found in unexpected, everyday places:

Half an hour's roaming about a street or village or railway station shows so much beauty that it is impossible to be anything but wild with suppressed exhilaration . . . In a flicker of sunlight on a blank wall, or a reach of muddy pavement, or smoke from an engine at night there's a sudden significance and importance and inspiration that makes the breath stop with a gulp of certainty and happiness.[30]

(The relevance of this in respect of Thomas's verse is clear.)

Others besides Brooke were changing the basis of their verse. For most it took the form of a return to simplicities of a Wordsworthian kind or a rendering of old truths in a new, direct manner. Thus Ralph Hodgson, in one of the most famous of Georgian poems, made Eve into a simple country girl tricked by a cunning serpent. Others took up the subject of modern life: Wilfrid Gibson's poems were set among the shipwrights, miners and fishermen of his native Northumberland, depicting hunger, unemployment, starvation, accidental death. For these verses he was christened by some 'poet of the common man', but he disputed this title with Masefield, who had followed 'The Everlasting Mercy' with other long narrative poems set among ordinary folk. Frost was also described in similar terms and although the title did not really fit any of the three, it is significant that only a few years earlier the idea of poetry encompassing the common man would have seemed a contradiction in terms.

The common voice was being heard too. Indeed, perhaps the most important change in poetry was the return to speech. Thus Gibson rendered the interior monologue of an unemployed girl:

> For she would rather drop stone-dead
> Than live as some . . . if she had cared
> To feed upon the devil's bread,
> She could have earned it easily . . .
> She'd pride enough to starve instead,
> Ay, starve than fare as some girls fared.
> But that was all behind . . .

Masefield had made a breakthrough by using the word 'bloody' in 'The Everlasting Mercy', even if it was printed with a dash. Lascelles Abercrombie was equally daring in his dialogue about the burghers of Calais, where the following exchanges take place:

> Pierre: I'm going to spew.
> Andrieu: Good lad! Why not?
> Jacques: For God's sake mind my legs—

and

> Eustache: Look out, behind!
> 'Ware turds! the street's a patch of muck.

Abercrombie set out his views on poetic language in a paper to the English Association, in which he said he was

> certain the whole of language must be left open to the poet. We cannot allow any pedantic hedgerows to fence him out of this tract or that, with notices stuck up alleging that it is too new for him or too old, or too scientific, or too commercial—or even too poetic.

and even advocated the use of slang:

> I even believe there is not only convenience but real and positive value for poetry in the use of forms like *don't* and *won't*: ... Don't is not simply a contraction of do not; it is somehow another and slightly different form of verbal life.[31]

This, then, is the context against which Edward Thomas's writing should be seen. Not everyone was happy with the trend towards collo-quialism. Many still felt that poetry was poetry precisely because it was not speech, not language used in an everyday manner, but in an elevated mode to express elevated feelings, to depict uncommon things. Gordon Bottomley criticised a new work on the grounds that in it words were used 'in the spirit of the prose writer and not freed from everyday syntax.'[32] John Drinkwater complained of an anti-romantic poem by Brooke, saying that though the fact that the beloved would certainly age was 'true in fact', it was not 'poetically true'[33]—meaning that poetic convention did not admit of such a theme in love poetry. Walter de la Mare, reviewing a verse play of Abercrombie's, claimed that 'Not even Mr Abercrombie can put a policeman into poetry without imperilling both.'[34] On language, even Abercrombie had his limits; he said sternly:

It would not do to make common speech into a sort of idol . . . It would be very difficult, for instance, to use the word 'bicycle' in poetry . . . It began empty, and an empty word takes a long time to fill.[35]

Oddly, he does not seem to have considered that poetry might sometimes need to use empty words.

Though they offered resistance, the traditionalists were in fact fighting a losing battle and it was not long before the argument was overtaken by events: first by the Imagists, who rejected both metre and rhyme, which turned the Georgians into conservatives, for they clung to established forms, and then by the war, whose all too real brutality made concepts of 'beauty' seem irrelevant. But the shifts that had taken place in the pre-war period were important, for without them war poetry might never have been possible. And it is interesting to note that even Ezra Pound, the originator of modernism, was himself influenced by the changes begun by the Georgians. Pound's early work was post-Victorian, looking back to an implicitly pastoral medieval or Provençal world, using frequent archaisms, but from 1909 his verse took on a contemporary cast, in line with many of the Georgians. And when in 1912–13 Edward Thomas began to alter the nature of his prose writing, relinquishing the quest for beauty and escape in favour of actuality and a plain, unrhetorical style, he was clearly mirroring the changes that were taking place elsewhere in literature, and preparing himself for his eventual appearance as a modern poet.

7

Wringing Rhetoric's Neck

Yes. I remember Adlestrop—
The name, because one afternoon
Of heat the express-train drew up there
Unwontedly. It was late June.

'Adlestrop'

On the edge of all the activity in poetry, Thomas had attained a position of some importance as a critic of new verse. He reviewed regularly for several papers: the *Daily Chronicle*, the *Nation*, the *Morning Post*, the *Saturday Review*, the *Bookman* and the *New Weekly*. He thus read much dross, the lists of slim volumes published at this period, frequently at the author's expense, being dismayingly long (according to Arthur Ransome, Thomas kept the very worst of these, that even the secondhand booksellers would not accept, beside the fire for additional fuel[1]), but he also kept in touch with new developments and, as time went on, helped to influence them by his judgments. There is evidence that he took this task seriously. He had high standards, and few poets won unqualified praise; among those whom he rated most highly were W. H. Davies and Walter de la Mare, whose *Peacock Pie* was one of his favourite books. Robert Frost became another such.

When Frost's first book, *A Boy's Will*, was published in 1913, Thomas needed to look no further than Frost's opening poem 'Into My Own' to sense a kindred spirit:

One of my wishes is that those dark trees,
So old and firm they scarcely show the breeze,
Were not, as 'twere, the merest mask of gloom,
But stretched away unto the edge of doom.

I should not be withheld but that some day
Into their vastness I should steal away
Fearless of ever finding open land
Or highway where the slow wheel pours the sand.

I do not see why I should e'er turn back,
Or those should not set forth upon my track
To overtake me, who should miss me here
And long to know if I still held them dear.

They would not find me changed from him they knew—
Only more sure of all I thought was true.

Here was a man who knew about the desire to run away, to lose himself walking in the woods, to escape from other people. His verse, subtle and often ambivalent, was the record of a struggle both with himself and with the outside world.

Thomas asked Ralph Hodgson to arrange a meeting with this new American poet. On 5 October 1913 he wrote to Eleanor explaining that he might not see her for tea the next day: 'I have an appointment of uncertain time with an American just before & may not be able to come.'[2] The meeting took place at the St George's restaurant in St Martin's Lane, where Thomas had met Arthur Ransome and where he still called to see his literary friends on his visits to town, but, as Eleanor noted,[3] he said nothing afterwards of his new acquaintance. The first recorded communication between Thomas and Frost is in fact a letter card from Thomas dated 17 December, arranging a second meeting, again at the St George's, in company with F. S. Flint, W. H. Davies and Ralph Hodgson.[4]

Meetings continued through the winter of 1913-14, which Thomas spent almost entirely away from home. In November he again went to stay with the Locke Ellises at East Grinstead, working on his book on Keats and, intermittently, on his autobiography. 'It's very lean', he told Eleanor in December, 'but I feel the shape of the sentences and alter continually with some unseen end in view.'[5] As the end approached he commented that it was time he looked forward rather than back. He continued to toy with the idea of fiction. In January he moved to stay in Clifford Bax's town apartment in West Kensington.[6]

He was clearly in a state of great tension, anxious for a decisive change in his life, yet unable to find the appropriate direction. Late in 1913 he contemplated a drastic move by applying for a lecturing job with the London County Council education department, but the application was no sooner submitted than withdrawn. Thomas apologised to Edward Garnett and W. H. Hudson, whom he had asked for references: 'The fact is knowing I had to do something I stupidly pretended to be brave when really lecturing was as impossible to me as sailoring . . . I am very sorry indeed that I troubled you before I discovered what I was really going to do.'[7]

The idea had perhaps been supplied by Frost, who had found greater maturity and self-confidence through his teaching job at Pinkerton

Academy, and soon came to understand Thomas's need. Indeed, as they got to know each other, the two men discovered remarkable similarities in their character and experiences, which gave their friendship a unique quality. Though inhabiting distant and different worlds—one in small-town New England and the other on the fringes of literary London—their lives had uncanny correspondences. [8]

Towards the end of his school career, Frost had shown signs of great literary promise, just as had Thomas, and had foreseen a successful future for himself. He had nurtured this ambition for twenty years before coming to Britain and at last finding the beginning of the rainbow. Thomas was still waiting for his breakthrough. He was just four years younger than Frost. The Frost and Thomas marriages had their similarities, too. At the age of seventeen Frost had fallen in love with his classmate Elinor White, and with her pledged a secret, open-air betrothal, though it was four more years before they were married. Founded on romantic idealism, the marriage had been in many ways a rough one, largely because of Frost's changeable moods and his refusal to settle for a secure, humdrum existence. There were four children and an insufficient income. Frost had started many projects and abandoned them for reasons known only to himself: he had left Dartmouth College after a term, and later failed to finish a course at Harvard. He had tried his hand at poultry farming and several other occupations, which were supposed to bring in easy money; to date teaching was the only one he had stuck to and succeeded in.

Temperamentally, Frost inclined towards flight; he had run away from several unpleasant situations. He had varying moods of delight and despair, and once or twice he had been gripped with immature suicidal intent; like Thomas, he had once brandished a revolver in front of his wife. The death of their first child in infancy had put great strain on the marriage. Elinor, who had abandoned a promising career of her own to marry Frost, tended towards the long-suffering, and her husband felt she punished him with silence. Unlike Helen Thomas, she did not flourish on motherhood, nor was she a natural homemaker; like Thomas, Frost blamed himself and took it out on his wife. Both women had married men they believed to be geniuses, only to find recognition a long time coming and daily life often trying.

In contrast to Thomas, however, Frost had a combative personality, prone to rages and sometimes violence against others. Once he had been in court for punching a neighbour in an imagined dispute. Gradually he had come to understand the emotional displacement in this and to learn from his quick temper. He evolved the personal philosophy that, in the words of his biographer, 'the best way out is often through.' From the quarrel with himself he had, slowly, created his poetry, and he had reached the age of thirty-eight with a small stock of around thirty verses. [9]

Thomas, by comparison, had virtually given himself up to self-pity and luxurious despair—'weakness was all my boast' he was to write later. He had lost all faith in himself and his writing. Yet through all the bad years he could no less than Frost relinquish his ambition: proud, defensive and spiky, he clung to the residual belief that he was worth something after all.

Recognising so many of his own feelings, Frost was able to offer just what Thomas needed. Hitherto Thomas's acquaintances had been either impatient with his troubles or too sympathetic, too ready to make allowances for his moodiness. Frost offered sympathy without indulgence, and positive advice.

The first form of advice was personal. Thomas was now more or less formally living away from his family, and according to Frost's biographer had 'become obsessed with the notion that he should divorce his wife.' Frost opposed this idea; as his biographer put it:

> Frost could tell Thomas a great deal about the vicissitudes of marital relations, but he was not willing to talk about them as grounds for divorce. If he had learnt the mistaken aspects of walking out, running away, escape, he was not yet convinced that the ambivalence of these terms should be reduced to one pejorative meaning . . .
>
> Marriage was only one kind of struggle involving alternations of love and hate—and not the most important. As long as he lived, he thought he'd be fighting a continuous battle on various fronts, and he felt he'd have to settle for nothing more or less than temporary victories. The wounds borne, the suffering, the anguish experienced in all these different conflicts could be survived if anyone possessed as ufficiently intense desire to accomplish one particular thing, come hell or high water . . .[10]

Perhaps, as Frost talked and admired Thomas's latest writings, Thomas began to feel that he could still take control of his life and hope to realise his ambitions. At any rate he dropped the idea of divorce although remaining convinced that love, as he remembered it, had vanished from his life for ever. In February 1914 he returned home to the new cottage in Steep; thanks to Geoffrey Lupton's generosity he still kept the study to work in.

Frost's advice appeared to have been sound. On 22 February Thomas wrote to Eleanor that he was 'glad to be back and to watch the plain and the downs from my study. We are all well and liking one another.'[11] He had finished his autobiography, which Eleanor typed, and now returned to the hated Omes and Aunts. But he did not complain: indeed his letters indicate an altogether more cheerful frame of mind. Most noticeable is the number of sentences in his letters from this period using the term 'we'— a verbal indication that he had once again returned to being and feeling a family man. 'Meantime we are most busy', he wrote in March, 'gardening, writing, typewriting for me from morning till 1 a.m. and on the whole it suits me, tho I feel thin at times.'[12]

On 25 March Thomas went to stay with the Frosts at their home at Beaconsfield in Buckinghamshire, and the friendship began to flourish; for the next few months the two men were seldom away from each other for more than a few weeks at a time. They had, they found, not only experiences in common but also opinions. Walking in the countryside, they discussed and confirmed each other's ideas—on literature particularly Frost's evolving notion that poetry should, as far as possible, conform to speech rhythms and follow normal syntax, rather than using an artificial 'poetic' mode whose chief feature was its lack of similarity to everyday spoken language. We have seen how this was returning to poetry; Frost was one of the first to work out a description and to some extent an analysis of this. Thomas urged him to publish his ideas in 'a book on speech and literature'. Otherwise, he warned, Frost would find him taking the ideas and doing it himself.[13] He was beginning to make use of them in his own work. We shall see later how Thomas's writing developed as a result of Frost's influence.

In the preceding twelve months, Thomas had tried out two new literary modes and in the process effected a subtle change in his literary style, though he did not yet know in what direction this would take him. Quite unaware of the fact, he was more than halfway to poetry. At the same time he had made several new friendships which either incidentally, in the case of the Bax/Farjeon circle, or directly, in the case of Frost, were to help him towards his emergence as a poet later in the year. Frost's influence was decisive, as many commentators have pointed out and as Thomas himself knew: the figure he had been long searching for in the shape of a young and beautiful maiden, who would change his life, had arrived in the shape of a nearly middle-aged American.

When Thomas first visited the Frosts, they were about to move from Beaconsfield, which they considered too suburban, to join Wilfrid Gibson and Lascelles Abercrombie in their rural retreat on the borders of Gloucestershire and Herefordshire. Frost was urged to come and see what true country life was like. The Abercrombies' home at Ryton, near Dymock, was much admired: a fine cottage, half thatched and timbered, and called The Gallows after a local legend. Some two miles away at Greenway was the Old Nailshop, also thatched and timbered, which Gibson took on his marriage in December 1913. The area is remote but gentle, a landscape of small fields, meadows and orchards, bounded on the north by the Malvern Hills, on the south by May Hill and the Forest of Dean, on the west by Wales and on the east by the River Severn. Here, as Mrs Abercrombie recalled,

the earth is a rich red loam, small hills covered with firs and birch, and acres of orchard, for we were in the midst of the cider making country. The sight of the blossoming of the apple and cherry trees in spring was unforgettable, with miles and miles of daffodils pouring over the ground (in medieval times they were grown as a crop for the dye.)[14]

Demographically, the area was static and tending towards decline. Socially it was a surviving outpost of near-feudal paternalism and deference towards landlord and gentry. The landowner and patron of Dymock itself was Lord Beauchamp (the title an ancient one resurrected in 1815), a civil and conscientious landlord but one whose presence was felt mainly through the bailiff and gamekeeper. These held considerable power over the villagers, who were not allowed to 'trespass' in the local fields and woods. At harvest and apple-picking time there were strong traditions of mutual help and co-operation, and the Frosts noted with pleasure that it was the local custom for each house to have a barrel of home-pressed cider to offer visitors. Other traditional attitudes survived in the shape of social divisions, which were visible and observed. Roughly a third of the community were farm labourers and their families. Rural depopulation had affected this area as others; the villages, never large, had suffered a net decline in inhabitants, one result of which was to make more than the usual number of cottages available for rent to impecunious poets. Not so many years before, the Gibsons' house had been the home and workplace of a thriving family of nailmakers.

The Frosts arrived in Dymock in April, welcomed by Gibson and Abercrombie, and rented a small black and white house called Little Iddens about a mile west of the Gibsons, in an area known as the Leadington, close to the river. Frost wrote home:

We are far from any town ... on a lane where no automobiles come. We can go almost anywhere we wish on wavering footpaths through the fields. The fields are so small and the trees so numerous along the hedges that, as my friend Thomas says in the loveliest book on spring in England, you may think from a little distance that the country was solid woods.[15]

Almost as soon as the Frosts were installed, Thomas arrived on a visit; on 24 April Gibson recorded him taking lodgings in the district for a week.[16] Thomas noted that it was 'a part of the country I had never known before', and later recalled:

In April here I had heard, among apple trees in flower, not the first cuckoo, but the first abundance of day-long calling cuckoos; here the first nightingale's song, though too far off and intermittently, twitched away by gusty night winds; here I found the earliest may blossom which, by May Day, while I still lingered, began to dapple the hedges thickly and no rain fell yet the land was sweet.[17]

During a few short months of fine weather in the summer of 1914, the literary fraternity in Gloucestershire led an idyllic existence. In May, June and July they spent their time exploring the countryside, tasting the local rough cider, walking, talking and writing poetry. It was, in some degree, a consummation of the pastoral ideal on the literary side of the Back to the Land movement, and it would be surprising if Thomas, a frequent visitor, had not found much to envy in the Dymock poets' life that summer.

Lascelles Abercrombie, like Thomas himself, had early decided on a career as a writer in the country. He had been a trainee quantity surveyor in Liverpool, until his first volume of poems, widely acclaimed, was published in 1908.[18] Later the same year he went to work as book reviewer and leader writer on the *Liverpool Courier* but as soon as he was able to negotiate a freelance arrangement with the *Courier* and two other papers whereby regular reviewing gave him an assured income, he left Merseyside and as he said 'bolted' for the country. With his wife Catherine he settled first at Much Marcle in Herefordshire and then a few miles away at Ryton. Two children were born in quick succession and a third in 1914. Abercrombie delighted in his new-found freedom; years later he wrote:

Now I could do what I liked. Or very nearly. At any rate now when I had finished writing for the night I could step out of doors and smell country air and hear the stream sounding and the owls calling. What great things I meant to do now I was my own man and living at last in the country![19]

In the mornings he worked at his reviews or on commissioned work such as his study of Thomas Hardy, published in the same series as Thomas's books on Pater and Swinburne. In the afternoons he was out walking, for his tenancy with Lord Beauchamp included express permission to ramble at will in the fields and coverts provided the game were not disturbed. In the evenings, he could sit before a great log fire reading for pleasure or writing his own poems. Catherine Abercrombie was equally delighted with life in the country. The Gallows had no mod cons—electricity and running water were extremely rare in country cottages at this date—and no servants, by her own choice, but she seems to have relished the simple life as much as her husband. As at the Thomases', life was lived out of doors as much as possible, as Mrs Abercrombie recalled in 1956:

'I had a permanent gipsy tent under the Seven Sisters, as the elms at the end of the garden were called and sometimes I would have an iron pot over the fire with a duck and green peas stewing in it, and Lascelles and John Drinkwater and Wilfrid Gibson would sit around and read their latest poems to each other, as I lay on a stoop of hay and listened and watched the stars wander through the elms and thought I really had found the why and wherefore of life. The Great Wars had not started then and one's mind could peacefully rest on loveliness and hopefulness as never again.[20]

The income needed to sustain such a pleasant life was relatively modest. In the four years from 1909 to 1913 Abercrombie calculated his earnings at around £210–220 per annum, about £4 per week. This may be compared with a farm labourer's 15s to 20s per week, and with Virginia Woolf's £600 a year. Edward Thomas was earning rather more—over £300 a year —but Abercrombie had as yet no school fees to pay and was content to be poor.[21]

More importantly, his poetry was highly regarded. Virtually unremembered today, Abercrombie was held to be among the foremost poets of his time; the *TLS* review of *Georgian Poetry* placed him at the head of the list, as having 'the most conspicuous union of breadth and intensity'.[22] He had also overcome some of the problems faced by poets whose work was lengthy or difficult to place in magazines by printing two of his own long poems in pamphlet form for sale by post. The success of *Georgian Poetry* convinced him that there was a paying market for verse.

And so, in the summer of 1913, Abercrombie and Gibson had got together with two fellow Georgians, Rupert Brooke and John Drinkwater, to publish their own new work in a quarterly magazine called *New Numbers*, sold on subscription from The Gallows. Brooke had been abroad, travelling in America and the Pacific, when the scheme was launched; at irregular intervals he mailed home packets of verse—one or two of which, it is interesting to note, were rejected by his fellow-editors as too crude even for their avant-garde tastes.[23]

When the Frosts arrived in Dymock, the second issue of *New Numbers* had just been printed. Thomas reviewed it in the *Daily Chronicle* on 29 April. The third issue was being planned when Brooke arrived home and at the end of June he paid a flying visit to the Gibsons. His visit coincided with that of Edward and Helen Thomas, who were on a short holiday. This was the first time Helen had met the Frosts; arrangements were being made for the whole Thomas family to return for the month of August.

The weather was still fine; later Thomas wrote of 'the consummation of midsummer, the weather radiant and fresh, yet hot and rainless, the white and pink wild roses, the growing bracken, and the last and best of the songs, blackbird's and blackcap's.'[24] The field next to The Gallows was covered in bright poppies, and Mrs Abercrombie recalled Brooke gazing at them as if intent on collecting images of England. He was the only one present to take the rumours of war seriously. There was a gathering of all the poets at the Gibsons' home, commemorated by Gibson in a poem called 'The Golden Room' and addressed to his wife Geraldine:

> Do you remember the still summer evening
> When in our cosy, cream-washed living room
> Of the Old Nailshop, we all talked and laughed—
> Our neighbours from The Gallows, Catherine
> And Lascelles Abercrombie; Rupert Brooke;
> Elinor and Robert Frost, living awhile
> At Little Iddens, who'd brought with them
> Helen and Edward Thomas? In the lamplight
> We talked and laughed, but for the most part listened
> While Robert Frost kept on and on and on
> In his slow New England fashion for our delight,
> Holding us with shrewd turns and racy quips
> And the rare twinkle of his grave blue eyes?
> We sat there in the lamplight, while the day
> Died from rose-latticed casements, and the plovers
> Called over the low meadows, till the owls
> Answered them from the elms, we sat and talked—
> Now a quick flash from Abercrombie, now
> A murmured dry half-heard aside from Thomas,
> Now a clear laughing word from Brooke; and then
> Again Frost's rich and ripe philosophy
> That had the body and tang of good draught cider
> And poured as clear a stream.

Thomas and Brooke were old acquaintances. They had first met while Brooke was at Cambridge and Thomas about to move into the new house at Wick Green. The reason had been Noel Olivier, youngest daughter of Sir Sydney Olivier, and a pupil at Bedales. Brooke had fallen in love with Noel but had been forbidden by her sisters to declare his love and had therefore to devise stratagems for meeting her by accident. One of these involved a careful plan for Brooke and a friend to be walking along the river Eden in Sussex when the four Olivier sisters happened to be on a camping holiday with Godwin Baynes and David Garnett. It was in this company that Thomas and Brooke had first met, and the acquaintance was renewed the following year when Brooke came down to Petersfield, before starting a Fabian speaking tour through Hampshire and Dorset by horse-drawn caravan, expounding the reform of the Poor Law to village audiences. Before setting off, Brooke asked the Thomases to fix a meeting with Noel. She was invited over to tea.

Later in 1910, in October, Brooke invited Thomas to stay with him at The Orchard, Grantchester, and shortly afterwards Brooke was back again at Wick Green, staying in the house while Helen was away. The two men cooked for themselves and in the evening sat talking; Thomas listened while Brooke read his latest poems.[25] A comparison of their work will show that Brooke and Thomas shared similar preoccupations: feelings for the countryside, dreams of idealised women and a longing to escape into oblivion. This, it may be said, was on the Swinburnian side; on the other, both shared an irreverent attitude towards society and its institutions, and both were confirmed atheists, albeit with Platonic tendencies. It is likely that Thomas admired the young man's good humour and ease of manner, the more so because he himself was in one of his low periods. Later, in an obituary notice of Brooke, Thomas wrote:

> He stretched himself out, drew his fingers through his waved fair hair, laughed, talked indolently and admired as much as he was admired . . . He was tall, broad and easy in his movements. Either he stooped, or he thrust his head forward unusually much to look at you with his steady blue eyes.[26]

When Brooke's first volume of poems was published at the end of 1911, Thomas reviewed it in the *Daily Chronicle*, calling it 'a symptomatic quintessence of the rebellious attitude today':

> Now and then he gives himself away, as when, in three poems close together, he speaks of the scent of warm clover. Copies should be bought by everyone over forty who has never been under forty. It will be a revelation. Also if they live yet a little longer they may see Mr Rupert Brooke a poet. He will not be a little one.[27]

The two met again in February 1913 when Thomas was invited to breakfast with Brooke and Edward Marsh, in whose Grays Inn apartment Brooke was a temporary lodger. The invitation must have been Brooke's, but the occasion was a disaster. Thomas was uncomfortable and morose and gave the impression of disliking both his hosts and the food.

It is not surprising that Thomas failed to hit it off with the urbane and cultured Marsh, who mixed with the titled reaches of London society. At the Grays Inn breakfast, Thomas probably had little to contribute to the gathering; his conversation was not amusing nor did he frequent first nights. He was not even very enthusiastic about *Georgian Poetry*. When, after Thomas's death, Marsh was compiling the third volume of *Georgian Poetry*, at least three of the contributors urged him to include

Thomas's work, and Walter de la Mare even offered to stand down in his favour.[28] Marsh refused, on the ostensible grounds that no poet should be represented posthumously, but had his critical judgment been better he might have waived this self-made rule. Had he done so, the name of Georgian might have stood higher, though it is also arguable that Thomas's reputation would have suffered by association. Overall, Thomas was better off for not being included in the Georgian anthologies.

Brooke was about to leave for North America and beyond; before he left he wrote to Thomas to see if they could meet in order that he 'could leave the muses of England in your keeping. I do that anyhow. Feed the brutes.'[29] This was a tribute to Thomas's position as critic of new poetry, the role in which he was best known to other poets in Gloucestershire. Thomas had admired Abercrombie's work; in his review of *Interludes and Poems* (1908) he had written:

in these poems a whole man, imaginative, intuitive, reflective, observant, passionate in his relations with life, is to be seen burning with original language, in towering and sweeping flames. . . . He has that most modern of modern qualities, the feeling for what is primitive . . . he has captured the rude sweet beauty of Nature . . .[30]

He had not been so polite about Wilfrid Gibson, of whose earlier work he had said:

Wilfrid Wilson Gibson long ago swamped his small delightful gift by his abundance. He is essentially a minor poet in the bad sense, for he is continually treating subjects poetically, writing about things instead of creating them.[31]

Of Gibson's later verse narrative Thomas remarked: 'He has merely been embellishing what would have been far more effective as pieces of rough prose . . . The verse has added nothing except unreality, not even brevity.'[32]

For their part, Abercrombie's and Gibson's attitudes towards Thomas probably reflected the common view—that he was a failed writer who made his living as a critic. Abercrombie, in his role as critic, had demolished Thomas's book on Swinburne with 'lusty derision',[33] but on a personal level the two men found they liked each other well enough. At the end of the summer Thomas was writing to Bottomley saying he had seen too much of Gibson and too little of Abercrombie.[34]

But it was Frost whom he had come to be with. And when the Thomas family returned at the beginning of August for a long visit, there was only one thing to hinder their enjoyment. War had been declared against Germany.

There was at first not much interruption of the holiday. War, though a serious matter, was not expected to concern the civilian population too directly. The poets' walks and picnics continued as planned, for Abercrombie and Gibson were keen to show Frost and Thomas as much of the countryside as possible. Frost planned for Thomas to return to New England with him, to see if a change would not work some alteration in his situation. Thomas was sceptical, but tempted; it was the friendship that was important to him.

This Thomas later recorded in his poem 'The Sun Used to Shine':

> The sun used to shine while we two walked
> Slowly together, paused and started
> Again, and sometimes mused, sometimes talked
> As either pleased, and cheerfully parted
>
> Each night. We never disagreed
> Which gate to rest on. The to be
> And the late past we gave small heed.
> We turned from men or poetry
>
> To rumours of the war remote
> Only till both stood disinclined
> For aught but the yellow flavorous coat
> Of an apple wasps had undermined;
>
> Or a sentry of dark betonies,
> The stateliest of small flowers on earth,
> At the forest verge; or crocuses
> Pale purple as if they had their birth
>
> In sunless Hades fields.

The cheerful rambling of the opening is gradually darkened by the references to the war which, from being a remote rumour, comes to dominate the poem:

> The war
> Came back to mind with the moonrise
> Which soldiers in the east afar
> Beheld then. Nevertheless, our eyes
>
> Could as well imagine the Crusades
> Or Caesar's battles. Everything

To faintness like those rumours fades—
Like the brook's water glittering

Under the moonlight—like those walks
Now—like us two that took them, and
The fallen apples, all the talks
And silences—like memory's sand

When the tide covers it late or soon,
And other men through other flowers
In those fields under the same moon
Go talking and have easy hours.

Frost's second book, *North of Boston*, had been published in May. As well as a small number of Frost's best-known lyrics such as 'After Apple-Picking', 'Mending Wall' and 'Birches', it contained long poems in blank verse—'The Death of the Hired Man', 'A Hundred Collars', 'The House-keeper' and others—domestic narratives based on the lives of New England hill folk and similar in conception, though not in sentiment or execution, to the Northumbrian dialogues Gibson had produced. Frost had cultivated his new friends with favour as well as friendship in mind, and he was rewarded with a number of good reviews—from Abercrombie, Gibson and Thomas (twice). Thanks to their conversations with the author, the reviewers were able to expand on his theories of poetry—and how, as Abercrombie noted, the verse sentences 'if spoken aloud, are most felicitously true in rhythm to the emotion.'[35] This was the spoken cadence, the speech rhythms which Thomas and Frost advocated for verse.

The theory of this may be understood from Frost's explanation:

A sentence is a sound in itself on which other sounds called words may be strung . . .
    The sentence-sounds . . . are apprehended by the ear. They are gathered by the ear from the vernacular and brought into books. . . . I think no writer invents them. The most original writer only catches them fresh from talk, where they grow spontaneously . . .
Remember that the sentence sound often says more than the words. It may even as irony convey a meaning opposite to the words.[36]

An easier way of describing what was meant was recalled by Eleanor Farjeon, who late in August came to stay in Dymock for a few days, on an occasion when she, Thomas and Frost were

strolling along a lane and Robert was talking of what he called the 'cadence' in the human voice which accompanied the speech that came natural to it . . . While we talked, we saw across two hedgerows a man's figure standing against the skyline on top of a cart; he had a fork in his hands with which he attacked some load, corn or manure, pitched from below. Frost stopped and shouted a question across the fields—it might have been 'What are you doing there, this fine afternoon?' but whatever the words the man could not have heard them. He too shouted some answer that rang through the air, and it was impossible for us to distinguish what he said. But the cadence of the answer was as clear as that of the question. Robert turned to Edward. 'That's what I mean', he said.[37]

In practice, the speech cadence resulted in poems of narrative and dialogue such as Frost's 'A Servant to Servants', which begins:

> I didn't make you know how glad I was
> To have you come and camp here on our land.
> I promised myself to get down some day
> And see the way you lived, but I don't know!
> With a houseful of hungry men to feed
> I guess you'd find. . . . It seems to me
> I can't express my feelings, any more
> Than I can raise my voice or want to lift
> My hand (Oh, I can lift it when I have to).

By now Thomas was quite sure of his views. Reviewing *North of Boston* in the *English Review* he said:

The result is a unique type of eclogue, homely, racy, and touched by a spirit that might, under other circumstances, have made pure lyric on the one hand or drama on the other . . . The language ranges from a never vulgar colloquialism to brief moments of heightened and intense simplicity. There are moments when the plain language and lack of violence make the unaffected verses look like prose.[38]

In the *Daily News*, he had opened his review with the words: 'This is one of the most revolutionary books of modern times, but one of the quietest and least aggressive.'[39]

Thomas's and Frost's ideas on verse were now virtually indistinguishable and had been amplified and developed in many conversations. How much was due to either man it is impossible to say, but it is clear that Thomas had as much to contribute as Frost on the subject of poetry and prose, plain speech and rhetoric.

He had, as we have seen, been moving in this direction for some time. His own writing had been fined down. He had abandoned the inflated

rhetorical language and style of his essays in the Aesthetic mode, in favour
of 'the truth or nothing', and in doing so he had been helped by his
critical books, in particular his study of Walter Pater, which had been
commissioned in 1911 by Martin Secker.[40] Reading this work, one can
almost watch Thomas moving from youthful admiration to disenchanted
impatience with the high-flown Paterian style. The book opens and closes
with lengthy, high-flown tributes to Pater as the 'half-hero, half-martyr
of Style', who

> as he begins to speak, a curtain falls upon the world; the light is
> changed ... clear and graceful forms appear in it, an architecture, a
> humanity, a race of animals and trees and plants, more exquisite than
> the eye has seen ... with a self-control and decorum beyond the dreams
> of virtue.

but inside the criticism is fierce:

> On almost every page of his writing words are to be seen sticking out,
> like the raisins that will get burnt on an ill-made cake.

and

> his prose embalms choice things, as seen at choice moments, in choice
> words.

He added that Pater must be seen, not read aloud, when his words 'betray
their artificiality by a lack of natural expressive rhythm.' Thomas was
already developing his thoughts on literature and speech when he remarked
elsewhere in the book that 'It is the last thing that many writers would
think of, to write as they speak'. He himself was only just beginning to do so.
    The attack on rhetoric was extended with Thomas's next critical book,
on Swinburne, also commissioned by Martin Secker and published in
1912.[41] He began by praising Swinburne's renowned musicality and
magic, saying that if the reader submitted to these elements he would be
enraptured by the poetry. Like his contemporaries, Thomas had read
Swinburne in adolescence, and no doubt succumbed to the hypnotic
rhythms and incantatory words. Now, however, his attitude was detached,
even contemptuous: 'He kept as it were a harem of words, to which he
was constant and absolutely faithful ... He used them more often out of
compliment than necessity.' He suggested that most could be 'safely
transposed in half a dozen ways without affecting the sense.' Rhyme, he
added, 'acted upon Swinburne as a pill to purge ordinary responsibilities',
and he claimed that any attempt to follow Swinburne's thought logically
led nowhere, for the sense was often 'extraordinary near nonsense'.

Finally, of Swinburne's rhythms he said that they tended towards 'a musical jargon that includes human snatches but is not and never could be speech.'

In fact, Thomas had long admired direct and simple verse, even while his own prose remained elaborate and laboured. Of W. H. Davies's *New Poems* (1906) he had written

> There is hardly a poem which is not a thing of entirely new beauty on account of its truth and imagination and above all the impression it leaves of coming straight from the spirit of a strange, vivid, unlearned, experienced man.[42]

Yeats's play *The King's Threshold* prompted him to say:

> In reading this play I seem to find with astonishment that verse is the natural speech of men, as singing is of birds.[43]

Of Synge's *Playboy of the Western World*, he said

> the talk has at once the character that seems almost to have caught an accent or brogue in it and a poetry that has nothing to do with invention but falls naturally out of the life of the speakers, as apples fall in a still night. The talk, all of it, is like poetry in its richness, its simplicity, its remoteness from the spoken print of towns.[44]

He had even praised Pound's *Personae* (1909) in the following terms:

> No remarkable melody; no golden words shot with meaning; a temperate use of images, and none far-fetched; no flattering of modern fashions in descriptions of nature; no apostrophe, no rhetoric, nothing 'Celtic'. It is the old miracle that cannot be defined: nothing more than a subtle entanglement of words, so that they rise out of their graves and sing.[45]

before being reprimanded by Bottomley and others, and recanting of his enthusiasm.[46]

Of the poet whose work Thomas's was most to resemble, he confessed that he preferred Mr Hardy's verse to his fiction[47] and found in *Time's Laughingstocks* (1909)

> a changing burden which is full if not of magic yet of a deep and strong suggestion of something which the intellect alone cannot handle. . . . Seldom does anything creep in from nature or the spirit of humanity to give his work a something not to be accounted for in what he actually says . . . He is not in the least afraid of colloquial prose.[48]

Through his criticism Thomas had come to identify what he most disliked in the literary style of the time, and by 1913 he was trying to apply it to his own writing. In his letters he referred more than once to his desire to 'wring all the necks of my rhetoric—the geese.'[49] The autobiography had been a start in this direction, and in the early months of 1914 he was trying out a new variety of essay, using direct narration, which he described as 'little Welsh pictures, of a plain perhaps lucid kind, in my later manner, if it is a manner.'[50]

This change in style reflected and required a change in treatment, being as much a new way of feeling as a new way of writing. In abandoning his high-flown approach he had not abandoned his favourite subjects, but rather altered his way of looking at them; his idealism gave way to a more sober and robust vision of the world as it was, not as imagination would have it. This fundamental change Thomas was to chronicle in one of his most crucial poems, 'Sedge-Warblers', which opens with a frank avowal of his past idealism:

> This beauty made me dream there was a time
> Long past and irrecoverable, a clime
> Where any brook so radiant racing clear
> Through buttercup and kingcup bright as brass
> But gentle, nourishing the meadow grass
> That leans and scurries in the wind, would bear
> Another beauty, divine and feminine,
> Child to the sun, a nymph whose soul unstained
> Could love all day, and never hate or tire,
> A lover of mortal or immortal kin.

Then, with a break, this vision is rejected:

> And yet, rid of this dream, ere I had drained
> Its poison, quieted was my desire
> So that I only looked into the water,
> Clearer than any goddess or man's daughter,
> And hearkened while it combed the dark green hair
> And shook the millions of the blossoms white
> Of water-crowfoot . . .

in favour of the actuality of nature in the sedge-warblers, with their 'quick, shrill, or grating' song:

> Their song that lacks all words, all melody,
> All sweetness almost, was dearer then to me
> Than sweetest voice that sings in tune sweet words.

> This was the best of May—the small brown birds
> Wisely reiterating endlessly
> What no man learnt yet, in or out of school.

Thomas's attitude to nature and the country had undergone a profound change. He no longer looked to the country as a paradisal source of tranquillity and bliss and divine beauty; rejecting the dream of the Golden Age 'long past and irrecoverable', he was now content with nature's reality, with the beauties that were to be found in the crowfoot flowers and the sedge-warblers' song, and to draw strength from their 'wisdom' without attributing metaphysical properties to them. As he had abandoned rhetoric in favour of plainness, so he had relinquished dreams for reality.

As 1914 progressed, he came closer and closer to the most significant change of his career, the move from prose into poetry. It was not, perhaps, altogether a new idea; certainly it had been suggested to him in the past, when the poetic nature of his writing had been remarked upon, but he had rejected it.[51] After reading *Light and Twilight* in October 1913, Eleanor Farjeon had been tempted to raise the subject:

> I asked 'Haven't you ever written poetry, Edward?'
> 'Me?' He uttered a short self-scornful laugh. 'I couldn't write a poem to save my life.'[52]

On reading Thomas's last country book *In Pursuit of Spring* (1914) a few months later, Robert Frost had recognised that it was full of poetry 'but in prose form where it did not declare itself.' Frost picked out paragraphs of the book 'and told him to write it in verse form in exactly the same cadence.'[53]

Frost's encouragement was important, but still Thomas hesitated. Returning home after his first long visit to Dymock, Thomas wrote to Frost saying 'I wonder whether you can imagine me taking to verse. If you can I might get over the feeling that it is impossible.'[54] Something more was needed before the feeling of impossibility could be removed, and that, as we shall see, turned out to be the war. At the end of July Thomas looked gloomily at his prospects as a writer in wartime, and remarked to Eleanor: 'I may as well write poetry. Did anyone ever begin at 36 in the shade?'[55]

The summer of 1914, then, had brought him to the brink of his last great departure. Friendship with Eleanor and Frost had restored his confidence and given him hope that perhaps, after all, he might find a means of expressing all that he still wanted to say about the country and himself. Perhaps, too, his acquaintance with the poets of the Georgian fraternity in Gloucestershire had suggested that he need not consider himself a failure for ever. If they could write poetry, why not himself? Certainly he had clear ideas about how he liked poetry to be.

The war's immediate impact on Thomas came in the form of a commission from the *English Review* for an article on what working people were saying about the war.[56] He disliked the jingoism of the popular press and was pleased with the commission, for he hoped to give the 'unvarnished truth' of what ordinary people felt and said. To collect copy, he set off early in September on a tour of the industrial north, through Coventry, Birmingham, Sheffield and Manchester, finishing at Newcastle, which he surprised himself by liking: 'In fact', he told Bottomley, 'I never enjoyed a night in any city so much, just for the city's sake & nothing but the city.'[57]

Other work was not so easy to find. At home once more, he thought vaguely about enlisting, more about going to America with Frost. A month later he was back in Dymock, making notes for another article on 'what country people say about the war.'[58] During this visit, he and Frost had an unpleasant encounter with Lord Beauchamp's unfriendly gamekeeper. Out for a walk one day, they came out of the woods (which the keeper was employed to preserve) onto a lane, meeting the keeper with his shotgun. In Frost's words, the keeper 'attacked me for going where he allowed the Gibsons to go as gentry. Me he called a "damn cottager" '.[59] A little frightened, but more angry, Thomas and Frost went round to the keeper's cottage and Frost threatened to beat the daylights out of him should he behave that way again. The incident got to the ears of Lord Beauchamp, who, apparently recognising the correct social standing of Frost and his friends, sent a note of apology.[60] This incident later found its way into Thomas's poem 'An Old Song' based on 'The Lincolnshire Poacher':

Since then I've thrown away a chance to fight a gamekeeper;
And I less often trespass, and what I see or hear
Is mostly from the road or path by day: yet still I sing:
'Oh, 'tis my delight of a shiny night in the season of the year.'

Soon after this, Thomas was home again, sitting glumly in his study wondering what he should do and irritated by having to read, for the purposes of another article for Monro's *Poetry and Drama*,[61] a large quantity of 'war poetry', virtually none of which succeeded, in his view, in expressing the nature of patriotism. Most was predictably rhetorical. Eventually his own emerging feelings about the war and his country—his countryside—brought him to verse. He followed Frost's advice, first composing a number of prose passages in his notebook. Then, at the beginning of December, he began to write poetry.

1 *Left* Helen Thomas in 1898, aged twenty-one

2 *Below* Shelgate Road, Battersea, where Edward Thomas spent his youth (the right hand house was the Thomases')

3 *Opposite top*   Elses Farm, Weald, Kent

4 *Opposite below*   The house built for the Thomases by Geoffrey Lupton at Wick Green, Hampshire

5   *Above*   The study cottage at Wick Green

6 *Left*   Edward Thomas in 1913, at Steep

7 *Overleaf*   View from the Shoulder of Mutton Hill, in the parish of Steep, looking towards the South Downs; in the foreground is the memorial stone to Edward Thomas erected in 1937; to the right, hidden by the yews, lies Berryfield Cottage, Thomas's first home in Hampshire

8 *Above* Robert Frost in 1915, shortly after his return to New Hampshire from Europe

9 *Left* Little Iddens, the Frosts' home at Leadington, on the Herefordshire-Gloucestershire border, as the house stands today

10 *Opposite top left* Rupert Brooke in 1913

11 *Opposite top right* Lascelles Abercrombie at Ryton, Gloucestershire, spring 1914

12 *Opposite below* Edward Thomas (second from left in middle row) in Lance-Corporal's uniform with a group in late 1915

13 *Above* The church at Priors Dean, Hampshire; view from Manor Farm—setting for the poem 'The Manor Farm'?

(See note 22 to Chapter 9):
'... I came down to the old Manor Farm,
And church and yew-tree opposite, in age
Its equals and in size.'

14 *Below* First three stanzas of poem 'I Never Saw that Land Before' (reduced from actual size), from Edward Thomas's manuscript notebook in the Bodleian Library

8

In It and No Mistake

Out of us all
That make rhymes,
Will you choose
Sometimes—
As the winds use
A crack in a wall
Or a drain,
Their joy or their pain
To whistle through—
Choose me,
You English words?
                    'Words'

The transformation was unexpected, even to Thomas himself. More remarkable still, the first few poems showed no beginner's traits. The technical and emotional maturity we associate with Thomas's verse was there from the beginning.

The first poem was completed on 3 December—'Up in the Wind', a dialogue based on a girl living in an unfrequented inn at a crossroads. It begins:

'I could wring the old thing's neck that put it here!
A public house! it may be public for birds,
Squirrels, and such-like, ghosts of charcoal-burners
And highwaymen.' The wild girl laughed. 'But I
Hate it since I came back from Kennington.
I gave up a good place. . . .'

Following Frost's advice the poem was rewritten from a prose sketch in Thomas's notebook dated 16 November. This gives a detailed description of the original for the inn.[1] The poem departs from the sketch in several important regards however and takes on its own shape and substance, as the dialogue between the girl and the narrator develops. Theme and treatment have clear affinities with Frost's tales in *North of Boston*, and a more distant relation to the verse dramas and dialogues of Abercrombie and Gibson. But the thoughts and language we recognise immediately as

Thomas's—here is his characteristic steady voice with a touch of humour
bringing together the contemporary and the timeless:

> For who now used these roads except myself,
> A market waggon every other Wednesday,
> A solitary tramp, some very fresh one
> Ignorant of these eleven houseless miles,
> A motorist from a distance slowing down
> To taste whatever luxury he can
> In having North Downs clear behind, South clear before,
> And being midway between two railway lines,
> Far out of sight or sound of them? . . .
> . . . the land is wild, and there's a spirit of wildness
> Much older, and crying when the stone-curlew yodels
> His sea and mountain cry, high up in Spring.
> He nests in fields where still the gorse is free as
> When all was open and common . . .

Here, too, is the movement from the girl's vigorous rejection of the inn at
the beginning of the poem to her acceptance of it towards the end:

> 'Not me:
> Not back to Kennington. Here I was born,
> And I've a notion on these windy nights
> Here I shall die. Perhaps I want to die here.
> I reckon I shall stay . . .'

Dramatically, the poem balances the ideas of the imagined past against the
actual present, and of the town against the country, concluding with a
picture of calves drinking from the pond which implicitly endorses the
country here-and-now. This endorsement is not sentimental, but achieved
through the slow revelation of the girl's sense of belonging.

The following day the second poem, 'November', was committed to the
notebook.[2] It begins:

> November's days are thirty:
> November's earth is dirty,

The title indicates, perhaps, that the idea for this poem had been in
Thomas's mind for a week or two before it was written. Again, the Thomas
voice is instantly recognisable, though this time with a free and swinging
rhythm, with a couplet rhyme scheme used to great effect yet never
obtrusively; there are no thudding end-stops. As Frost recommended, the
sentence meanings break across the metre in a taut but pregnant relation.

The theme is typically Thomas, too: a celebration of one of nature's least favoured aspects—mud:

> Few care for the mixture of earth and water,
> Twig, leaf, flint, thorn,
> Straw, feather, all that men scorn,
> Pounded up and sodden by flood,
> Condemned as mud.

But the poet

> loves earth and November more dearly
> Because without them, he sees clearly,
> The sky would be nothing more to his eye
> Than he, in any case, is to the sky;

So he can love even the mud. The sky, we note, is described in empty, inflated terms—'the pure bright of the cloudless heavenly light'—by contrast with the solid detail lavished on the mud, stressing the reality of earth against the insubstantiality of the heaven. The word 'earth' occurs seven times in the poem, and it is appropriate that one of the very first poems Thomas wrote should have been about the earth, the soil itself, for love of which he was later to lay down his life. Though he did not know it, mud was to become a kind of symbol of the Western Front.

The day after 'November' came 'March', with a more familiar subject for a nature poem. It begins:

> Now I know that Spring will come again,
> Perhaps to-morrow: however late I've patience
> After this night following on such a day.

The day is wintry, with hail and wind. An hour or so before sunset, however, the wind drops and the sun comes out, 'too late for warmth' but bright and tender. Then, with suddenness:

> What did the thrushes know? Rain, snow, sleet, hail,
> Had kept them quiet as the primroses.
> They had but an hour to sing. On boughs they sang,
> On gates, on ground; they sang while they changed perches
> And while they fought, if they remembered to fight:
> So earnest were they to pack into that hour
> Their unwilling hoard of song before the moon
> Grew brighter than the clouds. . . .

A similar moment is recorded in *In Pursuit of Spring*, and it may be that this was one of the passages Frost picked out to make his point about the inherently poetic nature of Thomas's prose:

> All the thrushes of England sang at that hour, and against that background of myriads I heard two or three singing their frank, clear notes in a mad eagerness to have all done before dark; for already the blackbirds were chinking and shifting places along the hedgerows.

Had 'March' simply recorded this moment, however, it had not been so memorable a poem. The thrushes' song is given more value:

> So they could keep off silence
> And night, they cared not what they sang or screamed;
> Whether 'twas hoarse or sweet or fierce or soft;
> And to me all was sweet: they could do no wrong.
> Something they knew—I also, while they sang
> And after. Not till night had half its stars
> And never a cloud, was I aware of silence
> Stained with all that hour's songs, a silence
> Saying that Spring returns, perhaps to-morrow.

Here is a theme we recognise as recurrent in Thomas's verse—what do the birds know? what is nature's secret? Many poems testify to the desire to reach across the gulf between the unconscious existence of nature and the conscious human mind, to express in words the essence of the natural world. Thrushes were Thomas's favourite birds, often chosen as a possible link between man and nature; here their use is more complex than at first appears.

In an ordinary nature poem of the Georgian period, the theme of 'March' would have been treated simply, with the thrushes' song being directly interpreted by the poet, through the poetic convention that such things were possible (incidentally a convention that Thomas himself had used in the past). By asking 'What did the thrushes know?', Thomas draws attention to the unrealism and then proceeds to assert that communication is possible—'Something they knew—I also, while they sang.' Yet this message is felt rather than understood; it cannot be rendered in words. It is therefore not the song itself which says that 'spring returns' but the later silence, and in that paradox of 'silence saying' lies the poem's kernel. Nature cannot speak to man—or can it? We may recall Thomas's comment on Hardy's verse, 'which is full if not of magic yet of a deep and strong suggestion of something which the intellect alone cannot handle.' The idea of reaching the edge of what can be known and—perhaps—touching what cannot appears frequently in Thomas's verse.

The fourth poem, completed on the fourth consecutive day, 6 December, was 'Old Man', the poem about the scent of wild clematis which was looked at briefly in Chapter 1:

> Old Man, or Lad's-love,—in the name there's nothing
> To one that knows not Lad's-love, or Old Man,
> The hoar-green feathery herb, almost a tree,
> Growing with rosemary and lavender.

It is a poem about memory and the past. In prose form, it had been written three weeks earlier in the notebook, under the more usual name 'Old Man's Beard'. Now the title was more suggestive. Apart from the opening lines, the poem is structurally similar to the prose, with virtually identical phrases, so that the notebook entry may be regarded as the first draft of the poem.[3]

It is an ambitious poem, attempting to describe a lost memory:

> As for myself,
> Where first I met the bitter scent is lost.
> I, too, often shrivel the grey shreds,
> Sniff them and think and sniff again and try
> Once more to think what it is I am remembering,
> Always in vain . . .
> I have mislaid the key. I sniff the spray
> And think of nothing; I see and I hear nothing;
> Yet seem, too, to be listening, lying in wait
> For what I should, yet never can, remember:

Literary references to things that suddenly bring back the past are fairly common; Thomas is conveying the more tantalising experience of a stimulus that evokes but does not bring back the past. Clearly, it comes from childhood, as the closing references to 'neither father nor mother, nor any playmate' indicate, but the negatives make the point: there is nothing there, the memory cannot be recalled. Again, we have reached the boundary of the knowable world; beyond memory lies 'Only an avenue, dark, nameless, without end.' It is a strange and disturbing image.

The fifth and last poem of this first group, dated 7 December, was 'The Sign-Post', which opens:

> The dim sea glints chill. The white sun is shy,
> And the skeleton weeds and the never-dry,
> Rough, long grasses keep white with frost
> At the hilltop by the finger-post;
> The smoke of the traveller's-joy is puffed

> Over hawthorn berry and hazel tuft.
> I read the sign. Which way shall I go?
> A voice says: You would not have doubted so
> At twenty. Another voice gentle with scorn
> Says: At twenty you wished you had never been born.

The unexpected but entirely natural transition from the external scene at the sign-post to the internal dialogue is yet another hallmark of Thomas's poetry, never more aptly achieved than in this instance, where the question 'Which way shall I go?' is both geographical and psychological.

The second part of the poem looks forward to the future, when the doubts and agonies of past and present will be equally irrelevant, when

> Whatever happens, it must befall,
> A mouthful of earth to remedy all
> Regrets and wishes shall freely be given;

and the present will appear desirable:

> your wish may be
> To be here. . . .
> To see what day or night can be,
> The sun and the frost, the land and the sea,
> Summer, Autumn, Winter, Spring,—

The free-flowing couplets are set against the measured, reflective pace of the opening; past and future are contained, and the question 'Which way shall I go?' is repeated in 'Wondering where shall he journey, O where?' There is no answer, for in Thomas's poetic world there are few certainties. Death—'a mouthful of earth'—is one. Another may be the elusive nature of contentment, only to be found in retrospect, never in the present. These, too, are themes that recur elsewhere in Thomas's poetry.

It is remarkable that at the age of thirty-six Thomas should have begun to write verse with five poems of such quality as this, and that between them these five poems cover most of the major themes with which his work was to be concerned. With the wild girl's tale of the inn in 'Up in the Wind' we can place the other poems about country characters and situations. With 'November' go all the many nature poems that choose neglected aspects of the countryside for special praise, and with 'March' all those that ponder on the meaning of nature's secret. 'Old Man' introduces us to the past and the impossibility of going back, while 'The Sign-Post' points forward to the poems about the quest for happiness and the need to accept death's finality.

This is not to say that every theme in Thomas's verse is covered in these first five poems, nor that they each deal definitively with the major themes. However, when one considers that they were the very first verses he wrote and that they were written in less than a week, their range and maturity are truly astonishing. The maturity is both technical, in terms of confident handling of verse structures and free metrical variations within established forms, and emotional, in the subjects chosen and the subtlety with which they are treated. 'Old Man', indeed, is among Thomas's most difficult and most successful poems—a fact he himself recognised in confessing it his favourite.[4]

He also recognised the decisiveness of his switch to poetry. On 15 December he wrote to Frost about his verse, saying he was 'in it and no mistake', adding that he was reluctant to trust his judgment lest his years of writing had simply made filling notebooks a habit with him, but affirming that at the same time he found himself 'engrossed and conscious of a possible perfection as I never was in prose.'[5] He had, one would guess, enough experience to recognise good work when he saw it. This is borne out by his immediate decision, while there were still only a few poems, to work towards a book. For on the same day that he sent the first poems to Frost, he sent copies too to Harold Monro, in his capacity as publisher, saying cautiously but firmly 'I enclose some poems which I should like you to look at. If you think anything of them the writer, who wishes to be very strictly anonymous, would like to see a small book of these and others.'[6] Monro sent them straight back with a negative response. Thomas, though disappointed, was not discouraged. He had in fact no higher opinion of Monro's critical judgment than of Marsh's and believed that in due course, on others' commendation, the Poetry Bookshop would publish his volume.[7]

Frost's immediate response was enthusiastic; he particularly liked 'Old Man'. Other close friends such as Bottomley and Garnett, as they read the poems, were less unqualified in their admiration. But whereas in the past Thomas had often accepted their criticisms and endeavoured to alter according to their suggestions, he now did neither. He was sorry his friends did not like the poems, but he hoped they would learn to appreciate them in time. He would not change them at their suggestion. Probably this confidence came from the feeling that other writers can confirm, that of knowing when something is good. When poor work is criticised the pain can be acute because it reinforces an inner knowledge of inferior quality; though praise is welcome, good work needs no approval from others.

So much is speculation, but what is clear is that by the very end of the year Thomas's state of mind was much improved. He had, he told Bottomley, 'given up groaning.'[8] Before the end of the year he had written several more poems, including 'The Other'.[9] This is one of Thomas's longest pieces, and is a key poem in terms of his sense of self. As it begins, the poet is coming out of a forest to an inn, where he is told that his double passed by the previous day. He sets off in pursuit:

> I travelled fast, in hopes I should
> Outrun that other. What to do
> When caught, I planned not. I pursued
> To prove the likeness, and, if true,
> To watch until myself I knew.

The quest continues through time and many places until, in the tenth stanza, the other is seen plain 'amid a tap-room's din' and heard, complaining of being followed; in shame the pursuer slips away, and the poem ends with the impossibility of reconciling identities, or of knowing oneself fully:

> And now I dare not follow after
> Too close. I try to keep in sight,
> Dreading his frown and worse his laughter.
> I steal out of the wood to light;
> I see the swift shoot from the rafter
> By the inn door: ere I alight
> I wait and hear the starlings wheeze
> And nibble like ducks: I wait his flight.
> He goes: I follow: no release
> Until he ceases. Then I also shall cease.

Again, an astonishingly complete and assured poem about a very complex and subtle subject. I am not sure I understand all its elements, but together they tell us more than anything else about Thomas's consciousness of self, and about his ability to render that consciousness in the language and images of poetry. The sense of dis-integration, or of different selves inhabiting the same mind, and the idea of knowing oneself from outside, may be said to be crucial themes in modern literature, but few works have conveyed them with such lucidity as Thomas's 'The Other'. The sustained but varied rhyme scheme, with three rhymes to each ten-line stanza, is impressive in itself, while within the poem is contained Thomas's own account of the elements which went to make up both his life and his writing:

> The last light filled a narrow firth
> Among the clouds. I stood serene,
> And with a solemn quiet mirth,
> An old inhabitant of earth.

Once the name I gave to hours
Like this was melancholy, when
It was not happiness and powers
Coming like exiles home again,
And weaknesses quitting their bowers,
. . .
And fortunate my search was then
While what I sought, nevertheless,
That I was seeking, I did not guess.

It was a remarkable end to the year.

9

An Ideal England

> He is fortunate who can find an ideal England of
> the past, the present and the future to worship,
> and embody it in his native fields and waters or
> his garden, as in a graven image.
>
> *The South Country*

On New Year's Day 1915 Thomas sprained his ankle badly. He was in bed for a week and then housebound still unable to walk. It was not until the beginning of March that the ankle was definitely on the mend. The enforced immobility made January and February good writing months, however, and verse began to flow. Within three weeks, nineteen poems were completed, a rate of virtually one a day; sending them to Eleanor for typing Thomas commented: 'This will prejudice you against them. A man can't do all that and be any good.'[1] Then there was a short break until February, during which seven more poems were completed (including two dated 11th and one each on 22nd, 23rd and 24th). It was an impressive output.

At the same time he was starting to compile an anthology of extracts of verse and prose which in his view best evoked the idea of 'England'. This followed naturally on from his *English Review* articles on the war and people's feeling for their country. It was Thomas's own idea and appears to have been meant as a contribution to the war effort. The idea was, he explained to Bottomley, 'to give as various an impression as possible of English life, landscape, thought, ambition & glory. The thing is to arrange it so that it will be as simple & rich as a plum pudding.'[2]

He was still thinking of going to America. The Frosts had decided to return home and had agreed to take Mervyn with them across the Atlantic, where he was to live with another friend of the Thomases. Before they left the Frosts paid a last visit to Steep, where Thomas was still disabled. He told Eleanor that 'I am sorrier than I would tell them that they are going because although I very much want to, I know how many things more likely than not will prevent my going out to them.'[3] Yet after the Frosts left (Helen travelling to Liverpool to see Mervyn off) Thomas told Bottomley that Frost had 'almost bound' him to go out in the summer. It was Frost's idea, he elaborated in his next letter, that 'helping him on the farm will set me up & set me free from English journalism & that I might find a market out there for what I really want to do.'[4] What that was, he added, was still uncertain; but the prospect of a fresh start was distinctly appealing—the more so because there did not seem too much of a market for his verse at home.

In mid-February, now with a stock of some thirty poems, he began to look again to publication. So far, only Helen, Eleanor and Frost had seen the manuscripts; he still hesitated to send them to friends like Bottomley, de la Mare or Garnett, lest it should look like begging for compliments, and he was determined to hide his identity from the public lest his poems be associated with the work of Edward Thomas, 'doomed hack'.[5] The solution was a pseudonym, and Thomas tried out various names on Eleanor before finally settling on Edward Eastaway.[6] The choice of name had its symbolic aspect. Not only was it a new name to suit the new voice and the new form that had emerged through the poetry, but it was an unmistakeably and significantly English name, taken from a Thomas family connexion in Devonshire. Previously, in his essays, Thomas had tended to adopt Celtic names and personae for his autobiographical figures: the would-be suicide in *Light and Twilight*, for instance, is called Morgan Treharon. Ten years earlier, in *Beautiful Wales*, he had said: 'I do not easily believe in patriotism in times of peace or war . . . unless I am in Wales.' 'Edward Eastaway' showed that he had at last cast off his nostalgia for the 'land of his fathers' and was ready and willing to identify with the country he knew and loved best—England.

Because it was awkward to have Edward Eastaway addressed c/o himself at Steep, Thomas asked Eleanor if he might be c/o the Farjeon home in Hampstead. Eleanor thus became responsible for mailing and returning all correspondence—mainly rejection slips—concerning the poems. In March, Thomas sent '8 lines of rhyme' to the *Times*.[7] The lines have not previously been identified, but it seems likely that they were in fact the final version of 'A Private', his only eight-line poem to date. This had been drafted early in January, as a poem about a homeless field worker, and then revised to make him a soldier dead in battle.[8] There is every reason to suppose that when this revision had taken place, Thomas thought of submitting the poem to the *Times* because its theme suited the patriotic mood of the day, its length suited a newspaper's exigencies of space, and because the *Times* had printed Hardy's war poem beginning ' 'Ere the barn cocks say Night is growing gray', which Thomas had remarked to W. H. Hudson was 'the only good one connected with the war'.[9] The *Times* did not care for his own poem, however, and returned it within a week; as Helen Thomas commented later: 'the profound love and knowledge of his country were too subtle in their patriotism for the nation's mood.'[10]

In April Thomas took courage and sent copies of his verses to several of his friends, including Walter de la Mare, W. H. Hudson, Edward Garnett, Gordon Bottomley, and Vivien Locke Ellis. He also sent them, or more probably showed them, to his friend the poet John Freeman, and mailed a second batch to Harold Monro, again with an eye to publication. Monro again rejected them. Thomas's friends were more generally encouraging, though with reservations, apart from Locke Ellis, who did not like them at all, on the grounds that 'their rhythm isn't obvious enough.'[11] Bottomley, his position as poet-and-critic with Thomas now reversed, gave as his opinion that while he liked several of the poems, especially 'Old Man', their language was still essentially that of prose, and not 'freed from everyday syntax'[12] as he considered poetry should be.

These two comments illustrate as well as anything the transitional phase poetry was in. For Ellis, like so many others brought up on the verse of Tennyson and Swinburne, poetry had to have a firm, flowing rhythm. For Bottomley, it had to lift language out of the everyday world. If it is surprising that these two men, who were among Thomas's few close friends, should have had views on poetry so different from his own, it must be remembered that Thomas's own views had changed: his aim was now exactly what Ellis and Bottomley deplored—the muffling of 'obvious' rhythm as speech cadences were allowed to play across metre and rhyme, and the use of 'everyday' syntax to distinguish poetry from prose not by inversion and elevation but by its being 'closer knit' and 'better than prose'.[13]

Disappointed that some of his friends failed to understand what he was trying to do, Thomas was modest—'What you say is very interesting & likely to be right', he wrote to Bottomley—but unmoved, 'but unless it happens to coincide with feelings I have about those particular poems all I can do is to try to discover reasons for agreeing.'[14] In fact, the poems were more liked than disliked, and although Thomas found himself surprised by the fluency with which they were written ('this unexpected ebullition', as he called it) and by the fact that they did 'not ask or get much correction on paper',[15] his letters show him to be interested and willing to discuss technique. The use of rhyme is a case in point. Early in January, when she had received the second batch of poems for typing, Eleanor evidently remarked that she preferred the blank verse poems, citing certain strained rhymes in 'After Rain':

> Throughout the copse
> No dead leaf drops
> On grey grass, green moss, burnt-orange fern,
> At the wind's return:
> The leaflets out of the ash-tree shed
> Are thinly spread

> In the road, like little black fish, inlaid,
> As if they played.

Thomas replied: 'As if they played I was anxious to have in. It describes the pattern of the fish but it comes awkwardly perhaps after inlaid'; and six days later: 'I wonder whether I can do anything with "inlaid" and "played". The inlaid, too, is at any rate perfectly precise as I saw the black leaves 2 years ago up at the top of the hill, so that neither is a rhyme word only.' He added: 'No, I don't believe rhyme is at all a *bad* trouble. I use it now more often than not and always fancy I leave the rhymed pieces as easy as the rest, but tho I am so young a versifier, I don't pretend to be sure.'[16] After his remarks on Swinburne's use of rhyme, Thomas was hardly likely to use it irresponsibly himself.

The poems from the New Year, far more than the first group, have the look of 'prentice work about them, almost as if Thomas was setting himself tasks. He drew heavily on his immediate environment of the high beech woods around Steep and the winter weather. 'The Source', dated 4 January, was close in theme and treatment to the earlier prose books, with its personification of natural forces:

> All day the air triumphs with its two voices
> Of wind and rain
> As loud as if in anger it rejoices,
> Drowning the sound of earth
> That gulps and gulps in choked endeavour vain
> To swallow the rain.
>
> Half the night, too, only the wild air speaks
> With wind and rain,
> Till forth the dumb source of the river breaks
> And drowns the rain and wind,
> Bellows like a giant bathing in mighty mirth
> The triumph of earth.

There is an awkwardness about this, both in the language ('choked endeavour vain') and in the imagery ('like a giant bathing in mighty mirth'). The next poems are less grandiose. 'Interval', for example, dwells on a lengthened twilight between day and night:

> The beeches keep
> A stormy rest,
> Breathing deep
> Of wind from the west.

The wood is black,
With a misty steam.
Above, the cloud pack
Breaks for one gleam.

This is an experiment in simplicity, with very short lines and a basic rhyme scheme. The simplicity is carried through to the end, where the woodman's cottage has

no care
For gleam or gloom:
It stays there
While I shall roam,

Die, and forget
The hill of trees,
The gleam, the wet,
This roaring peace.

and the larger statement being made about man and nature is contained in and understood through the simplicity.

'After Rain' takes a similar moment, as the winter sun emerges to find the last leaves off the trees, and:

What hangs from the myriad branches down there
So hard and bare
Is twelve yellow apples lovely to see
On one crab-tree.
And on each twig of every tree in the dell
Uncountable
Crystals both dark and bright of the rain
That begins again.

Here the slightly tricky use of the one long and one short rhyming line is successfully muted (except, as Eleanor noted, in the case of 'inlaid' and 'played') by the sense rhythms and run-ons—particularly if the lines are spoken rather than read. The rhyme scheme in fact serves to remind the reader of the structure on which the poem is built—a form which otherwise appears as naturally fitted to its subject as bark is to a tree trunk.

Other poems written in the New Year include 'A Private', 'Adlestrop', 'The Unknown Bird' and others that are discussed elsewhere. 'Swedes', dated 15 January, was again an experiment:

They have taken the gable from the roof of clay

On the long swede pile. They have let in the sun
To the white and gold and purple of curled fronds
Unsunned. . . .

The sight of the uncovered roots outdoes even that of the treasures of a
newly-discovered Egyptian tomb, with its

God and monkey, chariot and throne and vase,
Blue pottery, alabaster, and gold.

Nature has more to offer in the swede fronds' 'dream of spring' than have
long-dead lifeless treasures. But although the message of 'Swedes' is clear
and unencumbered, to my mind it has an air of contrivance, with the
swedes and Amenhotep yoked together in awkward rivalry. At the time,
the recent opening of Egyptian tombs no doubt made the comparison less
fanciful. Interestingly, Thomas commented of this poem: 'It is one of the
least like myself I fancy.'[17] As William Cooke has shown in his book
Edward Thomas: A Critical Biography (1970), 'Swedes' was one of many
poems whose origins are to be discovered in Thomas's prose books.[18] The
fluency and sure sense of judgment he found when he turned to poetry
were, in a sense, his reward for the many years' work in prose, in essays
and country books; in many cases verse was simply a new means of
expression for things he had been trying to say since he first began to
write. Except that form and content are inseparable, and the poetry is
both better than and different from the prose.

The slow change from winter to spring was an event Thomas had
watched many times. Now, in the early months of 1915, he wrote about
it in a new way, in 'But These Things Also are Springs's', when 'winter's
not gone':

The shell of a little snail bleached
In the grass; chip of flint, and mite
Of chalk; and the small birds' dung
In splashes of purest white.

Again, the plainest verse, and the plainest language, for an original idea.
The approach of spring is also the subject of 'March the Third' (completed 23 March) where an equinoctial twelve hours' daylight brings
twelve hours' singing for the birds

'Twixt dawn and dusk, from half-past six
To half-past six, never unheard.

It happens to be Sunday, too, and the church bells blend with the birds.
The day, the poems suggests, is unproclaimed—

> Or do all mark, and none dares say,
> How it may shift and long delay,
> Somewhere before the first of Spring
> But never fails, this singing day?

The lack of official recognition is, however, the day's best feature:

> This day unpromised is more dear
> Than all the named days of the year
> When seasonable sweets come in,
> Because we know how lucky we are.

This is almost a summary of Thomas's nature poetry: he praises the unseasonable sweets, the unexpected beauties. Nothing may be excluded by poetic prejudice, not even the farmyard dust in 'Tall Nettles', which is 'never lost Except to prove the sweetness of a shower.'

'March the Third', however, is not quite as straightforward as it at first appears. Apart from the fact that it is the 'singing day', the date 3 March is described as 'unnamed, unmarked', yet the poem does not tell us what is revealed in an editorial footnote—that 3 March was in fact Thomas's birthday. He was thirty-seven the month the poem was written. Perhaps there is a hint of something in the reference to 'all the named days of the year', but if so it is well concealed, and the reader is left in ignorance of the day's double significance. Why? Perhaps because it had none—the personal significance being concealed in the poem because it was not considered important in life. Now that he was writing poetry Thomas could (almost) ignore the fact that he was one year older, and allow the birds to celebrate his anniversary. Unpromised sweets had made him realise how lucky he was.

In other poems Thomas brought himself directly into the picture. 'Sowing' and 'Digging' were completed on 23 March and 4 April respectively, just as spring approached. They share the same reflective tone and quiet rhythms:

> To-day I think
> Only with scents,—scents dead leaves yield,
> And bracken, and wild carrot's seed,
> And the square mustard field;
> . . .
> The smoke's smell, too,
> Flowing from where a bonfire burns
> The dead, the waste, the dangerous,
> And all to sweetness turns.
>
> 'Digging'

> It was a perfect day
> For sowing; just
> As sweet and dry was the ground
> As tobacco-dust.
>
> I tasted deep the hour
> Between the far
> Owl's chuckling first soft cry
> And the first star.
>
> 'Sowing'

'Sweet' is the word most frequently used in Thomas's verse to praise nature and the countryside. It is today an overworked word, and was probably no less carelessly used in Thomas's day, but we may note how carefully and justly he uses it—'unseasonable sweets', 'all to sweetness turns', 'sweet and dry'. This is not the sweetness of saccharine or sentimentality.

By March the ankle was mending fast and Helen and Edward were busy in the garden of Yewtree Cottage, the second spring they had spent there together. Thomas was soon able to walk up to his study. After a short visit to London he told Eleanor that he was 'glad to get back here and go up to the study again and write and have fine days for sowing the garden.'[19] For what was to prove the last time in his life, he attained the life-style he had so long ago aspired to—that of the writer living in the country with a cottage vegetable garden and the freedom both to enjoy the country and write about it. As well as his verse, he was working on his anthology, *This England*. In a brief introduction he explained his purpose:

Building around a few most English poems like 'When icicles hang by the wall'—excluding professedly patriotic writing because it is generally bad and because indirect praise is sweeter and more profound—never aiming at what a committee from Great Britain and Ireland might call complete—I wished to make a book as full of English character and country as an egg is of meat. If I have reminded others, as I did myself continually, of some of the echoes called up by the name of England, I am satisfied.

Elsewhere he spoke of aiming at 'the antiquity and sweetness of England— English fields, English people, English poetry.'[20] It is a successful anthology, though for my taste rather too like the 'rich plum pudding' Thomas hoped it would emulate, for a little goes a long way, although as an anthology it is clearly meant for dipping into. The items range from extracts from the *Anglo-Saxon Chronicle* to Blake's 'Little Vagabond', from 'The Derby Ram' to Wordsworth's 'Ode to Duty'. The only living writers to be included were Thomas Hardy, W. H. Hudson, Walter de la Mare, Gordon Bottomley, Charles Doughty—and Edward Eastaway.

The final section of *This England* is entitled 'The Vital Commoners' and includes quotations from Chaucer, Fielding, Walton, Shakespeare and George Eliot in extracts designed to show the qualities of the common people of England. This theme was beginning to feature in Thomas's own work too, bringing with it the idioms of country speech. There was the old man, bent double raking leaves, in 'The New Year', who mutters: 'Happy New Year, and may it come fastish, too', and the ploughman 'dead in battle' of 'A Private', who used to tell all inquisitive enquirers that he slept 'At Mrs Greenland's Hawthorn Bush'. There is the charcoal burner boy playing 'The Penny Whistle', and the gipsy woman begging half a pipeful of tobacco in 'The Gypsy'.

'Man and Dog' is perhaps Thomas's most sombre poem of this kind, and it is worth looking at in some detail, since it shows how far Thomas had moved from his earlier idealisation of country life. It describes an encounter between the narrator and an old labouring man on a cold winter morning, and relates the story of the old man's life

> Since he left Christchurch in the New Forest, one
> Spring in the 'seventies,—navvying on dock and line
> From Southampton to Newcastle-on-Tyne,—
> In 'seventy-four a year of soldiering
> With the Berkshires,—hoeing and harvesting
> In half the shires where corn and couch will grow.
>   . . . the hoe
> And reap-hook he liked, or anything to do with trees.
> He fell once from a poplar tall as these:
> The Flying Man they called him in hospital.
> 'If I flew now, to another world I'd fall.'

Implicit in this account is a realistic understanding of the irregular and insecure nature of agricultural work at this period, following the depression. Now in his old age, the man is obliged to trudge twenty miles or more from one ill-paid job to another, pulling weeds, picking flints, his only bed a 'shakedown' in a farmer's barn or under a hedge. 'Flint-picking' was among the worst jobs on the land, usually undertaken by old people or children in the winter months when other work was scarce, and involved removing stones from ploughed fields.

In his country books, Thomas had presented such characters as archetypal figures of the landscape, 'half-converted' into the clay in which they toil. The man in 'Man and Dog' has individuality and dignity, despite his hard life. He has a stoical sense of humour, and accepts his situation, as he accepts his dog:

'No rabbit, never fear, she ever got,
Yet always hunts. To-day she nearly had one:
She would and she wouldn't. 'Twas like that. The bad one!
She's not much use, but still she's company,
Though I'm not. . . .'

He can even compare his situation favourably with others':

'Many a man sleeps worse tonight
Than I shall.' 'In the trenches.' 'Yes, that's right . . .'

The old man says farewell and plods off stiffly, while

the leaf-coloured robin watched. They passed,
The robin till next day, the man for good,
Together in the twilight of the wood.

In a superficially similar poem, 'Daffodils', about an old itinerant crockmender, Wilfrid Gibson depicts a country character making the best of hardship:

And he was glad he hadn't got a trade
That starched the mother-wit in you, and made
A man look silly in a field of flowers.
'Twas better mending crocks, although for hours
You hobbled on—ay! and, maybe for days—
Hungry and cold along the muddy ways
Without a job. And even when the sun
Was shining, 'twas not altogether fun
To lose the chance of earning a few pence
In these days: though 'twas well he'd got the sense
To see the funny side of things. It cost
You nothing, laughing to yourself. You lost
Far more by going fiddle-faced through life
Looking for trouble.

Thomas's poem conveys more about the vicissitudes of country life and renders country speech more acutely than does Gibson's, which is sentimental in conception and sloppy in writing. And when he too wrote about a country character who despite poverty and deformity can smile at life—as in 'The Huxter'—he did not do so by the patronising attribution of a fake cheeriness, but by a plain statement of facts:

> But the huxter has a bottle of beer;
> He drives a cart and his wife sits near
> Who does not heed his lack or his hump;
> And they laugh as down the lane they bump
>   This fine May morning.

In other poems, however, Thomas does attempt a larger statement about the nature and value of country life. One such is 'May the Twenty-third', where the central character is a figure called Jack Noman, who is

> Jaunty and old, crooked and tall,
> And stopped and grinned at me over the wall,
> With a cowslip bunch in his button-hole
> And one in his cap. Who could say if his roll
> Came from flints in the road, the weather, or ale?

Jack is a true countryman, who like the man with the dog sleeps in the open but unlike him appears to have no need to work for his living:

> Fairer flowers were none on the earth
> Than his cowslips wet with the dew of their birth,
> Or fresher leaves than the cress in his basket.
> 'Where did they come from, Jack?' 'Don't ask it,
> And you'll be told no lies.' 'Very well:
> Then I can't buy.' 'I don't want to sell.
> Take them and these flowers, too, free.
> Perhaps you have something to give me?
> Wait till next time. . . .'
> So off went Jack with his roll-walk-run,
> Leaving his cresses from Oakshott rill,
> And his cowslips from Wheatham hill.

There are several indications that this country figure is a symbolic one—the name 'Jack Noman' for one, and the references to perfection: 'there never was a finer day' and 'fairer flowers were none on the earth.' Like the best figures in fairytale, Jack vanishes into thin air at the end of the story, an aspect which was strengthened during the writing of the poem. An early draft has the last couplet as:

> A fine day was May the 20th,
> The day of Old Jack Noman's death.

In revision, the date was changed to rhyme with 'The day Jack Noman disappeared', a less mortal ending for a not altogether human figure. The poem belongs at least half to the world of pastoral. At the same time, Jack is a real enough person—slightly rascally, tending towards drink, whose cress and flowers come from real, named places. The balance between actual and ideal is finely kept: ultimately we are not sure if Jack is a person or a personification.

Yet as a whole 'May the Twenty-third' seems to me less than successful. Partly this is because of the jaunty almost doggerel rhythm, and the more than usually obvious use of rhyme, which lead the poem away from reality, towards the fanciful world of, for example, de la Mare's verse 'There was an old woman went blackberry picking'. Thomas was, as we know, a great admirer of de la Mare and of his handling of magic and mystery, but what he wanted to say about country life was not well suited to such a mode.

At the beginning of April 1915, just over a month after 'May the Twenty-third', Thomas returned to the subject of country life and in two days completed the 150 lines of his longest poem, 'Lob'. This is built around the quest for an old countryman, very like Jack Noman, who is introduced in terms that indicate the symbolic nature of the search while basing it firmly in reality:

> At hawthorn-time in Wiltshire travelling
> In search of something chance would never bring,
> An old man's face, by life and weather cut
> And coloured,—rough, brown, sweet as any nut,—
> A land face, sea-blue-eyed,—hung in my mind
> When I had left him many a mile behind.
> All he said was: 'Nobody can't stop 'ee. It's
> A footpath, right enough. You see those bits
> Of mounds—that's where they opened up the barrows
> Sixty years since, while I was scaring sparrows.
> They thought as there was something to find there,
> But couldn't find it, by digging, anywhere.'

The search begins in the villages, which

> All had their churches, graveyards, farms, and byres,
> Lurking to one side up the paths and lanes,
> Seldom well seen except by aeroplanes;

Although the same couplet rhyme scheme is used here as in 'May the Twenty-third', it is subordinated to the sense, unobtrusively disciplining the discursive verse, which goes on to describe the attitudes of village people:

> Ages ago the road
> Approached. The people stood and looked and turned.
> Nor asked it to come nearer, nor yet learned
> To move out there and dwell in all men's dust.
> And yet withal they shot the weathercock, just
> Because 'twas he crowed out of tune, they said:

The elusive figure is eventually identified by the next speaker, 'a squire's son Who loved wild bird and beast, and dog and gun', as 'one I saw when I was a child':

> 'His home was where he was free.
> Everybody has met one such man as he.
> Does he keep clear old paths that no one uses
> But once a lifetime when he loves or muses?
> He is English as this gate, these flowers, this mire.
> And when at eight years old Lob-lie-by-the-fire
> Came in my books, this was the man I saw.
> He has been in England as long as dove and daw,
> Calling the wild cherry tree the merry tree,
> The rose campion Bridget-in-her-bravery;
> And in a tender mood he, as I guess,
> Christened one flower Love-in-idleness . . .'

The reader now knows that the figure sought is not a real person but the essence of country life and tradition, but the transition has been so subtle that the illusion is maintained, and the balance between real and ideal carefully held, not least by the light touch, with its hints of humour, which keep ponderous symbolism at bay.

Part of the essence of the country lies in its place names: the Hog's Back, Mother Dunch's Buttocks, Totteridge, Totterdown, Juggler's Lane (when sending the poem to Blackwood's Magazine, Thomas proposed 'Happersnapper Hanger', a wooded coombe not far from Steep, in place of the impolite Mother Dunch's Buttocks—but the poem was rejected anyway).[21] Another aspect of the country is its expressive words and sayings:

> 'Lob has thirteen hundred names for a fool,
> And though he never could spare time for school
> To unteach what the fox so well expressed,
> On biting the cock's head off,—Quietness is best,—
> He can talk quite as well as anyone
> After his thinking is forgot and done.

He first of all told someone else's wife,
For a farthing she'd skin a flint and spoil a knife
Worth sixpence skinning it. She heard him speak:
"She had a face as long as a wet week"
Said he . . .'

Lob the countryman is kin to Shakespeare, Herne the Hunter, Hob, the
cobbler's boy who tricked the giant to make the Wrekin hill, Jack the giant
killer, and many other names in idiom or folk tale or history:

'The man you saw,—Lob-lie-by-the-fire, Jack Cade,
Jack Smith, Jack Moon, poor Jack of every trade,
Young Jack, or old Jack, or Jack What-d'ye-call,
Jack-in-the-hedge, or Robin-run-by-the-wall,
Robin Hood, Ragged Robin, lazy Bob,
One of the lords of No Man's Land, good Lob. . . .'

The spirit of village life these names represent is alive and flourishing,

'Although he was seen dying at Waterloo,
Hastings, Agincourt, and Sedgemoor too,—
Lives yet. He never will admit he is dead
. . .
Not till our weathercock crows once again
And I remove my house out of the lane
On to the road.'

Taken as a whole, 'Lob' is one of the finest evocations of English
country life in literature. Into its compressed yet rambling lines are
concentrated almost as many instances of 'English character and country'
as Thomas had included in his anthology. Notable too is the blend of the
ancient and the contemporary, for this version of pastoral is not merely
nostalgic, despite the device of a search, as the ending makes clear. 'Lob'
is not to be found 'by digging, anywhere', but recognised in country
features and figures, like the narrator, who disappears down the lane

In hazel and thorn tangled with old-man's-beard.
But one glimpse of his back, as there he stood,
Choosing his way, proved him of old Jack's blood,
Young Jack perhaps, and now a Wiltshireman
As he has oft been since his days began.

This is no lament for the lost paradise of Merrie England; the country
is resilient, able to encompass the kings and giants of the imagined past

and the aeroplanes of the very real present. The poem has these qualities, too: its rich allusiveness brings together disparate aspects of the same enduring reality, and the variety and lightness of the writing mean that the weight of the poem's message is never borne directly by the verse, saving it from pretentiousness. The several levels of meaning and allusion carry an unmistakeable message that is nowhere made explicit; in the words of another poem, it is a way of writing 'that hinted all and nothing spoke.' We may note, too, that the poem is set in England in war-time, though again this is not stated. Contained within the references to the ancient battles of Waterloo, Agincourt and the rest is an allusion to present wars and those who are dying in order that England may 'live yet'.

Thomas's first purpose in his writing had always been to create images of 'an ideal England of past, present and future' which would convey all he felt about the strength and continuity of country life. And when he began to write poetry, this was still very much to the forefront of his mind. One of his first poems, written on Christmas Eve 1914, was 'The Manor Farm', composed with a vision of England in view. It begins with a descriptive country scene, in winter:

> The rock-like mud unfroze a little and rills
> Ran and sparkled down each side of the road
> Under the catkins wagging in the hedge.

This might be the opening of any Georgian country poem. The setting is that of a country walk, in thin wintry sunlight, with nothing exceptional to be seen

> Till I came down to the old Manor Farm,
> And church and yew-tree opposite. . . .

The scene is caught in a moment of arrested time:

> The church and yew
> And farmhouse slept in a Sunday silentness.
> The air raised not a straw. The steep farm roof,
> With tiles duskily glowing, entertained
> The mid-day sun; and up and down the roof
> White pigeons nestled.

The blank verse moves with perfect assurance, creating a picture of quiet beneficence. The distinctive use of imagery in 'Sunday silentness' and 'entertained The mid-day sun' is hardly noticed, so naturally do the images fit the sense. It is the verbs that convey the feeling of enduring goodness and security. The church and farmhouse sleep, the tiles glow, the roof entertains the sun, the pigeons nestle: all is safe and well. The poem comes to rest with a description of the farmhorses looking over the gate, and then unexpectedly carries on into a coda. It is not often that Thomas steps forward, as it were, in his poems, to set out in an explicit manner the significance of what has been described. More often, as we saw in 'Lob', the message is implicit. But the Manor Farm is an emblem:

> The Winter's cheek flushed as if he had drained
> Spring, Summer, and Autumn at a draught
> And smiled quietly. But 'twas not Winter—
> Rather a season of bliss unchangeable
> Awakened from farm and church where it had lain
> Safe under tile and thatch for ages since
> This England, Old already, was called Merry.

This was what Thomas had sought in the country—a Golden Age of 'bliss unchangeable', surviving from the past into the present. Momentarily, such a vision might be seen, and described, as in this poem. It is clear, however, that in invoking the pastoral myth of the Golden Age or Merry England, it has been necessary to use words and images which belong to that myth—to personify the seasons, for instance—in a manner quite different from that used in the first part of the poem. In comparison, the catkins, the farmhouse and the horses are solid and real and it is only by virtue of their almost tangible vividness that we accept the assertion of the last four lines. To my mind, the scene of farmhouse, church and yew is diminished rather than enlarged by the association with 'bliss' and 'Old England', for the words are exhausted, too weak to carry the strength attributed to them, while those used to describe the manor are alive and potent, reflecting a real place rather than a vision.[22]

Seven months later, in July 1915, Thomas returned to this theme again in the poem 'Haymaking'. This time, the opening refers to the Golden Age:

> After night's thunder far away had rolled
> The fiery day had a kernel sweet of cold,
> And in the perfect blue the clouds uncurled,
> Like the first gods before they made the world
> And misery, swimming the stormless sea
> In beauty and in divine gaiety.

But the classical props are soon discarded. Again, the setting is a walk along a country road, a 'smooth white empty' road before the days of tarmac and modern traffic, and in chalk country. Every detail of the natural world is knowledgeably observed, from the June-fallen leaves of

the holly and the 'fir cones standing up stiff in the heat' to the thickets
where

> the nettle creeper
> And garden-warbler sang unceasingly;
> While over them shrill shrieked in his fierce glee
> The swift with wings and tail as sharp and narrow
> As if the bow had flown off with the arrow.

(We may note in passing the allusion to Swinburne's 'Hesperia'—'shrill
shrieks in our faces the blind bland sir'—and the adaptation of Hardy's
rather mechanistic image for swallows—'little cross-bows animate'.) The
poem continues its journey:

> Only the scent of woodbine and hay new mown
> Travelled the road. In the field sloping down,
> Park-like, to where its willows showed the brook,
> Haymakers rested.

If we are not alert we miss the hint of the smell of new-mown hay, for this
is the poem's destination. From a detail in the landscape, the haymakers
are enlarged:

> The tosser lay forsook
> Out in the sun; and the long waggon stood
> Without its team: it seemed it never would
> Move from the shadow of that single yew.
> The team, as still, until their task was due,
> Beside the labourers enjoyed the shade
> . . .
> The men leaned on their rakes, about to begin,
> But still.

Again, the moment of arrested time. Then the poem moves on towards
its conclusion almost without a break, through the use of two grammatically
similar sentences holding different sorts of meaning:

> And all were silent. All was old,
> This morning time, with a great age untold,
> Older than Clare and Cobbett, Morland and Crome,
> Than, at the field's far edge, the farmer's home,
> A white house crouched at the foot of a great tree.

The names invoked here stand for a vital tradition of regard for the countryside and of a way of depicting it, and the link they provide between past and present enables the poem to move to its final lines, which are again a direct statement of the scene's significance:

> Under the heavens that know not what years be
> The men, the beasts, the trees, the implements
> Uttered even what they will in times far hence—
> All of us gone out of the reach of change—
> Immortal in a picture of an old grange.

As well as being most firmly planted in the present (the haymakers are 'about to begin') the poem looks both forward and back, and holds past, present and future in one scene. That scene now represents not 'bliss unchangeable', but continuity and tradition; these are the enduring virtues of the country scene.

Like 'The Manor Farm', 'Haymaking' is pastoral in the sense that it creates an image of rural perfection, an instant of immortality, a vision of an idealised English countryside. But both are firmly based in reality and the present day, with vigorous description holding in check any tendency to sentimental nostalgia. Neither can be dismissed as escapist. In these poems Thomas achieved his clearest expression of his conviction that in its finest aspects the English countryside represented all that was best in earth or heaven.

This is borne out by the fact that it was these two poems which Thomas chose to include, somewhat surreptitiously, in his *This England* anthology. As the book reached its final stages, it became clear that there were two pages to spare, which Thomas filled by fitting his two most English poems at the end of the section entitled 'Her Sweet Three Corners', over the name Edward Eastaway.[23] They stood as his contribution to the indirect praise, which in his view was 'sweeter and more profound' than 'professedly patriotic writing', of England. They were, in a very real sense, poems for his country.

10

Country and Country

I found myself saying 'goodbye' ... It was a
signal not of a parting but of a uniting.
                                              'The Stile'

Thomas's poems in *This England* were placed immediately after Coleridge's
'Fears in Solitude', a poem which had much in common with Thomas's
mood. It was, according to its subtitle, 'written in April 1798, during the
alarm of an invasion' and in it Coleridge, after considering the political
and religious condition of Britain, confesses himself a believer who finds
religious meaning only 'in the forms of nature'. It ends with a hymn to
'dear Britain':

> How shouldst thou prove aught else but dear and holy
> To me, who from thy lakes and mountain-hills,
> Thy clouds, they quiet dales, thy rocks and seas,
> Have drunk in all my intellectual life
> All sweet sensations, all enobling thought ...

concluding

> There lives nor form nor feeling in my soul
> Unborrowed from my country.

Thomas's experiences and emotions were very similar to Coleridge's, as
was his response when England seemed once again threatened with
invasion. A large part of the initial patriotic response in the First World
War was aroused by the fear of an invasion, as the German Army overran
Belgium and swept into France, and at one level Thomas's immediate
response had been no different from that of the majority of his fellow
countrymen.

In September 1914 he had written an essay for *The Nation* on his
reaction to the declaration of war, entitled 'This England'—a phrase
which, with its Shakespearian echo, he was to use at least twice more in
the months that followed, in 'The Manor Farm' and as the title for his

English anthology. In the essay (which was later to be re-worked into the poem 'The Sun Used to Shine') he described his walks with Frost around Dymock and Ledbury, in a countryside which seemed as yet little affected by the war:

> Then one evening the new moon made a difference. It was the end of a wet day; at least it had begun wet and turned warm and muggy and at last fine but still cloudy. The sky was banded with rough masses in the north-west, but the moon, a stout orange crescent, hung free of cloud near the horizon. At one stroke I thought like many other people what things that same new moon sees eastward about the Meuse in France. Of those who could see it there, not blinded by smoke, pain or excitement, how many saw it and heeded? I was deluged, in a second stroke, by another thought, or something that overpowered thought. All I can tell is it seemed to me that either I had never loved England, or I had loved it foolishly, aesthetically, like a slave, not having realised that it was not mine unless I were willing and prepared to die for it rather than leave it as Belgian women and old men and children had left their country. Something I had omitted. Something, I felt, had to be done before I could look again composedly at English landscape, at the elms and poplars about the houses, at the purple-headed wood-betony with two pairs of leaves on a stiff stem, who stood sentinel among the grasses and bracken by hedge-side or wood's edge. What he stood sentinel for I did not know, any more than what I had got to do.[1]

This is a curious piece. Its tone is very much that of the contemporary apologia for war, particularly the kind that came from intellectuals who had hitherto opposed war and now felt themselves in the grip of an irrational patriotism; Gilbert Murray's pamphlet 'How Can War Ever Be Right?' is a case in point. Thomas admits the irrationality, in the 'second stroke . . . something that overpowered thought' and the emotional response that leads him to say: 'Something, I felt, had to be done before I could look again composedly at English landscape.' His patriotic response is not towards his country so much as towards the country, the landscape. In fact, as the passage progresses, it emerges that his feeling is concentrated on 'the purple-headed wood-betony with two pairs of leaves on a stiff stem, who stood sentinel among the grasses or bracken by hedge-side or wood's edge.' The use of 'who' rather than 'which' for the plant alerts us, as does the last sentence: 'What *he* stood sentinel for I did not know, any more than what I had got to do.' By anthropomorphising the wood-betony, Thomas has succeeded in justifying his emotional response: he is as ready to defend a single plant as he is to defend his nation. In a sense, there is barely a distinction: for him the wood-betony stands sentinel for the landscape, for England, demanding a response.

Thomas was not alone in feeling this way. Rupert Brooke described his reactions to the war in an essay written in the third person, strikingly similar to Thomas's, printed in the *New Statesman* in August. It was, he said, like an emotional crisis, with his mind divided into two parts:

the upper running about aimlessly from one half-relevant thought to another, the lower unconscious half labouring with some profound and unknowable change. . . . His consciousness was like the light scurry of waves at full tide, when the deeper waters are pausing and gathering and turning home. Something was growing in his heart and he couldn't tell what . . .

When he thought of 'England' and 'Germany' the word 'England' seemed to flash like a line of foam. With a sudden tightening of the heart, he realised that there might be a raid on the English coast. He didn't imagine any possibility of it *succeeding*, but only of enemies and warfare on English soil. The idea sickened him. He was immensely surprised to perceive that the actual earth of England held for him a quality . . . which, if he'd been sentimental enough to use the word, he'd have called 'holiness'.

Here is the same rush of emotion, the same need to redefine what is meant by 'England', as is present in Thomas's essay. Where Thomas, however, characteristically narrowed down his conception of England until it was compressed into the wood-betony flower at the wood's edge, Brooke's feeling takes him towards a litany in which the whole landscape of southern England is contained:

Grey, uneven little fields, small ancient hedges rushed before him, wild flowers, elms and beeches, gentleness, sedate houses of red brick, proudly unassuming, a countryside of rambling hills and friendly copses. He seemed to be raised high, looking down on a landscape compounded of the western view from the Cotswolds, and the Weald, and the high land in Wiltshire, and the Midlands seen from the hills above Princes Risborough.[2]

Thus for Brooke, too, love of the country was transformed almost naturally into patriotism. He, too, was ready and willing to die for 'the actual earth of England'. He did not need to wait to know what he 'had to do'; within a few weeks of the outbreak of war, he had enlisted in the Royal Naval Division and had taken part in the retreat from Antwerp.

Thomas was not so certain of what he should do. He was not under pressure to enlist, for although popular feeling was strong, it was directed at the young and single, not at those like himself nearing forty with a wife and family, and conscription had not yet been introduced. Apart from Brooke, Thomas knew few men who had joined up. Frost (who does not really count) was immediately anxious to get his family back to America. Abercrombie's income and inspiration dried up simultaneously (he was not to write poetry again until after the war was over—a curious reversal of Thomas's position) and after a bad year during which his wife underwent a serious operation, he left his beloved Gallows and returned to Merseyside to work as a shell inspector in a munitions factory—from paradise into inferno, as it were. Gibson initially regarded war as a dirty politicians' affair which interfered with his poetic career; after Brooke's death he twice tried to enlist but was saved from active service by his near-blindness. Gordon Bottomley was prevented from any kind of war service by chronic ill-health. Bertie Farjeon, unhappy in love, enlisted in September 1914 but was almost immediately invalided out with varicose veins and married to his beloved, after which he thought no more of the Army.[3] Arthur Ransome was in Russia as a war correspondent. And so it was that Thomas, as he later said, knew no-one in a comparable position with whom he might discuss options. To Hudson he wrote that the obvious thing was to join the Territorials, the home defence branch of the Army,[4] but he made no move to do so.

With one part of him Thomas wanted nothing to do with the war. It was after all the product, in Coleridge's words, of 'courts, committees, institutions' and Thomas detested the whole paraphernalia of the modern state, of commercial and imperial rivalry and of the popular clamour of jingoistic aggression. He was very tempted to join Frost in America and concentrate on his verse. 'It would be a good time for trying America', he wrote to Bottomley on 3 September, adding, 'if I could leave Helen & the children with a conscience.'[5] By the following June he was still talking of going out to join Frost in September.[6]

At the same time he felt he could not leave Britain. For one thing, it would be an abdication of his responsibility for Helen and the children; for another he had a duty to his country, though he could not yet see how to express it. Perhaps he could serve his country by writing? This was possibly his first hope, and certainly his essays on popular reactions to the war and on the nature of patriotism were undertaken in this light, as was the anthology *This England*. His verse, as we have seen, had been stimulated by the war, and his desire to see it published arose out of his knowledge that it was inspired by his patriotic feeling. In his article on war poetry for *Poetry and Drama*, Thomas had taken pains to analyse what he considered the crude deficiencies of most 'war poetry'; his own verse and anthology were designed to redress the balance.

Shortly after completing the anthology, he was commissioned by Chapman and Hall to write a life of the Duke of Marlborough, a subject very relevant to the present, now that British troops were once again

fighting in the fields of Flanders, as Thomas noted, several times mention-
ing the names of places which were already becoming familiar in the
newspapers—Mons, Armentières, La Bassée.

Previously, Thomas would have rejected such a commission—a pot-
boiling book dealing with an uncongenial subject and with a view of
history as the actions of heroes and generals which he had disliked since
his schooldays—and indeed he denounced it to both Eleanor and Bottomley.[7] It involved a good deal of reading and gutting of other books in
the British Museum Reading Room. Under the necessity of finishing it
by the end of June, he found less opportunity for his own verse and there
was a month (24 May—25 June) when he wrote no poems.

Beyond this commission, however, there were no immediate prospects
and as the life of the good Duke drew to an end, Thomas knew that he
would soon have to make a definite decision about the future. He did not
relish the thought of continuing to struggle along as a freelance writer.
He still had no assured income. He could not, he told Eleanor, be certain
of being able to make even £150 a year, despite his willingness to work.[8]
Moreover, although his writing was, he knew, inspired by patriotic feeling,
it was a private rather than a public declaration, and there was in him a
need to commit himself publicly. Something, he felt, 'had to be done.'

Enlistment had been a possibility from the outset: as early as November
he had told W. H. Hudson that he might have enlisted 'had I been in
company that had encouraged me. At least I think so. Not that I pretend
to be warlike . . .' He mentioned Brooke's presence at Antwerp with muted
admiration as 'the most I've heard of a poet so far', adding with a little
malice, 'there are so many we could have sacrificed too.'[9] A week later he
announced that he had acquired the enlistment forms, but still hesitated.
It was, he concluded, 'an insoluble problem till one has some really strong
impulse one way.'[10]

In January he outlined to Eleanor a proposed visit to the National
Service League in London, where he hoped to get advice on what he
might do in the way of war service. His ankle was still bad and it is not
certain whether he kept the appointment, although a week later he reported
that he was thinking of joining the cyclists' corps, and this may have been
one of the suggestions made to him. He could not take a definite decision
until the sprain was fully healed, and as late as May was still hesitating.[11]

Thomas's indecision persisted for several months. Hitherto this state
of mind, knowing a decisive move had to be made but unable to bring
himself to the point, had been associated with acute tension. Now, it
appears, he was much calmer and able to consider the options open to
him. There was America, civilian life, and the Army. Which should he
choose? Perhaps he knew all the time, for there is little sense of anxiety
in his letters. Indeed, he was more sanguine than he had probably ever
been, as this extract from a letter to Bottomley shows:

God bless us all, what a thing it is to be nearing 40 & to know what one likes & know one makes mistakes & yet is right for oneself. How many things I have thought I ought to like & found reasons for liking. But now it is almost like eating apples. I don't pretend to know about pineapples and persimmons, but I know an apple when I smell it, when it makes me swallow my saliva before biting it. Then there are pears, too, & people who prefer pears. It is a fine world & I wish I knew how to make £200 a year in it without sucking James Milne's——[12]

For a man about to volunteer his life in the service of his country, Thomas was remarkably cheerful.

Almost from the outset, his poetry had included the war. On 8 January 1915 he completed a poem called 'Tears', which opens with a memory of watching a pack of hounds stream past

> In Blooming Meadow that bends towards the sun
> And once bore hops:

and moves on to another memory of the Tower of London on an April morning, when

> They were changing guard,
> Soldiers in line, young English countrymen,
> Fair-haired and ruddy, in white tunics. Drums
> And fifes were playing 'The British Grenadiers'.

The first image dates from the time the Thomases lived in Kent, the second from an unknown day prior to the outbreak of war. They are brought together with no other explanation than that the scenes

> told me truths I had not dreamed,
> And have forgotten since their beauty passed.

The truth was that Thomas's love of the country and love of his country were very close; images from pastoralism and patriotism came together by force of feeling, foreshadowing a 'truth' he was not yet ready to act on.

In other poems, the war is, as it were, offstage, but never forgotten. We have already seen how the harsh conditions of the casual labourer's life are favourably compared with those of the soldiery in 'Man and Dog'. A similar comparison is made, this time more humorously although the final message of the poem is sombre, in 'A Private', which ends:

> And where now at last he sleeps
> More sound in France—that, too, he secret keeps.

The theme is explored again in 'The Owl', where the measured celebration of good fortune is held in check by the recognition of those less
well off. As the poem begins, the poet is coming to the end of a long
winter tramp:

> Downhill I came, hungry, and yet not starved;
> Cold, yet had heat within me that was proof
> Against the North wind; tired, yet so that rest
> Had seemed the sweetest thing under a roof.
>
> Then at the inn I had food, fire and rest,
> Knowing how hungry, cold and tired was I.
> All of the night was quite barred out except
> An owl's cry, a most melancholy cry

The owl, which enjambement carries on to the next stanza, forms the link
between the first half of the poem with its gratitude for the fulfilment of
basic needs—food, fire and rest—and the second half with its knowledge
of others' need. The owl's melancholy cry is a sound

> telling me plain what I escaped
> And others could not, that night, as in I went.
>
> And salted was my food, and my repose,
> Salted and sobered, too, by the bird's voice
> Speaking for all who lay under the stars,
> Soldiers and poor, unable to rejoice.

In my opinion this is one of Thomas's finest poems, all the more
impressive for its quietness and brevity. The diction is very plain yet it
holds a wealth of meaning, as in the use of 'salted', which is repeated as if
to savour its full ambiguity as both seasoned or heightened and made
bitter or stinging. The knowledge of 'what I escaped' increases the sense
of comfort, while knowing that 'others could not' modifies and sobers it.
Salted is the opposite of 'sweet', following on from 'rest had seemed the
sweetest thing under a roof.' Metre and rhyme are also very simple, yet a
sustained and subtle rhythm plays across the lines, breaking most in half,
and carrying the sense forward through the form, so that it might (almost)
be prose.

In another poem the choice of the owl as the voice speaking for 'those
others' (as in a variant title[13]) might have been a deliberate symbol; here
it seems only natural that the bird's melancholy cry should have brought
to mind all those spending the night 'under the stars, Soldiers and poor,
unable to rejoice.' One is perhaps a little surprised at the social under-

standing displayed in this poem, for Thomas often seems, as he himself believed, altogether too self-conscious and self-regarding, capable of the most sensitive recording of his own feelings but not so concerned with the larger world. Yet clearly he was aware of the society around him (and not only through the war) and of his relation to it; something of this is seen in 'Man and Dog'. In 'The Owl' it is made more direct, with the poet's enjoyment of simple pleasures at the end of a hard day's walking being compared with others' lack, so that what seems at the beginning the mere satisfaction of basic needs comes to be seen as a privilege, a benefit made possible only by others' sacrifice.

Perhaps it needed the war to make Thomas aware of his blessings. Certainly by the beginning of April 1915 it had become a constant echo in his verse. Few poems ignore the war entirely. In 'Lob', for instance, it is strongly present, though unspoken. In 'Wind and Mist' one of the speakers, fancifully, imagines England and Germany playing at chess on the chequered landscape below the hills (an image that reflects the literalness of Thomas's patriotic feeling). At Easter the war came to the forefront of Thomas's poetry in 'In Memoriam':

> The flowers left thick at nightfall in the wood
> This Eastertide call into mind the men,
> Now far from home, who, with their sweethearts, should
> Have gathered them and will do never again.

The poem is poignant and touched with an entirely proper sentimentality.

Up to this point, Thomas's perspective on the war is that of the civilian onlooker, not yet personally engaged but conscious and chastened by what is happening. He does not protest: death is a matter for regret, not for indignation: the waste of young men's lives is an inevitable aspect of war. As he came closer to taking a decision on his own course of action, Thomas's relation to war began to figure more prominently, as in 'Fifty Faggots', written on 13 May where he considers the wood-pile he has cut and stacked for winter fuel and, by extension, the future of both himself and it. As regards the wood-pile,

> Next Spring
> A blackbird or robin will nest there,

thinking it a permanent fixture. He knows their destiny, but not his own:

> 'Twas a hot day for carrying them up:
> Better they will never warm me, though they must
> Light several Winters' fires. Before they are done
> The war will have ended, many other things

Have ended, maybe, that I can no more
Foresee or more control than robin and wren.

At the end of June he was still uncertain as to what he should do. With
Marlborough finished (seven and a half thousand words written in twenty-
six days) he had set off on a short cycling holiday to Gloucester and back
through Coventry. He intended to use this trip to come to a definite
decision: 'Now I am going to cycle & think of man & nature & human
life & decide between enlisting or going to America before I enlist', he
told Bottomley. 'Those are the alternatives unless something turns up out
of the dark.'[14] On the road between Gloucester and Coventry[15] he composed the only poem in which he refers to himself as a poet—'Words',
which begins

> Out of us all
> That make rhymes,

and goes on to praise English words, 'light as dreams, tough as oak,
precious as gold' and 'as dear As the earth which you prove That we love',
ending

> Let me sometimes dance
> With you,
> Or climb
> Or stand perchance
> In ecstasy,
> Fixed and free
> In a rhyme,
> As poets do.

Some months later he was to use a similar form to express his deep-seated
fondness for roads and travelling in the poem 'Roads' which begins:

> I love roads:
> The goddesses that dwell
> Far along invisible
> Are my favourite gods.

but proceeds, more sombrely, to

> Now all roads lead to France
> And heavy is the tread
> Of the living; but the dead
> Returning lightly dance:

On his return from the cycling trip, Thomas went up to London, where he applied to join the Artists' Rifles, a territorial corps which undertook initial officer training. His medical examination on 13 July was satisfactory and he returned home in order to arrange his affairs before being attested on 19 July.

His old fear of failure had made him conceal his decision lest he be rejected on medical or other grounds. To Helen, he had pretended that he was going up to town to look for work, and then sent a telegram announcing his enlistment. When they met at Steep station, Edward was already a soldier, in uniform and with his hair cropped. Initially and understandably dismayed, Helen persuaded herself that what was right for him was right for her, though she cannot but have regarded the future with foreboding. They took one long and glorious walk together in the familiar and loved countryside around Steep, and, as she recalled later:

> Sometimes, walking through familiar country which we loved, we talked of that, and sometimes in the old way we walked silently. I remember thinking 'Oh, if only we could walk on like this for ever, and for ever it be summer, and for ever we be happy!' And then I remembered that after all the war was itself the reason of this very walk, and had its part in the depth of our deep content with the English country and with each other.[16]

On hearing the news, Eleanor's first response was 'I don't know why, but I am glad.' Edward replied, 'I am too, and I don't know why either.'[17] A week later, following his first day's drill during which his Achilles tendon became so inflamed by the new boots that he had to be given an immediate week's sick leave, Edward told Eleanor he was about to see the doctor: 'I only hope he won't give me leisure to think why I joined. Several people *have* asked me, but I could not answer them yet.'[18]

Part of the answer can be read from the poetry. Earlier in the year Thomas had written 'Health', an intensely self-regarding poem about ambition and chronic dissatisfaction:

> had I health I could not ride or run or fly
> So far or so rapidly over the land
> As I desire: I should reach Wiltshire tired;
> I should have changed my mind before I could be in Wales.
> I could not love; I could not command love.
> Beauty would still be far off
> However many hills I climbed over;
> Peace would still be farther.

He had given up seeking medical cures for his melancholy and come to

believe it was in his nature to be sorrowful and dissatisfied, never knowing
contentment or peace of mind. This, at least, is the message of 'Aspens',
a poem committed to the notebook on 11 July,[19] just two days before he
went for a soldier. The chief subject is the trees:

> All day and night, save winter, every weather,
> Above the inn, the smithy, and the shop,
> The aspens at the cross-roads talk together
> Of rain, until their last leaves fall from the top.

In the last two stanzas the connection between trees and man is made:

> Over all sorts of weather, men, and times,
> Aspens must shake their leaves and men may hear
> But need not listen, more than to my rhymes.

> Whatever wind blows, while they and I have leaves
> We cannot other than an aspen be
> That ceaselessly, unreasonably grieves,
> Or so men think who like a different tree.

The comparison, or identification, of Thomas with the aspens is delicately
done, and defies paraphrase, yet so unmistakeable is the meaning that one
is surprised to learn that Eleanor misunderstood the poem. 'You missed
just the turn that I thought essential', Thomas told her. '*I* was the aspen.
"We" meant the trees and I with my dejected sadness. Does that clear it
up, or do you think in rereading it that I have not emphasised it enough?'[20]

A couple of days later, Thomas wrote 'For These':

> An acre of land between the shore and the hills,
> Upon a ledge that shows my kingdoms three,
> The lovely visible earth and sky and sea
> Where what the curlew needs not, the farmer tills:

> A house that shall love me as I love it,
> Well-hedged, and honoured by a few ash trees
> That linnets, greenfinches and goldfinches
> Shall often visit and make love in and flit:

> A garden I need never go beyond,
> Broken but neat, whose sunflowers every one
> Are fit to be the sign of the Rising Sun:
> A spring, a brook's bend, or at least a pond:

For these I ask not, but, neither too late
Nor yet too early, for what men call content,
And also that something may be sent
To be contented with, I ask of Fate.

This needs virtually no explication, being among the most lucid of poems, using the familiar means of establishing desires only to deny them. What is (or is not) being denied are all the ideals of Thomas's country life. The first three stanzas may stand as an emblem of the ideals of Back to the Land, while the kingdoms three of earth and sky and sea take us back to Richard Jefferies' writing, with the birds and the house and garden belonging to Thomas's own dream world. But they are ideals, unattainable. Thus the reversal of reality in 'what the curlew needs not, the farmer tills', or the impossible 'house that shall love me as I love it', or the fairy garden 'I need never go beyond', and the final recognition that what is needed is not fantasies but satisfaction in things as they are. This represents a coming to terms with the mortal world, and an understanding of what the country can and cannot give. Yet Thomas is not entirely subdued; he asks not only for 'what men call content' but also for 'something to be contented with'.

It is curious that Thomas appears to put himself in the hands of Fate in this poem at the very time when he was doing that in life. Once he had joined the Army there was no going back and no discharge except in the case of injury or death. He would have no chance to regret or rescind his decision. This he understood from the beginning. Less than a month after he had joined, he wrote to Eleanor saying, 'Part of me envies you getting about and envies me of 12 months ago at Ledington, without a pang though. I have to learn to keep my buttons bright . . . I have conspired with God (I suppose) not to think about walks and walking sticks or 6 months or 6 years hence. I just think about when I shall first go on guard etc.'[21] He was already learning something about contentment.

Although Thomas became a soldier because of his deep feeling for his country, he was anything but conventionally patriotic. This brought him into conflict once more with his father, in whose house he was billeted. Philip Henry Thomas shared with the majority of the nation the patriotism which had instantly turned to hating Germans and to elevating the courage and heroism of the British in battle. His son, fresh from studying the realities of war under Marlborough and disinclined to believe the newspapers, argued against this simplistic notion of Goodies vs Baddies. He suggested, to his father's rage, that German soldiers were as brave as British, or conversely, that the British tommy was as likely to be scared of being killed as any German. Nothing, perhaps, was more calculated to annoy his father than such unmilitary sentiments expressed by one in uniform, a volunteer who refused the reflected glory.

The argument was bitter and unresolved. Thomas returned to his training in a disturbed and grumpy frame of mind,[22] and attempted to work the bitterness out of himself by putting his views into verse:

> This is no case of petty right or wrong
> That politicians or philosophers
> Can judge. I hate not Germans, nor grow hot
> With love of Englishmen, to please newspapers.

He claims to love even the Kaiser better than 'one fat patriot' (hints of war profiteering lurking in this image) and then says that the issue is not Britain versus Germany:

> But I have not to choose between the two,
> Or between justice and injustice. Dinned
> With war and argument I read no more
> Than in the storm smoking along the wind
> Athwart the wood. Two witches' cauldrons roar.
> From one the weather shall rise clear and gay;
> Out of the other an England beautiful
> And like her mother that died yesterday.

It is surprising to find Thomas adopting the contemporary view, seen also in the image of 'swimmers into cleanness leaping' in Brooke's war sonnet 'Peace', of war as a cleansing or purifying process. But we know how much he disliked the modern England of cities and industrialism, and how he dreamt of restoring and returning to Old England 'that was called Merry'—'her mother that died yesterday'. Nostalgia remained a potent force.

The remainder of the poem, however, takes us beyond nostalgia, to the core of his feeling for his country:

> Little I know or care if, being dull,
> I shall miss something that historians
> Can rake out of the ashes when perchance
> The phoenix broods serene above their ken.
> But with the best and meanest Englishmen
> I am one in crying, God save England, lest
> We lose what never slaves and cattle blessed.
> The ages made her that made us from dust:
> She is all we know and live by, and we trust
> She is good and must endure, loving her so:
> And as we love ourselves we hate her foe.

'She is all we know and live by': all his adult life Thomas had lived by his idea of England, the England of field and furrow, copse and cottage, the England of 'The Manor Farm' and 'Haymaking'. With Coleridge he believed:

> There lives nor form nor feeling in my soul
> Unborrowed from my country.

Whatever the intellectual or political arguments might be, if England was at war, under threat, possessed of enemies, he could do nothing else but go to her defence.

The literal patriotism that drove Thomas to identify his beloved rural landscape with his nation at war has parallels in other war poetry of the time, most notably in that of Rupert Brooke, whose most explicitly patriotic poem was 'The Soldier'. In this, the poet identifies himself with the soil of England, a being:

> whom England bore, shaped, made aware,
> Gave, once, her flowers to love, her ways to roam,
> A body of England's, breathing English air,
> Washed by the rivers, blest by suns of home.

In a fragment of verse composed as his troopship steamed towards the Dardanelles in the spring of 1915, Brooke began a long poem about England,[23] containing the line 'She is all we have loved and found and known.' This is strikingly similar to Thomas's 'She is all we know and live by.' Brooke would have understood what Thomas meant when, walking in the country with Eleanor later in the war, he answered her question 'Do you know what you are fighting for?' by bending down to pick up a crumble of earth and saying 'Literally, for this.'[24]

After his first week's training, Thomas wrote no more verses until the end of the year. He was busy with basic soldiering—drilling, route marches, guard duty. It was, as he had anticipated, an entirely new life, with entirely new values, that he had resolved to accept. By September, his letters show him becoming a little bored with Army life. There was no sign of the commission for which he had enlisted, despite the fact that the demands of the war meant that the Artists' Rifles were producing two hundred and fifty new officers a month. He was hoping for weekend leave, anxious to lift the potatoes in the garden at Steep to see Helen through the winter.

At the end of September he moved to 'camp' at an Army base near Epping Forest in Essex, not far from London. At first he found it unpleasant and uncomfortable, living with the men of his company in huts rather like dormitories, with no privacy and nowhere to relax after the day's work except the draughty, noisy canteen. He was trying to learn the contents of the various army manuals required by potential officers, and learning to get on with his fellow soldiers, an assorted bunch of men. In October the company was moved back to headquarters for a fortnight, and spent some of its time practising map-reading on Hampstead Heath. Thomas showed some talent for this, acquired as a result of his years of walking throughout southern England and Wales, and when the company moved back to camp near Romford, also in Essex, he was promoted to lance-corporal and appointed assistant instructor in map-reading. As well as teaching recruits how to read and follow a map, instruction also involved sketching and rough map-drawing of unfamiliar terrain; most of the work was practical and out of doors.

Though strenuous—early in December Thomas taught one five-day course from 7.30 a.m. to 4.30 p.m.—it was pleasant to be out in the autumn countryside. Life was made easier by the regular weekend leaves every fortnight, when he could get home and continue to sort out his affairs. It was, after all, not so different from previous occasions when he had lived away from home—except that now his visits were rationed and he came· willingly. His relationship with Helen had rarely been better, and Thomas's biographer states that 'they hoped in vain for another child during his last year in England.'[25] One of Thomas's satisfactions was the regular separation allowance paid to Helen as a result of his enlistment—a little ironic, in view of his earlier refusal to take a regular paid job. Mervyn was due back from America at Christmas.

Towards the end of November Thomas found his poetic impulse returning, firstly with 'There's Nothing Like the Sun', celebrating a simple sense of contentment but ending on an ominous note:

> No day of any month but I have said—
> Or, if I could live long enough, should say—
> 'There's nothing like the sun that shines to-day.'
> There's nothing like the sun till we are dead.

Ten days later, he wrote 'Liberty', perhaps his most considered account of his present situation. The poem is set at night, we may imagine looking out from an Army hut:

> The last light has gone out of the world, except
> This moonlight lying on the grass like frost
> Beyond the brink of the tall elm's shadow.

The poet compares himself with the moon:

> Both have liberty
> To dream what we could do if we were free
> To do some thing we had desired long,
> The moon and I. There's none less free than who
> Does nothing and has nothing else to do,
> Being free only for what is not to his mind,
> And nothing is to his mind.

'Freedom' had been a watchword in Thomas's youth, associated with the escape from home and the city, with living naturally and loving without constraint. By refusing to take a regular job, Thomas had believed himself free to do what he really wanted—to write and dream. But he had learnt that this was a delusion, that 'There's none less free than who Does nothing.' He now dreamt of turning this wisdom into wealth:

> If every hour
> Like this one passing that I have spent among
> The wiser others when I have forgot
> To wonder whether I was free or not,
> Were piled before me, and not lost behind,
> And I could take and carry them away
> I should be rich;

or into greater wisdom:

> or if I had the power
> To wipe out every one and not again
> Regret, I should be rich to be so poor.

The poem ends on different note:

> And yet I still am half in love with pain,
> With what is imperfect, with both tears and mirth,
> With things that have an end, with life and earth,
> And this moon that leaves me dark within the door.

This is in some ways an opaque poem, with the form of a night-time reverie, moving from thought to thought. It is a renunciation of his search for perfection and an acceptance of things as they are, mixed, uncertain, mortal. It expresses the maturity of relinquishing the dream of absolute liberty, riding with the moon in pursuit of vain desires, and of being content to remain 'dark within the door'.

Thomas had described his decision to enlist as 'the natural culmination of a long series of moods and thoughts.'[26] Having impelled him to identify his deep and abiding love of the countryside with his love of his country, and to act in accordance with his feeling, the war had brought Thomas to a sort of satisfaction.

I I

Whatever It Is I Seek

> It is not out of reach, yet it is never attained. It
> is not forbidden, and nevertheless something
> withholds or indefinitely delays it. Some day—
> somehow—we shall be there and not leave it
> again; but not yet.
>
> 'The Island'

Thomas had spent many years searching for happiness, for 'something to be contented with.' He had thought to find it in the country. Several poems testify to Thomas's hope that, somehow, he could unlock the key to nature's secret and share in its happiness. Birds' song was most often seen as the instrument: if only it could be translated, nature's meaning might be revealed. 'What did the thrushes know?' he asked in 'March', answering 'Something they knew—I also, while they sang.' The distracted woman in 'She Dotes'

> has fancied blackbirds hide
> A secret, and that thrushes chide
> Because she thinks death can divide
> Her from her lover:
> And she has slept, trying to translate
> The word the cuckoo cries to his mate
> Over and over.

The woman is plainly deranged, is she not? to imagine that the birds are talking to her. To believe in the possibility of direct communication with nature is to fantasise and dream.

But it was this mystery at the heart of the relationship between man and nature that Thomas had set out to elucidate when he dreamt of being a country writer. As the poem 'Sedge-Warblers' made clear, he had begun with fancies drawn from the myth of the Golden Age, and it was not until he was

> rid of this dream, ere I had drained
> Its poison,

that he came to appreciate the sedge-warblers' song despite the lack of melody, for its wisdom beyond that of human kind:

> This was the best of May—the small brown birds
> Wisely reiterating endlessly
> What no man learnt yet, in or out of school.

Nature's wisdom is secret, hidden, concealed. But it is there all the same, and something of its meaning can be absorbed by man, if he can respond to nature as it is, without dreams and illusions.

The same message is contained in 'I Never Saw that Land Before', a poem about an unidentified landscape which has been known only briefly. It is a pastoral scene of the kind that pleased Thomas most in the country, the epitome of his country books, and that which he had most wanted to 'transmute into words'. Here is

> the valley and the river small,
> The cattle, the grass, the bare ash trees,
> The chickens from the farmsteads, all
> Elm-hidden, and the tributaries
> Descending at equal interval;

The exact location is not important. Here is felt the essence of the country, the essence which could be felt but not known, from the breeze 'That hinted all and nothing spoke', and all that Thomas wanted to say but could not find adequate words for:

> I neither expected anything
> Nor yet remembered: but some goal
> I touched then; and if I could sing
> What would not even whisper my soul
> As I went on my journeying,
>
> I should use, as the trees and birds did,
> A language not to be betrayed;
> And what was hid should still be hid
> Excepting from those like me made
> Who answer when such whispers bid.

The goal touched, intuitively felt but not to be verbally rendered, is a private one. The ambition to convey nature's inner meaning, to reach through into the other world, to translate the trees' and birds' language, is here recognised as an impossible one, yet not without its rewards. Nature's secret remains inaccessible.

The quest for happiness continued. It was found mainly in retrospect as if it were something that belonged to the past. In 'It Rains', the poet looks out on the orchard and back on the past:

> And I am nearly as happy as possible
> To search the wilderness in vain though well,
> To think of two walking, kissing there,
> Drenched, yet forgetting the kisses of the rain:

In 'The Unknown Bird', the remembrance of a strange bird stimulates similar reflections:

> Three lovely notes he whistled, too soft to be heard
> If others sang; but others never sang
> In the great beech-wood all that May and June.
> . . .
>   Was it but four years
> Ago? or five? He never came again
> . . .
>   I never knew a voice,
> Man, beast, or bird, better than this. I told
> The naturalists; but neither had they heard
> Anything like the notes that did so haunt me,
> I had them clear by heart and have them still.
> Four years, or five, have made no difference.

The bird's voice was sweet, sad and joyful all at once, suggesting a happiness 'too far off for me to taste it'. Yet is memory to be trusted?

>   I cannot tell
> If truly never anything but fair
> The days were when he sang, as now they seem.

The unknown bird, it has been suggested, was the golden oriole,[1] a rare summer visitor to Britain, but for the poem's sake it is better that it remain unidentified, mysterious,

> As if a cock crowed past the edge of the world,
> As if the bird or I were in a dream.

for it stands as a symbol of the elusive joy Thomas could never quite capture in the present moment.

Haunted by memories of past, irrecoverable happiness, Thomas continued 'to search the wilderness' for something that always proved

unknowable and inexpressible. Sometimes, in his despair, he felt himself
doomed to an endless, hopeless yearning, as when in 'The Glory' he turned
from nature to ask:

> Shall I now this day
> Begin to seek as far as heaven, as hell,
> Wisdom or strength to match this beauty, start
> And tread the pale dust pitted with small dark drops,
> In hope to find whatever it is I seek,

and carried on in a desperate spiral of unanswered, unanswerable questions:

> Or must I be content with discontent
> As larks and swallows are perhaps with wings?
> And shall I ask at the day's end once more
> What beauty is, and what I can have meant
> By happiness? And shall I let all go,
> Glad, weary, or both?

At other moments, he felt himself close to his goal, as when in 'The
Ash Grove' he recalled entering an empty, half-dead grove of trees where

> nothing at all,
> Not even the spirits of memory and fear with restless wing,
> Could climb down in to molest me

and

> the moment unveiled something unwilling to die
> And I had what most I desired, without search or desert or cost.

What was it Thomas most desired? Even at the moment when he approaches it, he cannot put it into words.

This sense of endless, unsatisfied searching—for what? contentment,
certainty, a feeling of belonging?—constitutes the undeniable modernity
of Thomas's verse. It expresses more than the simple nostalgia for lost
childhood, rather all the mobility, aspiration, rootlessness, insecurity and
self-consciousness of the individual in modern society, a state of mind
which neither memory nor dream can console, a despair that, like the
aspens, 'ceaselessly, unreasonably grieves' for what cannot, given the
absence of social or religious belief, ever be found. In Housman's words,
the modern individual is doomed to wander 'a stranger and afraid In a
world I never made.'

All his life Thomas had sought to make a world for himself, to find a place where he would be at home, at rest. Such is the message of 'Home', a poem in which he describes a sense of being at one with his environment:

> Often I had gone this way before:
> But now it seemed I never could be
> And never had been anywhere else;
> 'Twas home; one nationality
> We had, I and the birds that sang,
> One memory.
>
> They welcomed me. I had come back
> That eve somehow from somewhere far:
> . . .
>
> The thrush on the oaktop in the lane
> Sang his last song, or last but one;
> And as he ended, on the elm
> Another had but just begun
> . . .
>
> Then past his dark white cottage front
> A labourer went along, his tread
> Slow, half with weariness, half with ease;
> And, through the silence, from his shed
> The sound of sawing rounded all
> That silence said.

That others could sometimes absorb this sense from Thomas himself is indicated by Walter de la Mare's remark that 'to be with him in the country was to be in one's own native place, and even a Cockney's starven roots may thirst for the soil.'[2] But such assurance as this was not permanent. In his life in the country Thomas had moved many times, always in search of somewhere that would banish his melancholy and make him feel at home at last. As he grew older he came to realise that nothing in the external world could satisfy what was essentially an inner need. At the same time, he also understood that to look for dreams and ideals in the real world could only aggravate his sense of dissatisfaction. In this respect the poem 'Wind and Mist', quoted in Chapter 5, has a dual message, being about both the house built for the Thomases on the ridge at Wick Green, where they hoped to make their home permanently, and the dreams that prevented him from coming to terms with reality:

> 'But flint and clay and childbirth were too real
> For this cloud-castle. . . .'

At the very end of the poem, however, the speaker stops suddenly, and says:

> 'But one word. I want to admit
> That I would try the house once more, if I could;
> As I should like to try being young again.'

If one could live one's life again, without illusions, one might learn from one's mistakes.

But there is no going back. In another poem, again with 'Home' as the title, Thomas returned to the theme of the necessity of coming to terms with the past. It is written in simple quatrains, the rhythm broken by short terse statements conveying a feeling of having come to a stop:

> Not the end: but there's nothing more.
> Sweet Summer and Winter rude
> I have loved, and friendship and love,
> The crowd and solitude:
>
> But I know them: I weary not;
> But all that they mean I know.
> I would go back again home
> Now. Yet how should I go?
>
> This is my grief. That land,
> My home, I have never seen;
> No traveller tells of it,
> However far he has been.
>
> And could I discover it,
> I fear my happiness there,
> Or my pain, might be dreams of return
> Here, to these things that were.
>
> Remembering ills, though slight
> Yet irremediable,
> Brings a worse, an impurer pang
> Than remembering what was well.
>
> No: I cannot go back,
> And would not if I could.
> Until blindness come, I must wait
> And blink at what is not good.

In this poem, Thomas's long sense of searching, always in vain, for nature's secret, happiness, or home, is stilled. His desire to 'go back home' is strong, but without an object: the goal is unknown, a land he has never seen. 'Home' is a way of describing heaven, beyond the edge of the world. And, if it could be reached, it might hold both happiness and pain, like the present, and make him dream of 'returning' to what he now wants to leave behind. The sense, using the metaphor of travelling, looks towards the past, in the sense of 'going back', and moves towards the future— 'could I discover it'—when the present will seem the 'these things that were'. To go home is both a retreat and an advance, and a journey into the unknown. The verse, although most simple in its words and phrases, holds these subtleties of meaning in perfect suspension: thought and language are fused. The conclusion is unqualified—the poet gives up the desire to go back and resolves to await death ('blindness', not the expected illumination of heaven) with all the fortitude he can muster.

There were many things to 'blink' at in army life, and Thomas was stoically resolved not to complain or regret. He spent the first six months of his enlistment adapting himself to the military way of life, aiming to do so without ostentation or inner conflict. On one occasion he was mortified to find that he had unintentionally let his hair grow too long, by soldiers' standards. By the beginning of 1916 he had, he felt, fitted himself to his new life. He thought of staying on as a map instructor, especially if he was promoted and given a higher separation allowance. The alternative was to seek a commission. Beyond that he still saw France.

The off-duty hours Thomas found dismal and tedious, particularly at weekends when he could not get leave. He had little in common with most of his fellow soldiers and although not unfriendly he could not easily join in their conversation or leisure activities. He made a determined effort to be more sociable, hitting upon the method of finding some district known to him and each of the men in his hut. In the evenings he kept largely to himself, reading or writing letters. Partly at least to escape from boredom, he began writing consistently again in 1916, completing twenty-eight poems in the first five months of the year, compared with only eight since his enlistment the previous July. One, written in March, was a third poem with the word 'home' for a title, although this time it was set in quotation marks, ' "Home" ', as an ironic comment on its subject. It opens with three men returning from an exercise in the snow-covered country.

> Fair was the morning, fair our tempers, and
> We had seen nothing fairer than that land,
> . . .
> Fair too was afternoon, and first to pass
> Were we that league of snow, next the north wind.

There was nothing to return for, except need,
And yet we sang nor ever stopped for speed,
As we did often with the start behind.
Faster still strode we when we came in sight
Of the cold roofs where we must spend the night.
Happy we had not been there, nor could be,
Though we had tasted sleep and food and fellowship
Together long.

       'How quick', to someone's lip
The words came, 'will the beaten horse run home!'

The word 'home' raised a smile in us all three,
And one repeated it, smiling just so
That all knew what he meant and none would say.
Between three counties far apart that lay
We were divided and looked strangely each
At the other, and we knew we were not friends
But fellows in a union that ends
With the necessity for it, as it ought.

Never a word was spoken, not a thought
Was thought, of what the look meant with the word
'Home' as we walked and watched the sunset blurred.
And then to me the word, only the word,
'Homesick', as it were playfully occurred:
No more.

      If I should ever more admit
Than the mere word I could not endure it
For a day longer: this captivity
Must somehow come to an end, else I should be
Another man, as often now I seem,
Or this life be only an evil dream.

This is a bleak conclusion, sparely written, to Thomas's only poem directly about army life, and it shows clearly that whatever peace of mind he may have gained from the decision to enlist, he did not enjoy the consequences—notwithstanding the pleasure of the snow-covered landscape—and that he schooled himself not to complain. He had taken a decision and meant to see it through, but it was 'captivity', the opposite of freedom, and his companions were not friends 'but fellows in a union that ends with the necessity for it.' To survive meant to suppress a large part of himself. The war was an evil dream and he was only sustained by the fact that it must end one day.

Hitherto Thomas had been determined not to look beyond the immediate future, or at least not beyond the next leave. But the war was becoming inexorable in its demand for men and those passing through the Romford training camp were steadily being transferred into front-line units, whose fate was in everyone's minds. Several men were on one occasion detailed without warning for France and sent to fighting units without the option. Even the instructors might be drafted, it was rumoured.

Thomas did not volunteer; he was not yet ready to go. Yet the future was very much in his mind, and he had begun to contemplate it obliquely in his verse. In February he wrote the two poems to his parents discussed in Chapter 1. 'P.H.T.', to his father, was completed on 8 February, barely two months since they had argued so fiercely and unpleasantly about patriotism. Perhaps the unsettling effect of this had urged Edward towards what was to be his final reckoning of the filial relationship:

> I may come near loving you
> When you are dead
> . . .
> But not so long as you live
> Can I love you at all.

Three days later followed the poem to his mother, for whom his feelings were very different. She had recently been in hospital for a cataract operation, and Thomas was anxious on her behalf. In the poem, however, it is not her death which is envisaged (as it is his father's in 'P.H.T.'— with a touch of oedipal feeling perhaps) but his own:

> No one so much as you
> Loves this my clay,
> Or would lament as you
> Its dying day.

Two months later, this eventuality is implicit in the poems to his children, which have the flavour of a bequest, disguised as make-believe fantasy: 'If I should ever by chance grow rich' and 'If I were to own this countryside' standing almost for 'If I should die'.

Instead of property or wealth, Thomas is leaving his children their shared delight in nature and the countryside, flowers, birds and country place names:

> Shellow, Rochetts, Bandish, and Pickerells,
> Martins, Lambkins and Lillyputs,
> Their copses, ponds, roads, and ruts,
> Fields where plough-horses steam and plovers
> Fling and whimper . . .

In 'giving' these portions of the countryside to his children, Thomas was expressing one of his deepest ideas, that the true owners of the land were those who loved and appreciated its beauty, those who dreamt of its immortality and who were prepared to die for it. Thus the conceit of ownership, though appropriately 'make-believe', has a serious base.

The fact that the four family poems, to Bronwen, Mervyn, Myfanwy and Helen, were written in sequence[3] suggests a certain deliberation, as if Thomas knew what he meant to do. Only in the third poem, however, is there as much as a hint that in these verses he was, poetically speaking, drawing up his will—and even the hint is ambiguous:

> What shall I give my daughter the younger
> More than will keep her from cold and hunger?
> I shall not give her anything.
> . . .
> But leave her Steep and her own world
> And her spectacled self with hair uncurled . . .

In this context, 'leave' can mean either 'bequeath' or 'not alter'—or, most probably, both.

Although Thomas had not tried sending his verses to any editors since joining the Army, he still retained his pseudonym, trusting the friends who knew to keep confidence regarding the authorship. As it happened, it was an unintentional breach of this confidence that led to the first major appearance of the poems in print. In July 1915 Bottomley had discussed the possibility of publishing an anthology of new verse with Lascelles Abercrombie and R.C. (Bob) Trevelyan—a now forgotten contributor to *Georgian Poetry* who was also known to Thomas. The idea was to collect half a dozen poets and print a selection of their latest work in an annual anthology. The plan clearly owed much to *Georgian Poetry* and *New Numbers*. Having a number of Thomas's poems in the house, Bottomley brought them out to show the others, suggesting that Thomas be invited to be a contributor. Abercrombie and Trevelyan were at once interested and of like mind. Bottomley wrote to tell Thomas, who replied that he was still intending to keep his poems secret from all but a few close friends but that he was so pleased at Abercrombie's liking them that he should 'not dream of complaining.'[4]

The other contributors to *An Annual of New Poetry* (1917) were W. H.

Davies, John Drinkwater, Wilfrid Gibson, T. Sturge Moore and Robert Frost, together with Bottomley and Trevelyan. All the work was previously unpublished. When the selection was to be made, Thomas sent forty poems for consideration, out of his total stock to date (March 1916) of nearly a hundred. He was clearly hopeful of the opportunity of publication, anxious lest inclusion in an anthology should make his verse indistinguishable from the rest, and wishing for recognition on his own merits.[5] Today, knowing how Thomas's reputation has grown by comparison with that of the Georgian commonalty, and how instantly distinguishable his work is, this fear may seem foolish, but it serves as a reminder that he had as yet had no recognition and could not know how his verses would be received by the public and the critics. It was this that made him retain the pseudonym. With eighteen poems 'Edward Eastaway' had the largest and most impressive section in the book.[6]

From the correspondence concerning this selection some of Thomas's own preferences can be seen. At first he approved of Bottomley's choice, but a month later he sent 'Aspens' and 'After Rain', urging that they replace 'Wind and Mist', on the grounds that it was too long and too like 'The New House', also included in the *Annual*. Bottomley argued strongly in favour of 'Wind and Mist', and it stayed. Thomas wrote again, suggesting that 'After Rain' replace 'The Glory', a suggestion apparently adopted, for the latter poem does not appear in the book. At the same time Bottomley agreed to include 'Aspens' after all, it is not known at the expense of which poem if any.[7] It is no surprise to learn that 'Aspens' was a favourite poem; more so to learn that 'After Rain' with its contentious rhyme of 'inlaid/played' was so favoured. Altogether, Bottomley's choice was a good one, including several poems important to a judicious understanding of Thomas's poetic work such as 'Old Man', 'Beauty', 'Sedge-Warblers', 'For These' and 'Roads'.

Among the others was the recent 'The Word', a poem with distinct similarities to 'Old Man'. It opens with an easy, almost rambling reflection on memory:

> There are so many things I have forgot,
> That once were much to me, or that were not,
> All lost, as is a childless woman's child
> And its child's children, in the undefiled
> Abyss of what will never be again.
> I have forgot, too, names of the mighty men
> That fought and lost or won in the old wars,
> Of kings and fiends and gods, and most of the stars.
> Some things I have forgot that I forget.

and moves on to a more tantalising matter:

> One name that I have not—
> Though 'tis an empty thingless name—forgot
> Never can die because Spring after Spring
> Some thrushes learn to say it as they sing.
> There is always one at midday saying it clear
> And tart—the name, only the name I hear.
> While perhaps I am thinking of the elder scent
> That is like food; or while I am content
> With the wild rose scent that is like memory,
> This name suddenly is cried out to me
> From somewhere in the bushes by a bird
> Over and over again, a pure thrush word.

Thrush, we know, was a language Thomas longed to learn, fancying it might unlock the key to nature. Its 'empty thingless name' represents one, or all, of the things forgotten or lost in the past, the 'undefiled abyss of what can never be again'. As a child, Thomas had been distressed by a strange sense of loss—for the book called *The Key of Knowledge* in particular—which could not be repaired in later life: 'Some things I have forgot that I forget.' The past, like the dark avenue in 'Old Man', is impenetrable, impassable.

The future was another matter. Should Thomas apply for a commission and the front, or remain 'safe' as a map instructor for the duration? There were arguments on both sides. Helen was talking of leaving Steep and finding a house in Essex to be near Mervyn, who was about to take an engineering apprenticeship with the London United Tramway Co. at Walthamstow, north-east of London, which had been arranged through the good offices of one of Edward's brothers and suited Mervyn's mechanical aptitudes. Thomas was conscious of his responsibility to his family, and of Helen's impulsive and disorganised approach to financial matters. But map-instructing had been, as he explained to Bottomley, 'first too comfortable & then too uncomfortable a job'.[8] Not surprisingly, the instructors were regarded by the other soldiers as 'truants', avoiding the risks, and Thomas no more wished to save his own skin than he wished to kill the Kaiser himself. His state of indecision, however, proved poetically productive, and many of the poems written in the summer of 1916 reflect Thomas's immediate concerns, illustrating the thoughts and feelings that accompanied what was to be his last major decision in life.

On 25 and 26 May he considered his uncertain future directly in ten lines inspired by the sound of a bugle call:

> 'No one cares less than I,
> Nobody knows but God,
> Whether I am destined to lie

Under a foreign clod,'
Were the words I made to the bugle call in the morning.

But laughing, storming, scorning,
Only the bugles know
What the bugles say in the morning,
And they do not care, when they blow
The call that I heard and made words to early this morning.

He did care, however. A couple of days later he pursued the theme in 'As the Team's Headbrass', a longer poem using the now familiar device of dialogue to voice the different, contradictory aspects of the matter under consideration—whether or not to volunteer for France.

The poem is set in a field that is being ploughed by a team of horses at a slow, immemorial pace. The narrator, evidently in uniform, is sitting on a fallen elm.[9] At each turn the soldier exchanges a word with the ploughman, 'about the weather, next about the war'. The ploughman asks if he has 'been out', that is in France:

'No.' 'And don't want to, perhaps?'
'If I could only come back again, I should.
I could spare an arm. I shouldn't want to lose
A leg. If I should lose my head, why, so,
I should want nothing more . . .'

The ploughman voices a natural reluctance. The narrator responds with a sober assessment of the risks involved, not only that of death but also those of mutilation, which were considerable.

At the next turn the ploughman starts to talk of the impact of the war on himself and the land:

'Only two teams work on the farm this year.
One of my mates is dead. The second day
In France they killed him . . .'

and speculates on what might have been:

'if
He had stayed here we should have moved the tree.'

If it were not for the war, the narrator replies, still cool and philosophical:

'Everything
Would have been different. For it would have been
Another world.'

'Ay, and a better', counters the ploughman, voicing the most direct criticism of the war to be heard in this or any other poem of Thomas's. It is, however, immediately modified by the stoical 'If we could see all all might seem good' expressing a countryman's resignation to fate.

The tension in this poem lies between the ploughman's restrained but real bitterness towards the war and the narrator's controlled determination to accept it—a necessary attitude for a combatant to adopt. The poem, however, has more than a personal application: it is about necessary and contradictory attitudes towards the war. It contains, too, a recognition of war's transitoriness, in its implicit understanding that the land will still need to be ploughed, whatever happens. In this it is similar to Hardy's 'In Time of the Breaking of Nations'. Compare Hardy's opening:

> Only a man harrowing clods
> In a slow silent walk
> With an old horse that stumbles and nods
> Half asleep as they stalk.

with Thomas's ending:

> The horses started and for the last time
> I watched the clods crumble and topple over
> After the ploughshare and the stumbling team.

He had almost made up his mind to go out. He prepared himself with 'Early One Morning', a jaunty song based on Rio Grande, with the refrain:

> I'm bound away for ever,
> Away somewhere, away for ever.

This statement is, of course, not to be taken seriously; the folksong mode is being employed. The first line stresses the naïf quality: 'Early one morning in May I set out'—before the second undercuts it with a strange deflationary realism: 'And nobody knew I was about.' The verses continue in this double movement, the jolly rhythm accompanied by a mocking undertow:

> There was no wind to trouble the weathercocks.
> I had burnt my letters and darned my socks.
>
> No one knew I was going away,
> I thought myself I should come back some day.

> I heard the brook through the town gardens run.
> O sweet was the mud turned to dust by the sun.

until they reach a turning point:

> A gate banged in a fence and banged in my head.
> 'A fine morning, sir', a shepherd said.

From now on the poem's tone is serious, though not solemn. The gate in the poet's head is shut on the past; as in 'Home' there is a refusal to look backwards, a deliberate cutting loose from the past, leaving the town gardens, the brook, youth, love and misery, good and bad. The final couplet looks mercilessly at the past, and sets off into the future with a carefree air:

> The past is the only dead thing that smells sweet,
> The only sweet thing that is not also fleet.
>   I'm bound away for ever,
>   Away somewhere, away for ever.

Read as an oblique statement of intent, the mode of this poem expresses a crucial element in the decision to volunteer for France: the uncertainty of the outcome. It was necessary to act both as if the decision were final ('burnt my letters') and as if it were not ('I thought myself I should come back one day'). The only possible attitude is that of the wanderer setting off into the unknown.

A fortnight later, on 21 June, Thomas returned again to the theme in a burst of fluency caused by three days' sickness and confinement. 'It Was Upon' looks more sombrely at the future. It relates directly to the past, too, looking back to a moment twenty years earlier when Thomas had noted a mown hayfield in Wiltshire. It was recorded as the entry for 30 June 1895 in the 'Diary in English Fields and Woods' in *The Woodland Life*, and reads thus:

> Grass of the rising aftermath or 'lattermath' beautifully green after a quickening rain, while the thistled pastures are grey.

The poem mistakes the month, but not the memory:

> It was upon a July evening.
> At a stile I stood, looking along a path
> Over the country by a second Spring
> Drenched perfect green again.

The words uttered on that occasion—'the lattermath will be a fine one'—come back to mind now:

> after the interval
> Of a score years, when those fields are by me
> Never to be recrossed, now I recall,
> This July eve, and question, wondering,
> What of the lattermath to this hoar Spring?

'Hoar' is the only hint of what is envisaged. The poem's power lies almost entirely behind the lines in what is understood rather than stated in the unspoken image of the mown meadows—other, older images: all flesh is grass, death the mower, scything men. These echoes connect the past and present green fields with the war and bring together the cutting of the hay and the infantry in battle. The lattermath or second hay crop is green and spring-like; what of war's aftermath? No answer is ventured, but the foreboding is registered.

Two days later came 'There Was a Time', another poem looking back towards youth:

> There was a time when this poor frame was whole
> And I had youth and never another care,
> Or none that should have troubled a strong soul ...

and concluding

> But now that there is something I could use
> My youth and strength for, I deny the age,
> The care and weakness that I know—refuse
> To admit I am unworthy of the wage
> Paid to a man who gives up eyes and breath
> For what would neither ask nor heed his death.

Eleanor thought these lines sick. Thomas replied that they were 'more than a shade heroic'.[10]

He had in fact made up his mind to go. He put his name down for a commission in the Royal Garrison Artillery or the Anti-Aircraft division. Gunnery of this kind required a good deal of specialised knowledge, and he began to re-learn maths he had not looked at since schooldays in order to be accepted. There were tests and interviews, and he became anxious lest he be rejected. It was just a year since he had joined the Army.

On 1 July he went home on leave to Steep, where changes were also afoot. With her husband away at the front, Mrs Geoffrey Lupton had given Thomas notice to quit the hill-top study, which meant bringing all the books down to Yewtree Cottage. This done, Edward and Helen set off to walk from Hampshire to London, staying overnight with the Guthries, the Ellises and the Hootons consecutively, in what were almost farewell visits. On 5 July Thomas reported back to camp. He was home again on 16 July, to sort out more books and discuss the future with Helen, who had become determined to leave Steep as soon as possible. She was estranged from her former friends on the staff of Bedales, for collectively the school adopted a pacifist position and disapproved of Thomas's enlistment. 'By degrees', she wrote,

> I became antagonistic towards the school people and all they stood for. I felt stifled—especially at that agonising time—by the self-confident righteousness, by the principles which proved so irresistible to hypocrisy, by the theories which remained in the head and never reached the heart.

She went on to add a final comment on the school and its progressive ideas:

> A meeting was called at the school at which it was decided that, as the men of the village were all at the war, the cottagers' gardens should be dug and planted by pacifist members of the staff, 'for we realise', they said to the women who composed the audience, 'how much you depend on your gardens and that the soil is too heavy for you to tackle.' The women clapped for the vote of thanks, but were not much impressed with the magnanimity of this offer, for being wiser than their betters they knew that if they did not dig their gardens themselves no one else would. And so indeed it turned out.[11]

This was a sad ending to Helen's youthful enthusiasm, but it was the loss of the study which finally drove her from Steep. The letter from Mrs Lupton had been short and curt and when Helen wrote back explaining the unconditional terms on which Edward had been granted use of the room the reply she received was equally sharp. Now bitterly angry at the unkindness, Helen wrote again, saying exactly what she thought of Mrs Lupton. Her fury was compounded the following day when a Bedales teacher came to the cottage with the letter in his hand, asking Helen to withdraw it. He was rewarded with a verbal flood of all the hatred and scorn Helen felt towards everyone, aroused not only by this incident but also by the indifference of all concerned to Edward's future.[12] In the autumn of 1916 she found a new home at High Beech in Essex, and within cycling distance of Mervyn's garage at Walthamstow.

Thomas took the loss of his study with a stoicism that made Helen's rage look slightly ridiculous. For him there were greater changes ahead.

He had been accepted by the Artillery. 'I wanted a change', he explained to Bottomley. 'Nobody perhaps is quite as pleased as I am myself & shall be when I am gazetted.'[13] His transfer to the RGA training school in London was to take place at the end of August. Where it would lead he was only too well aware but, as he told Eleanor, he was now able to shut his eyes to many things, even without trying, and in his outward behaviour there was no sign of the momentous change he had anticipated in his verse. Back again at Steep, he began preparing for the move, packing belongings, burning papers and selling books—a great clear-out during which his correspondence, from Bottomley, Garnett and others, perished He was newly ruthless with the past. In mid-July he had composed this aphoristic quatrain:

> When he should laugh the wise man knows full well:
> For he knows what is truly laughable.
> But wiser is the man who laughs also,
> Or holds his laughter, when the foolish do.

A month later, in hospital with an infected arm, this brief poem on the swift's seasonal departure was written:

> How at once should I know,
> When stretched in the harvest blue
> I saw the swift's black bow,
> That I would not have that view
> Another day
> Until next May
> Again it is due?
>
> The same year after year—
> But with the swift alone.
> With other things I but fear
> That they will be over and done
> Suddenly
> And I only see
> Them to know them gone.

What other things was he conscious of seeing for the last time?

A few days later he was staying with his mother, his father being away in Wales. On 15 August he went up to town, as he had done so often in the past, to meet some literary friends for tea. They were John Freeman, Walter de la Mare and Roger Ingpen, who was de la Mare's brother-in-law and a publisher with Selwyn and Blount Ltd. They discussed the possibility of publishing a volume of 'Edward Eastaway'. This became a serious proposal, and the most substantial sign of recognition so far. On 27 August Thomas wrote to ask Eleanor to return all the recent poems he had sent her, in order that he could send a full complement (127 poems to date) to Ingpen. He had not leisure to do much more, for his off-duty hours were still spent trying to master the necessary mathematical formulae for the artillery school. He understood a good deal less of these than Mervyn, who was spending the summer holiday at home, and who was usefully able to help his father with his homework. This, in Thomas's last months, offset some of the friction that existed between him and his son.[15]

On 3 September, as a break from logarithms, he composed the eight stanzas of 'Gone, Gone Again' in which he compared himself to a deserted house:

> Look at the old house,
> Outmoded, dignified,
> Dark and untenanted,
> With grass growing instead
>
> Of the footsteps of life,
> The friendliness, the strife;
> In its beds have lain
> Youth, love, age, and pain:
>
> I am something like that;
> Only I am not dead,
> Still breathing and interested
> In the house that is not dark:—
>
> I am something like that:
> Not one pane to reflect the sun,
> For the schoolboys to throw at—
> They have broken every one.

He was beginning to sign off: not yet dead, but withdrawing. The poem was written at a new address—the Royal Artillery School in Handel St, WC, where he had reported two days earlier. He was now Cadet P. E. Thomas, destined to go as an officer with a gun battery to France.

12

The Dark Haunts Round

Where were those young men scattered? Where
had their war march on that April morning led
them?

'Home'

Like his earlier decision to enlist, Thomas's decision to join the Royal
Garrison Artillery was the culmination of a long period of inner reflection.
He might, as we have seen, have elected to spend the war in comparative
safety; instead, he chose to deny his age and literally offer his 'eyes and
breath For what would neither ask nor heed his death'—his country. It
was a virtually suicidal step: the survival rate on the Western Front was
notoriously low.

Thomas knew this and, as his poems clearly show, contemplated the
prospect of death, in verses written shortly after he took the decision to
proceed to France. The first of these is 'The Green Roads'. It is in couplets
and complements the half-serious, half-humorous lines of 'Early One
Morning', written less than three weeks previously. Though unrhymed,
the couplets have a sinister repetition. Death is approached obliquely:

> The green roads that end in the forest
> Are strewn with white goose feathers this June,
>
> Like marks left behind by someone gone to the forest
> To show his track. But he has never come back.

The forest is a constant symbol of death in Thomas's verse; it may have
been an image picked up from Frost, if we recall the latter's poem 'Into
My Own' about stealing away into the forest vastness. The strewn goose
feathers are also an indirect death/war image. The green roads leading to
Thomas's forest are the rarely-used country tracks he loved so well—and
life:

> Down each green road a cottage looks at the forest.
> Round one the nettle towers; two are bathed in flowers.

THE DARK HAUNTS ROUND

An old man along the green road to the forest
Strays from one, from another a child alone.

In the thicket bordering the forest,
All day long a thrush twiddles his song.

The images are very careful and precise, as is the verse, with its unusual
internal rhyme scheme. There is a strange sense of foreboding. Nature is
represented by Thomas's favourite bird, the thrush. Death is both a new
experience and an eternal one:

It is old, but the trees are young in the forest,
All but one like a castle keep, in the middle deep.

That oak saw the ages pass in the forest:
They were a host, but their memories are lost,

For the tree is dead:

This is the only direct reference to the poem's theme. The poet stands
poised on the margin, looking both ways:

all things forget the forest
Excepting perhaps me, when now I see

The old man, the child, the goose feathers at the edge of the
    forest,
And hear all day long the thrush repeat his song.

A sense of deep control, on the verge of an irrevocable act, informs this
poem and is emphasised by the rhymes and the rhythms that go with
them, moving one way and then the other.

The next poem, written while Edward and Helen were walking from
Hampshire to London, also contemplates death, as it befell the victims
of a gamekeeper: weasel, crow, magpie. The title, 'The Gallows', refers
to the keepers' custom of stringing up the bodies of vermin either as a
sign of competence or as a warning to other animals. There is an echo of
Jefferies in the subject. The poem was suggested by stories Thomas had
once told his daughter, which no doubt accounts for the 'child's story'
element in the opening lines of each stanza:

There was a weasel lived in the sun
With all his family,
Till a keeper shot him with a gun
And hung him up on a tree,
. . .

There was a crow who was no sleeper,
But a thief and a murderer
Till a very late hour . . .
. . .

There was a magpie, too,
Had a long tongue and a long tail;
He could both talk and do—

This child's eye view, however, is appropriate to the unemotional approach
to death. The weasel and the rest pass swiftly from life to death, simply
made 'one of the things that were' by the keeper's gun, and the outcome
is recorded dispassionately. The weasel

swings in the wind and rain,
In the sun and in the snow,
Without pleasure, without pain,
On the dead oak tree bough.

The crow and the magpie hang and flap identically in the wind and rain,
and by the fourth stanza, the repetition has ceased to be that of the nursery
and is ominous in its insistence:

many other beasts
And birds, skin, bone, and feather,
Have been taken from their feasts
And hung up there together,
To swing and have endless leisure
In the sun and in the snow,
Without pain, without pleasure,
On the dead oak tree bough.

Knowing that this was written during the First World War, it is impossible
to read these lines without thinking of the soldiers who died on the barbed
wire of No Man's Land. Dead bodies swinging in the wind, disregarded:
'The Gallows' is aptly named and is a grim poem, looking forward without
illusions. Thomas had no religion in the conventional sense and did not

believe in any form of life after death. As this poem shows, he was prepared to face up to the implications of atheism. Beyond death there is no pleasure or pain, only shrivelled skin and bone, for animals and men alike.

The third poem on death took the same image as the first—'The Dark Forest':

> Dark is the forest and deep, and overhead
> Hang stars like seeds of light
> In vain . . .
>
> . . . evermore mighty multitudes ride
> About, nor enter in;
> Of the other multitudes that dwell inside
> Never yet was one seen.
>
> The forest foxglove is purple, the marguerite
> Outside is gold and white,
> Nor can those that pluck either blossom greet
> The others, day or night.

Here the edge of the forest is more than a boundary: it is a divide across which there is no communication. Death is dark and unknowable. Thomas confessed to Eleanor that he thought the poem was probably 'no good' because the forest was too obvious a metaphor,[1] but the imagery is in fact vivid and original, with the shadowy picture of 'mighty multitudes' circling the forest and unseen others within. The movement of the poem is disturbing, soothed at the end by the emblematic contrast between the bright marguerite or daisy and the narcotic foxglove.

After the Artillery School in London Thomas was transferred to the main training centre at Trowbridge in Wiltshire, where he spent a month learning about heavy guns and their accoutrements. In addition there were regular drill, marches, night operations, together with learning the duties and skills of an officer. He was fully occupied. Poems came irregularly, jotted down in the half dark of a late evening train or the privacy of the hut while the men were in the mess. He was shy of letting his fellow soldiers know he wrote verses, and one poem was sent to Eleanor for typing on a sheet of paper covered in calculations and written out with only capitals to mark the lines, so none should suspect what he was writing.[2]

This poem was 'The Trumpet', the poem placed so misleadingly at the beginning of the first and subsequent editions of the *Poems*, giving readers and critics an erroneous impression of Thomas as a 'war poet' in the mould of Rupert Brooke or Julian Grenfell. 'The Trumpet' is written to the tune of the reveille call:

> Rise up, rise up,
> And, as the trumpet blowing
> Chases the dreams of men,
> As the dawn glowing
> The stars that left unlit
> The land and water,
> Rise up and scatter
> The dew that covers
> The print of last night's lovers—
> Scatter it, scatter it!
>
> While you are listening
> To the clear horn,
> Forget, men, everything
> On this earth new-born,
> Except that it is lovelier
> Than any mysteries.
> Open your eyes to the air
> That has washed the eyes of the stars
> Through all the dewy night:
> Up with the light,
> To the old wars;
> Arise, arise!

The sentiments are hardly warlike. The central message, that the earth is 'lovelier Than any mysteries', belongs, one would think, to Thomas's pastoral period. But the emotion expressed is clearly expectant and similar in theme to Brooke's 'Peace':

> Now, God be thanked Who has matched us with His hour,
> And caught our youth, and wakened us from sleeping

and suggested that Thomas now felt fully integrated with the aims and purpose of the Army and the war. 'I hope I shall always be as eager to risk my life as I have these last few months', he told Eleanor in November.[3]

The same month he was commissioned as a Second Lieutenant, and went to visit the Bottomleys on the southern edge of the Lake District, talking, listening to music, singing folksongs with his hosts and teaching them rowdy army ones. One afternoon there was a spectacular storm in the mountains, and Thomas remarked that for all his ill-health Bottomley was the luckier man. On leaving the Lake District, Thomas composed a poem to Bottomley's house, 'The Sheiling', as a memorial to their friendship:

It stands alone
Up in a land of stone
All worn like ancient stairs,
A land of rocks and trees
Nourished on wind and stone.

And all within
Long delicate has been;
By arts and kindliness
Coloured, sweetened, and warmed
For many years has been.

He then returned to High Beech, where Helen and the children were now installed. It was a 'horrible house on the top of a high hill . . . ugly, cold and inconvenient.' Perhaps in unconscious protest against what was happening, Helen had barely attempted to make it home-like. There was no stove, so that cooking had to be done on a primus, but more significant was her frame of mind. She recalled how she would 'sit by the fire not thinking, not reading, emptied of all emotion, even loneliness' and how 'an icy chill' had taken possession of her heart, making her feel she was simply marking time until something should happen.[4]

When he arrived on leave, Thomas did little to help. Eleanor, visiting the family that same week, remarked on his perverse mood, which was clearly not attuned to the domestic scene, but rather to the routines of camp life; psychologically the Army had become the centre of his reality. Perhaps he was preparing Helen as much as himself for the long separation to come: once embarked for France there would be no weekend leaves, no daily letters; she would have to cope alone. He chopped a new woodpile to last them through the winter, and began to make a list of things he would need at the front—sleeping bag, gauntlets, a lined waistcoat, which was ear-marked as Eleanor's parting gift.

He was systematically saying goodbye to his friends. Frost was too far away but there were old friends like the Guthries in Sussex, Jesse Berridge in Brentwood, John Freeman in south-east London and several others who could be met in town. All remarked on the air of gentle finality Thomas brought to these farewells, usually without overt mention of what all feared.

He was leaving his poetical affairs in some sort of order. *The Annual of New Poetry* was now nearly ready. He had corrected the proofs of his section from Bottomley and returned them, while for the volume of his own, Roger Ingpen was making a preliminary selection. During his last leave Edward prepared the final contents of the sixty-four allotted pages—sixty-four poems, including some most recent ones.

The prospect of annihilation was very close, and may have prompted the retrospective look at his writing life contained in 'The Long Small Room', the poem which remembers Ivy Cottage, the second of the Thomas homes in the country. It was twelve years ago, but

> One thing remains the same—this my right hand
>
> Crawling crab-like over the clean white page,
> Resting awhile each morning on the pillow,
> Then once more starting to crawl on towards age.
> The hundred last leaves stream upon the willow.

In a letter to Eleanor, Thomas explained that he had started this poem with the last line and built up from there[5]—a rare insight into his process of composition. He had also written about the departure from Hampshire, in 'When First', the poem recalling the hope he felt on his arrival there

> as if my feet
>
> Only by scaling its steps of chalk
> Would see something no other hill
> Ever disclosed. And now I walk
> Down it the last time. Never will
>
> My heart beat so again at sight
> Of any hill although as fair
> And loftier.

That hope 'for I knew not what' has vanished now for ever.

> Perhaps
> I may love other hills yet more
> Than this: the future and the maps
> Hide something I was waiting for.
>
> One thing I know, that love with chance
> And use and time and necessity
> Will grow, and louder the heart's dance
> At parting than at meeting be.

Now that he was leaving home for what might be the last time, he felt regret.

The next poem to be sent to Eleanor for typing was in an entirely

different mode, that of children's verses. 'The Child in the Orchard'
dramatises a child's questions about three white horses. The first

> rolls in the orchard: he is stained with moss
> And with earth, the solitary old white horse.

The second is from nursery rhyme:

> Who was the lady that rode the white horse
> With rings and bells to Banbury Cross?

and the third is cut out of chalk:

> the Westbury White Horse
> Over there on Salisbury Plain's green wall?

In style, this is close to Walter de la Mare's verse, which Thomas admired
for its simplicity and sense of magic. With a few other poems, such as
'To-Night', the dialogue between 'Harry' and 'Kate' agreeing to meet in
Castle Alley, this shows Thomas's ability to handle the notoriously
difficult faux naïf manner with a skill approaching Wordsworth's. In
bringing together themes from prehistory, folk rhyme and the countryside,
'The Child in the Orchard' is reminiscent of 'Lob'. It also, in a quite
different way, recalls a previous poem about death, 'The Child on the
Cliffs'. The child is lying on a cliff in Wales with his mother, chattering:

> Mother, the root of this little yellow flower
> Among the stones has the taste of quinine.
> Things are strange to-day . . .

He hears a bell ringing, out in the bay, which puzzles him:

> Fishes and gulls ring no bells. There cannot be
> A chapel or church between here and Devon,
> With fishes or gulls ringing its bell,—hark!—
> Somewhere under the sea or up in heaven.

His mother eventually explains that the bell is on a buoy, but the child's
fantasy runs on:

> Sweeter I never heard, mother, no, not in all Wales.
> I should like to be lying under that foam,
> Dead, but able to hear the sound of the bell,

And certain that you would often come
And rest, listening happily.
I should be happy if that could be.

This poem takes its title from Swinburne's 'On the Cliffs' and has its
origin in Swinburne's evocation of waves and water, dream and death, the
true escapism of 'The Triumph of Time':

I will go back to the great sweet mother,
Mother and lover of men, the sea.
I will go down to her, I and none other,
Close with her, kiss her and mix her with me
. . .
I shall rise with thy rising, with thee subside;
Sleep and not know . . .

and affinities with Brooke's 'Retrospect':

O infinite deep I never knew,
I would come back, come back to you,
Find you, as a pool, unstirred,
Kneel down by you and never a word . . .

Earlier in his life, Thomas had experienced his own wish for oblivion
and for a nostalgic return to pre-natal unconsciousness as expressed in
prose poems like the essay 'The Flower Gatherer' about the child drowning
in the stream. It was a sort of death wish. In 'The Child On the Cliffs' he
gives rein to this yearning, but puts it into the mouth of a child to indicate
that it is not an adult emotion. Comparing both the sense and speech
rhythms of Thomas's poem with those of Brooke's, we can see how
Thomas's verse takes the Georgian mode away from the baleful Swinburnian influence. When he faced the prospect of real as opposed to dream
death, it was without poetic trappings or fantasies. One of his first poems
on this theme, 'Rain', had been written early in January 1916, shortly after
the argument with his father had left him feeling low-spirited and depressed. He was back at camp, lying awake at night listening:

Rain, midnight rain, nothing but the wild rain
On this bleak hut, and solitude, and me
Remembering again that I shall die

This has its origin in the passage Thomas had written some years earlier
in his book *The Icknield Way*[6] mentioned in Chapter 5, when, at one of

his most melancholic periods, he had abandoned himself depressively to thoughts of rain and death:

> There is nothing else in my world but my dead heart and brain within me and the rain without ... The rain has drowned the splendour. Everything is drowned and dead, all that was once lovely and alive in the world, all that had once been alive and was memorable though dead is now dung for a future that is infinitely less than the falling rain ... Now there is neither life nor death, but only the rain. Sleep as all things, past present and future, lie still and sleep, except the rain, the heavy black rain falling straight through the air that was once a sea of life ... In a little while or in an age—for it is all one—I shall know the full truth of the words I used to love, I knew not why, in my days of nature, in the days before the rain: Blessed are the dead that the rain rains on.

The poem has a harder centre:

> Blessed are the dead that the rain rains upon:
> But here I pray that none whom once I loved
> Is dying to-night or lying still awake,
> Solitary, listening to the rain,

But there is a grammatical looseness in the last eight lines which betrays the unresolved feeling that ends in ambiguity:

> Either in pain or thus in sympathy
> Helpless among the living and the dead,
> Like a cold water among broken reeds,
> Myriads of broken reeds all still and stiff,
> Like me who have no love which this wild rain
> Has not dissolved except the love of death,
> If love it be for what is perfect and
> Cannot, the tempest tells me, disappoint.

This is the most striking example of what has long been known about Thomas's work, namely his habit of reworking earlier prose passages in verse.[7] He had a wealth of experience to draw on but had in the past suffered from the same deficiencies that he diagnosed in Brooke, when after Brooke's death he commented: 'He lacked power of expression. He was a rhetorician, dressing things up better than they needed.'[8] Thomas had suffered from the same faults, from an inability to balance sense and feeling. Thought, he said, gave him indigestion.[9] 'Rain' is in some ways a transitional poem. Death is no comforting cradle beneath the waves: it is cold water among broken reeds, with a foreshadowing of the corpses on the battlefield. Yet love of death is still seen, somehow, as a solvent, and death itself as a goal to be desired, being 'perfect' and beyond disappointment. The poem is powerful but unsatisfactory, because the contradictory ideas are not adequately resolved. This is reflected in the confused syntax of the long second sentence.

Ten months later, Thomas wrote the poem 'Lights Out' in full and unflinching expectation of death. His commission was about to be gazetted and his fate, as it were, sealed. Like 'No One Cares Less than I' and 'The Trumpet', the poem was inspired by a camp bugle call, and Thomas told Eleanor that he wished it could have been as brief as the two pairs of long notes that comprise the Last Post call.[10] In the poem sleep is a metaphor for death:

> I have come to the borders of sleep,
> The unfathomable deep
> Forest where all must lose
> Their way, however straight,
> Or winding, soon or late;
> They cannot choose.
>
> Many a road and track
> That, since the dawn's first crack,
> Up to the forest brink,
> Deceived the travellers,
> Suddenly now blurs,
> And in they sink.
>
> Here love ends,
> Despair, ambition ends;
> All pleasure and all trouble,
> Although most sweet or bitter,
> Here ends in sleep that is sweeter
> Than tasks most noble.
>
> There is not any book
> Or face of dearest look
> That I would not turn from now
> To go into the unknown
> I must enter, and leave, alone,
> I know not how.
>
> The tall forest towers;
> Its cloudy foliage lowers
> Ahead, shelf above shelf;

> Its silence I hear and obey
> That I may lose my way
> And myself.

Again, the forest is an image of death, suddenly engulfing the unwary, but of a compelling power. Twenty years earlier, in his first book,[11] Thomas had seen a southern woodland in full leaf towering up the hill 'ledge beyond ledge'; now the image returned unconsciously.

There is little that commentary can add to 'Lights Out'; criticism is silenced by its vivid solemnity and unblinking readiness to meet death. It is an austere poem, powerful yet full of grace too. It is entirely without self-indulgence, poetically or emotionally. Both release and horror hover in the wings of the poem, but the gaze and movement are steady and firm: there is no escape, and no desire to do so.

Laudable though such courage is in the face of death, we may pause to wonder why it was that Thomas had chosen to put himself in the firing line. On his last visit Bottomley had asked Thomas why he had chosen to join the Artillery with its special training and special risks. Gun batteries were obvious targets for enemy shells and, apart from the idiotic infantry attacks across No Man's Land which the Allied generals were so fond of, there can hardly have been a more dangerous job to choose. Thomas's answer was brief: to get a larger pension for Helen.[12] But this suggests only a commendable desire to minimise the cost for those he left: of the likely cost to himself he can have been in no doubt.

To speak of suicide would perhaps be misleading. Thomas had fantasised about suicide in the past, as an escape from frustration and failure, and it may be that the desire lay deep in his soul. Maybe with one part of him he did wish to die, to die defending the soil of England he loved so dearly, becoming one with the earth and the ages. Maybe with another part of him he was playing dice with death, putting himself at risk to see if he was 'destined to lie' in a foreign grave, or to survive. Unhappily for him, Helen and posterity, the First World War was a fatal game weighted inexorably against the players.

On 3 December Thomas reported to his new base at the RGA camp named Tintown (composed of corrugated tin huts) at Lydd on the flat sea-marshes of southern Kent. Within four days there was a call for volunteers to proceed at once to the Front, and 'I made sure of it by volunteering', Thomas told Eleanor, asking her not to tell Helen until it was definite.[13] But there was no turning back. He was assigned to 244 Siege Battery, a unit halfway through its training and expected to leave for France sometime in January. It comprised four howitzers, seven officers and a hundred and fifty men. The officers were all relatively junior—a Captain, a Lieutenant and five Second Lieutenants—and Thomas soon discovered that he was three years older than the most senior and twice as old as the youngest member of the battery, who would thus have been nineteen.

Helen took the news as stoically as she could manage, but was devastated to learn that there would be no prospect of leave over Christmas. The family had always celebrated festivals with seasonal enthusiasm, and the promise of six days' embarkation leave in the New Year was no compensation. She must have looked back sadly to the old days at Berryfield Cottage and Wick Green, where there was no dream of such a dark and fearful future.

Alone in his hut one evening, Thomas too cast his mind back to the days at Steep, musing

> Some day, I think, there will be people enough
> In Froxfield to pick all the blackberries
> Out of the hedges of Green Lane . . .

'The Lane' recreates an enduring picture of the natural world, explicitly located close to the place that had been his home for ten years and encapsulating spring, summer, autumn and winter in one scene. The war is not mentioned, but it is tempting to think that Thomas wrote this poem as a reminder of what he was fighting for—nature and the English countryside, where in the hedge 'the chaffinch tries His song' and dark holly leaves glint.

At the last moment, Christmas leave was granted after all, from Friday 22 to Tuesday 26 December. At the same time Eleanor was given £20 from a benevolent literary fund to forward to Helen, who travelled excitedly up to London to buy presents, including several practical items for Edward, and then returned home to prepare the feast. On the day of Edward's homecoming, Bronwen completed a story about a horse to give her father, while Myfanwy, now six and a half, embroidered a wool butterfly on a card that Helen had pricked with holes. It was a snowy Christmas and with joy the uncomfortable house in the forest was transformed into 'a festive bower of holly and ivy and fir boughs' amidst a sparkling landscape.[14] Myfanwy longed for a real Christmas tree, and with the two older children Helen dug up a tiny fir tree and secretly decorated it with toys and candles supplied by Eleanor. It was a complete success on the day when Myfanwy, as Edward wrote to tell Eleanor, 'went pale with surprise as she came into the room and found it.'[15]

By 27 December Thomas was back at Tintown, and content to be so. He remarked on the curious fact that although he had been pleased to be with the family, he felt no resentment or anxiety at having to return to camp.[16] In his Christmas letter to Eleanor he had ended by hoping they would meet at the same time next year,[17] a conventional wish made poignant by the circumstances, but one which we can also see was sincerely meant. If he was prepared to die, he also hoped that he might survive, and as the date of embarkation drew closer this hope became more overt.

Perhaps as a hostage to fortune, Thomas began a diary on 1 January 1917. After his death it was returned to Helen with the rest of his belongings but not rediscovered until 1970, when it was found by his grandson among Mervyn's papers. *The Diary of Edward Thomas: 1 January—8 April 1917* was published in book form in 1977, sixty years after it was written. It was not a printed diary with days and dates, but a leatherbound notebook 8 in. × 4 in. which Thomas filled with short entries, four or five days to a page, a factual record of movements and observations, both military and natural, written under conditions of little leisure and less comfort, particularly towards the end. It has the authentic flavour both of army life, with its tedium, irritations and dangers, and of the man who wrote it, determined not to be beaten by any of these. There is a sad irony in the fact that both the first and the last books by Thomas to be published should have been in diary form; the brief observations of wild life amid the devastated countryside of northern France, though very different from those of southern England in *The Woodland Life*, provide an emblem of continuity that shaped Thomas's life as a country lover and country writer.

Back in Lydd the Battery had commenced firing practice with the big guns and its departure was fixed for the end of January. Thomas found to his relief that he did not mind the deafening sound of the guns at close quarters, and felt that with this and a pair of good field-glasses for observing enemy positions he would be able to acquit himself adequately in action. He was to be in charge of a section of two guns, and to take his turn in proceeding to the observation posts to calculate enemy positions.

On 5 January he left Lydd for his last six days' mobilisation leave, spending the night at his parents' home and accompanying his mother on a shopping trip the next morning. He then collected Bronwen from Chiswick and arrived at High Beech in the early evening. This last visit home he used to arrange all his and Helen's affairs in as good order as he could manage, signing cheques to cover the next six months' bills. For one night Eleanor came to stay; it was, as she recorded, a visit like many others, with Edward singing Welsh songs as he bathed Myfanwy in front of the fire, and with the adults sitting up talking after the children were in bed. They spoke as usual of people and poetry, and of Edward's forthcoming book, to be dedicated to Robert Frost.

Helen went upstairs first; then Eleanor, shyness preventing her even now from showing her feelings, until Edward came upstairs too and she opened the door of her room, saying goodnight, and offering her face to him. They kissed and that, she felt, was the real goodbye, a timid token

of the depth of her love for him. The following morning he accompanied
her to the station, and they parted with the usual handshake. It was the
last time they met.[18]

The next day Thomas went up to London to see his dentist and meet a
number of friends, including W. H. Davies, Ivy Ransome and Roger
Ingpen, before returning for what was to be his last night at home. Helen
related the agony of the final day in *World Without End*[19] and the eventual,
dreaded farewell in the snow-covered, misty forest. The *Diary* records
that he left with Bronwen, delivering her to his parents' house where he
stayed the night, once more for the last time, with all his brothers gathered
together for the occasion.

He then returned to Tintown, expecting to entrain immediately for the
mobilisation depot at Codford on Salisbury Plain, but remaining to make
the formal handover to the incoming unit. That evening, with the camp
partly deserted, he wrote his last verses, on love and parting, printed for
the first time in the *Diary*. The poem begins with an echo from *Romeo
and Juliet*:

> The sorrow of true love is a great sorrow
> And true love parting blackens a bright morrow.

and goes on to argue that in fact such sorrow equals joy, since it contains
hope; greater sorrow comes from less love, when there are no extremes
of mood, but only

> a frozen drizzle perpetual
> Of drops that from remorse and pity fall
> And cannot ever shine in the sun or thaw,
> Removed eternally from the sun's law.

The almost Elizabethan phrases and rhythms of the opening are no prepara-
tion for the body of the poem, where the couplets run on in a series of
descending and increasingly agonised clauses, with little punctuation,
until they reach the despairing final line. Despite a number of words
associated with light—bright, blinded, shine, sun—the poem laments the
loss of love, of youth, of feeling, and records the bleakness of a cold heart.
Is it too much to see the effect of the war in this? Perhaps as a necessary
defence against feeling Thomas had so stifled and repressed his emotional
responses that he no longer felt any kind of love or sadness at parting.
Although the lines seem complete, it is possible that had he lived Thomas
would have revised the piece, for the rhymes are uncharacteristically
dominant, and the long second part is grammatically untidy, reflecting
imperfectly controlled thought.

But there was no leisure for revision. Within a couple of days Thomas moved to Codford in Wiltshire, where the Battery was to collect its stores and ammunition before embarking. With sombre appropriateness, Thomas's last residence in England was in his favourite county, not far from the Downs which he and Jefferies, his first hero, had loved so well, and on the plain where Hardy's Tess came to the end of her story. There were some beautiful walks to be had, he told Eleanor, sometimes disguised as route marches, map operations or night manoeuvres, and whenever possible Thomas and his fellow officers called at country inns for tea, strumming out tunes on rustic pianos. On his first Sunday Thomas missed church parade (had he, like Bertie Farjeon, given his religion as 'pagan' on enlistment, and thus been excused the ordinary services?) and walked alone across the downs to visit Sir Henry Newbolt and his wife. It was cold, with a freezing drizzle reminiscent of his last poem; on the way he passed two travelling families in a green road, roasting a small animal on an open fire. The landscape of southern England had not changed: how much did Thomas reflect on the changes in his own situation since he had last walked this way, gathering material for his country books?

The following day he appears to have got some leave, for he left his men sorting stores and went to Gloucester to pay a farewell visit to John Haines, a friend he had met at Dymock in the summer of 1914. Haines reminisced about Frost and gave Thomas a copy of Frost's new book *Mountain Interval*. This began with 'The Road Not Taken', a poem close in spirit to Thomas's 'The Sign Post':

> Two roads diverged in a wood and I—
> I took the one less travelled by,
> And that has made all the difference.

and ended with 'The Sound of Trees', inspired by the Frosts' stay at The Gallows in Dymock, concluding with a farewell:

> I shall make the reckless choice
> Some day when they are in voice
> And tossing so as to score
> The white clouds over them on.
> I shall have less to say
> But I shall be gone.

Thomas stayed overnight with Haines and then returned to camp. The Battery was due to leave on 29 January. The guns and equipment were loaded onto trucks, the paperwork completed, and kit packed. On the 27th he received a telegram to say that Myfanwy had gone to stay with Ivy Ransome at Tisbury, and Thomas walked over and spent his last but one night in England with his youngest child. She hoped he would have a safe crossing, not knowing of the dangers he was really going to face. The next morning he cycled back across frosty downs, along juniper-lined tracks, arriving only twelve hours before departure time. The troops entrained for Southampton at 6.30 a.m. but had to wait all day before sailing, with several other military units, for Le Havre, where they docked at 4 a.m. on 30 January. Ashore, they proceeded to a camp outside the town, where tents accommodated twelve men each, snow fell like sugar and the water froze in the pipes. Thomas escaped to bed early and read Shakespeare's sonnets, Helen's parting gift. It was a bleak arrival, and the first time he had been out of England.

A few weeks earlier, during his Christmas leave, he had composed the poem 'Out in the Dark', suggested by something Myfanwy had said about the deer in Epping Forest. It was his last poem on death; the forest is again invoked, though subsumed in the darkness of night, which is drawing closer:

> Out in the dark over the snow
> The fallow fauns invisible go
> With the fallow doe;
> And the winds blow
> Fast as the stars are slow.
>
> Stealthily the dark haunts round
> And, when the lamp goes, without sound
> At a swifter bound
> Than the swiftest hound,
> Arrives, and all else is drowned;
>
> And star and I and wind and deer,
> Are in the dark together,—near,
> Yet far,—and fear
> Drums on my ear
> In that sage company drear.
>
> How weak and little is the light,
> All the universe of sight,
> Love and delight,
> Before the might,
> If you love it not, of night.

The fear, which is very real, is kept at bay by the steady rhythms and the sustained rhymes in each stanza, which hold the long and short lines together and delay the inevitable end. There is an awkwardness in the inversion of the last line of the third stanza, which may seem to mar the

poem as a whole, but when Eleanor objected to it, Thomas replied that
he wished she could have liked that verse 'because, do you know, I like it
best.'[20] It is the only place where he admits fear, fear of the dark, fear of
death, yet not with panic, as it approaches him. The images of death in the
going out of the lamp, the hound and the deer and the extinction of sight
are combined with delicate mastery, and the verse moves from simplicity
through a series of intense poetic images, growing in power yet never
losing its lucidity. It is a fine poem to have written on the verge of departure
for the trenches.

Six months before Thomas arrived in France, the British Army had
lost half a million men in the Battle of the Somme. The Western Front,
with temporary alterations in outline, still stretched across France and
Belgium. A new French assault on the line at Noyon was being planned,
with the British to provide support through a preliminary attack at Arras,
in the north. Perceiving this plan, the Germans began to withdraw
strategically to the carefully prepared Hindenburg Line, confident that the
Allied armies would exhaust themselves in any attack and that in any case
the intensive U boat attacks on Atlantic shipping would prove decisive, as
indeed they almost did. Allied plans went ahead regardless of the withdrawal, which made a break in the line much less likely. New British troop
arrivals, Thomas among them, were destined to take part in the build-up
behind Arras.

After more cold days in the Havre camp full of men coming and going,
and with his ankles chafing from new boots, Thomas and his companions
entrained for the front. They were billeted in abandoned farms, officers
in the house, men in the barns. On 10 February he went into the trenches
for the first time, up as far as the forward observation posts. 'I could not
see a living thing', he told Eleanor, 'only snow, posts and barbed wire, a
dark shadowline marking the enemy trench, a line of trees and houses
along a road behind. The only men we saw were around corners of the
trenches as we passed, and there was one dead man lying like a monument
covered with sacking.' But he 'enjoyed the exercise, the work with map
and field glasses, the scene, the weather, and the sense of being able to do
a new job.'[21] On 14 February he recorded in his diary a tour of observation
posts on the front line:

Fine sunny day—snow melting. Black-headed buntings talk, rooks
caw, lovely white puffs of shrapnel round planes high up. Right section
does aeroplane shoot in afternoon. Dead campion umbels, and grass
rustling on my helmet through trenches. Pretty little copse in deep
hollow high up between Ficheux and Dainville, where guns look over
to Berneville and Warlus.[22]

He spent the evenings censoring the men's letters home, writing his own, reading and listening to popular songs on a wind-up gramophone. One of his fellow officers was a dismal, irritating fellow, who objected to the bawdy talk and held himself aloof and suffering. In comparison Thomas found himself at ease with the men, a pleasant discovery to one who had rarely liked company. The men in his Battery found him likeable, steady and reliable, looking to him as to a kind of father figure, impressed by his quiet cheerfulness and refusal to complain.

After a short transfer to the local HQ at Arras, Thomas moved up to the line with 244 Battery, which was now in action. The preliminary bombardment was under way. Thomas had his first real taste of life in the trenches, being on duty twenty-four hours without rest in the front line:

20th. Stiff mud all the way up and shelled as we started. Telegraph Hill as quiet as if only rabbits lived there. I took revolver and left this diary behind in case. For it is very exposed and only a few Cornwalls and MGC about. But Hun shelled chiefly over our heads into Beaurains all night—like starlings returning 20 or 30 a minute. Horrible flap of a 5·9 a little along the trench. Rain and mud and I've to stay till I am relieved tomorrow. Had not brought warm clothes or enough food and had no shelter, nor had telephonists. Shelled all night. But the MGC boy gave me tea. I've no bed. I leant against wall of the trench. I got up and looked over. I stamped up and down. I tried to see patrol out. Very light—the only sign of Hun on Telegraph Hill, though 2 appeared and were sniped at. A terribly long night and cold. Not relieved till 8. Telephonists out repairing line since 5 on the morning of the

21st. At last 260 relieved us. Great pleasure to go, be going back to sleep and rest. No Man's Land like Goodwood Racecourse with engineers swarming over it and making a road between shell holes full of blood-stained water and beer bottles among barbed wire. Larks singing as they did when we came up in the dark and were shelled. Now I hardly felt as if a shell could hurt, though several were thrown about near working parties. Found letter from Helen, Eleanor and Julian. Had lunch, went to bed at 2 intending to get up to tea but slept till 6.30 on the . . .

22nd. (Beautiful was Arras yesterday coming down from Beaurains and seeing Town Hall ruin white in sun like thick smoke beginning to curl. Sprinkle of snow today in sun.)[23]

All knew the big attack was due to begin soon. Thomas was both apprehensive and excited; he told Eleanor, 'I keep feeling that I should enjoy it more if I knew I would survive it.'[24] He wrote several farewell letters, telling Bottomley that Frost had found an American publisher for his

Poems, and that the Chicago magazine *Poetry* wanted to print a selection.[25] Bottomley replied that the *Annual of New Poetry* was out and appeared to be doing well; some inquiries had been received about the identity of 'Edward Eastaway', but Thomas was not yet ready to reveal it.[26] In London, the preparations for Eastaway's own volume continued.

The spring assault on the German lines went ahead more or less on schedule. The French Army was in difficulties, with governmental changes reflecting military problems; some elements believed the attack ill-advised in view of the consolidated German line, but the generals in charge were confident of an immediate breakthrough, and the British support manoeuvre to the north was an essential ingredient. The bombardment began in earnest on 1 April, along a fourteen-mile front north and south of Arras. Some eighty-eight thousand tons of shell were fired, more than at the battle of the Somme. On 2 April, 244 Battery fired a hundred rounds blind, amid sleeting snow. On the 4th it was six hundred rounds. Between the 5th and 8th they practised firing the rolling barrage which was to be used to cover the infantry advance. The 8th was Easter Sunday, bright and warm, Thomas noted in his diary, but the shelling continued. He went over to the Battery in the afternoon, and as he stood by the guns, which were unprotected, a shell fell within a few yards of him. It was a near escape, and that evening his luck was remarked on in the billet.

He dared not think of what might happen. In a letter to Helen written on the 6th he had explained that he could not be very forthcoming:

> I know that you must say much because you feel much. But I, you see, must not feel anything. I am just, as it were, tunnelling underground and something sensible in my subconsciousness directs me not to think of the sun, at the end of the tunnel there is the sun . . . If I could respond to you as you would like me to to your feelings I should be unable to go on with this job in ignorance whether it is to last weeks or months or years. I never even think will it be weeks or months or years . . .[27]

He had very little time left. On the morning of 9 April the Battle of Arras began, with a massive bombardment and infantry attack. The day was successful and around Arras the Allied armies advanced three and a half miles, the furthest in any one day since 1914. But Edward Thomas knew nothing of that. He had been killed by a shell at 7.30 in the morning.[28]

The dismal officer wrote stiffly to inform Helen, and on the following day his Captain wrote too, expressing more fully the Battery's grief:

> Your husband was very greatly loved in this battery, and his going has been a personal loss to each of us. . . . He was always the same, quietly cheerful, and ready to do any job that was going with the same steadfast

unassuming spirit . . . I wish I could convey to you the picture of him, a picture we had all learnt to love, of the old clay pipe, gum boots, oilskin coat, and steel helmet.[29]

Thomas was buried in the small military cemetery of Agny only a few hundred yards from where he was killed. The war on the Western Front went on. Before the battle of Arras was over, another hundred and fifty thousand British troops had also died. By 1918 a million and a half lives had been taken. Like the others, Thomas had sacrificed his life in France to save his country, and in his death his country lost one of her finest poets.

Postscript

When one comes to consider Edward Thomas's place in the history of English poetry, one recognises immediately his debt to the literary tradition. His own knowledge of literature, acquired through his work as critic and editor and through wide reading, was deep and thorough, ranging from the medieval to the modern. Quotations from lyric, ballad and epic are scattered throughout his prose books, while his two anthologies form an eclectic collection of all the pieces, from the anonymous to his own, that he liked best.

It is the same with his verse, where echoes and allusions to virtually the whole past of English poetry may be found. There is a hint of the medieval lyric 'sumer is icumen in' in the 'loudly rings "cuckoo" ' of 'April', and an echo of Chaucer in the 'as I guess' of 'Lob'. Also in 'Lob' is an explicit reference to Shakespeare's 'tall Tom that bore the logs in . . . when icicles hung by the wall', and verbal allusions in 'There's nothing like the sun' and other poems. The spirit of George Herbert seems to lie behind 'Home' ('Not the end . . .') while Clare and Cobbett are deliberately invoked to set the scene of 'Haymaking'. Echoes of Wordsworth are numerous: the opening of 'There was a time' comes directly from 'Ode on Intimations of Immortality' and the line 'the gossamers wander at their own will' in 'October' from 'Upon Westminster Bridge'. Keats is present in the language and feeling of several poems such as 'Liberty' ('half in love with pain') and 'Ambition' ('the end fell like a bell') and in the texture of 'October' and 'Melancholy'. Shelley lurks behind 'The Clouds that are so Light' and 'After You Speak'. Allusions to Swinburne have already been noted; there are others from the late Victorian period, notably the work of William Morris and Charles Doughty, which Thomas admired.

This allusiveness is unobtrusive and natural in Thomas's verse, as if he were conscious of no division between his and earlier uses of language: all inhabit the same world. It illustrates his belief in the vital English tradition that 'lives yet', and enriches his own lines with a sense of that tradition, all the more powerful for being so easily integrated into his own verse. At the same time, his voice is distinctly modern in its speech rhythms and discursive patterns; with the exception of the occasional use of ' 'twas' and ' 'twixt', it is the language of the twentieth century.

Edward Thomas was a poet of his time, both in his choice and treatment of themes. His closeness to Frost is evident and needs no further explication here,[1] while some aspects of his relationship with English poets of his own generation such as W. H. Davies, Walter de la Mare and Gordon Bottomley, have already been described. Strictly speaking, Thomas is neither a Georgian nor a non-Georgian poet, in much the same way as he is neither a war poet nor a non-war poet. In his work he attained and went beyond many of the aims of Georgian poetry such as have been described as the 'rejection of large themes and the language of rhetoric' and the rendering of 'immediate experience, sensuous or imaginative, in a language close to common speech.'[2] He understood what Abercrombie and Brooke were trying to do in poetry, though he admired Davies and de la Mare more. In several of his own poems Thomas employs a form of childlike rhyming reminiscent of de la Mare, though without de la Mare's whimsicality. In turn, some of de la Mare's later verse seems to show the influence of Thomas.

Of the poets of his time, however, Thomas is closest in spirit to Thomas Hardy. It is no accident that Thomas should have preferred 'Mr Hardy's poems to his novels'.[3] He made explicit allusion to Hardy's poem on the blackbird, 'The Spring Call', by quoting its phrase 'pretty dear' in 'Lob'. Both poets shared a fondness for solitary walks, for putting new words to old country tunes, and for the character sketch in verse. There is a striking similarity between certain of Thomas's poems, such as 'A Gentleman' and 'The Gypsy', and ones in Hardy's collection of 1913, *Time's Laughing-stocks*, such as 'The Dark-Eyed Gentleman' and 'A Trampwoman's Tragedy'.

Thomas's most obviously Hardyesque poem is one that is rarely quoted: 'February Afternoon'. It ends:

> Time swims before me, making as a day
>   A thousand years, while the broad ploughland oak
>   Roars mill-like and men strike and bear the stroke
>   Of war as ever, audacious or resigned,
> And God still sits aloft in the array
>   That we have wrought him, stone-deaf and stone-blind.

Intriguingly, there is a curious resemblance, too, between Thomas's last poem, 'Out in the Dark', and Hardy's 'The Fallow Deer at the Lonely House' (which incidentally also echoes the rhymes of another Thomas poem on death, 'Lights Out'). The first stanza of 'The Fallow Deer' reads:

> One without looks in to-night
>   Through the curtain-chink
> From the sheet of glistening white;

> One without looks in to-night
>   As we sit and think
>   By the fender-brink.

First printed in *Late Lyrics and Earlier* (1922), Hardy's poem was almost certainly written after Thomas's[4] and it is interesting to speculate on whether or not he had read Thomas's poem, first published in *Last Poems* in 1918. Imagery, tone and feeling are remarkably close, in this stanza at least.

With the hint of a ghost looking in at those around the fireside, 'The Fallow Deer', like so many of Hardy's poems, tacitly invokes the past. And it is in this concern with the past, and with memory, that Thomas's verse has most affinity with Hardy's.[5] We may compare two poems on the theme of a recurrent memory: Hardy's 'Under the Waterfall' and Thomas's 'Over the Hills'. In Hardy's poem the recollection of a lovers' picnic, when a drinking glass was rinsed in a stream

> Where it slipped, and sank, and was past recall,
> Though we stooped and plumbed the little abyss
> With long bared arms

is triggered off whenever the action of plunging the arm into a bowl or basin of water is repeated. In Thomas's poem the memory of crossing a ridge to 'a new country' has 'become almost a habit' when the poet, digging, leans on his spade and sees the scene again in his mind's eye. But

>   Recall
> Was vain: no more could the restless brook
> Ever turn back and climb the waterfall.

Hardy's sense of the past is generally both more positive and more pathetic than Thomas's: he can recall easily, only to regret the loss. Thomas finds recall more difficult, less satisfactory, like the figure in 'Celandine'—'Gone like a never perfectly recalled air'—and knows that memory is not always to be relied on—'Some day I shall think this a happy day'—nor welcomed —'So memory made Parting today a double pain'.

Nevertheless, the correspondences between two poems about recollection, Hardy's 'On a Midsummer Eve' and Thomas's 'It Rains', are almost as striking as the two with fallow deer. The first begins:

> I idly cut a parsley stalk,
> And blew therein towards the moon;
> I had not thought what ghosts would walk
> With shivering footsteps to my tune.

> I went, and knelt, and scooped my hand
> As if to drink, into the brook,
> And a faint figure seemed to stand
> Above me, with the bygone look.

Thomas's poems opens

> It rains, and nothing stirs within the fence
> Anywhere through the orchard's untrodden, dense
> Forest of parsley.

and ends

> When I turn away, on its fine stalk
> Twilight has fined to naught, the parsley flower
> Figures, suspended still and ghostly white,
> The past hovering as it revisits the light.

The verbal echoes are uncanny. Thomas's poem was written in May 1916, Hardy's published in *Moments of Vision* one year later.

The dominant poetic mode in the years following Hardy's death in 1928 was, in the words of Donald Davie, 'bardic and exalted' or 'mythological', rather than personal. It offered a symbolic transformation of reality, not a detailed rendering of the doubts and ironies of everyday life; the poet customarily wore a mask and seldom spoke with his own voice. But, as Davie has argued,[6] there is a sense in which the mainstream of English (as opposed to American) poetry has remained recognisably Hardyesque in tone and feeling. Yeats, Pound and Eliot have been major influences, but they are on the wane; re-emerging is a characteristically English modesty, which appears almost as diffidence, avoiding the grand manner to concentrate on local achievements and the honest confession of human weakness. This connects Thomas with the present landscapes of English poetry.

R. S. Thomas's character Iago Prytherch, for instance—'Just an ordinary man of the bald Welsh hills, Who pens a few sheep in a gap of cloud'—is close kin to the old men met in Edward Thomas's poems, and his bird in 'A Blackbird Singing' has links with Thomas's thrushes. The response to place is also similar; consider the opening of R. S. Thomas's 'The Village':

> Scarcely a street, too few houses
> To merit the title; just a way between
> The one tavern and the one shop

> That leads nowhere and fails at the top
> Of the short hill . . .

A feeling for the relationship between men and the land is shared by both poets: R. S. Thomas's second volume of verse was entitled *An Acre of Land*, like the first line of Edward Thomas's 'For These'—'An acre of land between the shore and hills'. R. S. Thomas, however, has roots in, and a long familiarity with the land of Wales in a way that Edward Thomas, displaced suburbanite, had not, and from these come a sense of solidity and contentment that eluded the author of 'For These', who asked only but in vain 'for what men call content'. R. S. Thomas's is a cold country, but it can be more comforting than Edward Thomas's lush southern landscapes.

Religion of course is a crucial difference between the two, and yet it is interesting to note how close the Christian sense of the one comes to the agnostic natural piety of the other. One may compare Edward Thomas's response to the timeless moment in 'The Ash Grove', or his apprehension of eternity in 'The Mountain Chapel' (which might, incidentally, belong to R. S. Thomas's parish) with R. S. Thomas's religious sense expressed in 'The Moor'. 'The Moor' begins:

> It was like a church to me.
> I entered it on soft foot,
> Breath held like a cap in the hand.
> It was quiet.
> What God was there made himself felt,
> Not listened to, in clean colours
> That brought a moistening of the eye,
> In movement of the wind over grass.

'The Mountain Chapel' opens:

> Chapel and gravestones, old and few,
> Are shrouded by a mountain fold
> From sound and view
> Of life. The loss of the brook's voice
> Falls like a shadow. All they year is
> The eternal noise
> Of wind whistling in the grass . . .

Here the use of irregular rhyme and half-rhyme, and the rhythms cutting across the lines, point forward to Larkin as well as R. S. Thomas. Striking echoes of Edward Thomas are heard too in R. S. Thomas's 'No Through Road', which begins 'All in vain. I will cease now', and in 'the Lonely

Farmer', which rehearses the search for a natural or divine message:

> There was a sound of voices on the air,
> But where, where? And once when he was walking
> Along a lane in spring he was deceived
> By a shrill whistle coming through the leaves:
> Wait a minute, wait a minute—four swift notes;
> He turned, and it was nothing, only a thrush
> In the thorn bushes easing its throat.
> He swore at himself for paying heed,
> The poor hill farmer, so often again
> Stopping, staring, listening, in vain,
> His ear betrayed by the heart's need.

The present-day poet who has perhaps most in common with Thomas is Philip Larkin, despite the great gaps of time and verse that divide them. Thomas, we may think, would have recognised the awkward honesty of Larkin's 'Talking in Bed':

> It becomes still more difficult to find
> Words at once true and kind,
> Or not untrue and not unkind.

and the piety of 'Water':

> If I were called in
> To construct a religion
> I should make use of water.
>
> Going to church
> Would entail a fording
> To dry, different clothes;

In 'Sad Steps', Larkin regards the moon and concludes, with Thomas, that

>   the plain
> Far-reaching singleness of that wide stare
>
> Is a reminder of the strength and pain
> Of being young; that it can't come again . . .

Although the landscapes they describe are very different, Thomas and Larkin display a similar sensibility, moving freely between the overall and the particular. Larkin's view is characteristically from a train, as in 'Here':

> swerving through fields
> Too thin and thistled to be called meadows,
> And now and then a harsh-named halt, that shields
> Workmen at dawn . . .
>
> . . .
>
> Here domes and statues, spires and cranes cluster
> Beside grain-scattered streets, barge-crowded water,
> And residents from raw estates . . .

Eventually, like 'Haymaking', his poem reaches its destination, the out-lying villages on the coast:

> Here silence stands
> Like heat. Here leaves unnoticed thicken,
> Hidden weeds flower, neglected waters quicken,
> Luminously-peopled air ascends;
> And past the poppies bluish neutral distance
> Ends the land suddenly beyond a beach
> Of shapes and shingle. Here is unfenced existence:
> Facing the sun, untalkative, out of reach.

The landscape of 'The Whitsun Weddings' where

> —An Odeon went past, a cooling tower,
> And someone running up to bowl . . .
> . . .
> I thought of London spread out in the sun,
> Its postal districts packed like squares of wheat:

may be compared with the 'angled fields of grass and grain' seen from a height in 'Wind and Mist', or the villages of 'Lob', which

> All had their churches, graveyards, farms, and byres,
> Lurking to one side up the paths and lanes,
> Seldom well seen except by aeroplanes;
> And when bells rang, or pigs squealed, or cocks crowed,
> Then only heard.

In their different ways, both poems are about the common people. And the ending of 'The Whitsun Weddings' is very close to Thomas both in feeling and structure:

> it was nearly done, this frail
> Travelling coincidence: and what it held
> Stood ready to be loosed with all the power
> That being changed can give. We slowed again,
> And as the tightened brakes took hold, there swelled
> A sense of falling, like an arrow-shower
> Sent out of sight, somewhere becoming rain.

The unfolding clauses here, holding the present moment yet expanding to encompass greater meaning, seem to me to form a living link with the poetry of Edward Thomas. If there is a mainstream of modern English poetry, Thomas cannot be denied a major place in it.

Sources

The main events of Edward Thomas's life are thoroughly covered in a number of biographical studies and published collections of letters. Professor R. G. Thomas is currently working on a definitive and official biography of Edward Thomas. For the present study the main sources of biographical information are as follows:

The Childhood of Edward Thomas, with a Preface by Julian Thomas (London, 1938)
Helen Thomas, *As It Was* (London and New York, 1926) and *World Without End* (London and New York, 1931; reissued in one volume, London, 1956)
The Diary of Edward Thomas, 1 January–8 April 1917 (The Whittington Press, Cheltenham, 1977)
R. P. Eckert, *Edward Thomas: A Biography and Bibliography* (London and New York, 1937)
John Moore, *The Life and Letters of Edward Thomas* (London, 1939)
Eleanor Farjeon, *Edward Thomas: The Last Four Years* (London, 1967)
Lawrance Thompson, *Robert Frost: The Early Years* (New York, 1966; London, 1967)
R. G. Thomas (ed.), *Letter from Edward Thomas to Gordon Bottomley* (London and New York, 1968)
William Cooke, *Edward Thomas: A Critical Biography* (London and New York, 1970)
R. G. Thomas, *Edward Thomas* (University of Wales Press, Cardiff, 1972)

Letters from Edward Thomas quoted in the present study are from Moore, Farjeon, R. G. Thomas, R. G. Thomas (ed.), and Cooke above-cited, and also:
'Edward Thomas's Letters to W. H. Hudson', edited by James Guthrie, *London Mercury*, Vol. II, No. 10 (August 1920)
Edward Garnett, 'Edward Thomas', *Athenaeum*, 16 and 23 April 1920.

Sources for other background material will be found in the Notes. Critical studies of Edward Thomas's work are not numerous, although there are a number of interesting articles. The most substantial books of criticism are as follows:

H. Coombes, *Edward Thomas* (London, 1956; New York, 1973)
Vernon Scannell, *Edward Thomas* (*Writers and their Work* series, London, 1962)

William Cooke, *Edward Thomas: A Critical Biography* (London and New York, 1970)

Edna Longley (ed.), *Edward Thomas: Poems and Last Poems* (Macdonald and Evans Annotated Student Texts, London, 1973)

Other critical works are cited in the Notes to the Postscript.

Notes

Abbreviations used in the Notes are as follows:

Childhood *The Childhood of Edward Thomas* (1938)
WWE Helen Thomas, *As It Was* and *World Without End* (1956)
EF Eleanor Farjeon, *Edward Thomas: The Last Four Years* (1967)
GB R. G. Thomas (ed.), *The Letters of Edward Thomas to Gordon Bottomley* (1968)
Diary *The Diary of Edward Thomas, 1 January–8 April 1917* (1977)

Chapter 1: CHILDHOOD AND YOUTH

1 *Childhood*, p.17.
2 *ibid.*, p. 143.
3 See Cooke, p. 23.
4 *Childhood*, pp. 105, 137.
5 P. H. Thomas, *A Religion of This World: A Selection of Positivist Addresses* (London, 1913), p. 8.
6 *ibid.*, p. 7.
7 *Childhood*, preface, p. 8.
8 *ibid.*, p. 135.
9 *ibid.*, p. 144.
10 *The Woodland Life* (London, 1897), pp. 167 and 188.
11 *ibid.*, p. 220.
12 See *WWE*, pp. 80 and 99.
13 *GB*, p. 282 and John Moore, *The Life and Letters of Edward Thomas* (London, 1939), p. 290.
14 *WWE*, p. 23.
15 *Childhood*, pp. 18–19.
16 The five younger Thomas boys were as follows: Ernest, who became a commercial artist; Theodore, who was Traffic Manager of the London Public Transport Board (later London Transport); Reginald, who went into the theatre and later joined the Army, dying of influenza during the war epidemic; Oscar, who became a businessman with theatrical interests; and Julian, a civil servant who wrote in his spare time (see *WWE*, 1972 edn,

p. 186). In his autobiography Thomas claims to remember little of his
brothers in childhood except an ongoing feud with the next eldest (*Childhood*, p. 77); while in his preface to the same work, Julian Thomas states
that Edward, 'like all his brothers, was the despair of his parents, a mystery
to both father and mother' (*Childhood*, preface, p. 91).

17 See Cooke, p. 37. Helen Thomas identified the poem as having been
    addressed to her mother-in-law in a radio broadcast, BBC Third Pro-
    gramme, 8.4.67.
18 *Childhood*, p. 26.
19 *ibid*.

Chapter 2: LOVE AND MARRIAGE

 1 *WWE*, p. 21.
 2 *ibid*., pp. 18–19.
 3 *ibid*., p. 22.
 4 *ibid*., pp. 24, 63, 64.
 5 *ibid*., pp. 38–48.
 6 *The Letters of Rupert Brooke*, ed. Geoffrey Keynes (London, 1968), p. 273.
 7 *WWE*, p. 38.
 8 *ibid*., p. 44.
 9 Manuscript notebook vol. XIX (1897) in Berg Collection, New York Public
    Library, quoted in Cooke, p. 28.
10 *WWE*, p. 58.
11 *ibid*., p. 62.
12 *Oxford* (1903), p. 117.
13 H. W. Nevinson, *Changes and Chances* (London, 1923), p. 195.
14 See Cooke, p. 33.
15 *WWE*, p. 82.
16 *ibid*., p. 88.
17 'Isoud with the White Hands', *Horae Solitariae* (London, 1902).
18 For these and other details of meetings between Thomas and Bottomley,
    see *GB, passim*. Although Bottomley was an invalid who was never confident
    of living through the next winter, his health improved spectacularly after
    1920, and he survived Thomas by over thirty years.
19 *GB*, p. 282.
20 *ibid*., p. 53.
21 *WWE*, p. 92.
22 Manuscript letter from Helen Thomas to Janet Hooton, now in the posses-
    sion of Mrs Patricia M. Rogers, quoted in Cooke, pp. 35–6.
23 *WWE*, p. 99.
24 See Lawrance Thompson, *Robert Frost: The Early Years* (London, 1967)
    for details of the Frost relationship and the births of the Frost children,
    pp. 224, 252, 285, 286, 289, 339. The first child, Elliott, died in infancy and
    the sixth, Elinor Bettina, shortly after birth. Frost blamed himself for both
    deaths; see pp. 258 and 340.
25 *GB*, p. 64.

26 *ibid.*, p. 68. At this time Thomas spelt his son's name with an f in the Welsh manner, although later he reverted to the spelling Mervyn, which is the form used throughout this book for the sake of consistency.

27 See, for example, *EF*, p. 30.

28 R. G. Thomas, *Edward Thomas* (University of Wales Press, 1972), p. 59.

29 See *GB*, pp. 129–30, and 'July' in *Light and Twilight* (1911); see also the poem 'These Things that Poets Said'.

30 *WWE*, p. 101.

31 See *EF*, p. 20 and *WWE*, p. 153.

32 See *WWE*, pp. 116–7.

33 *GB*, p. 172.

34 *ibid.*, p. 173.

35 See Lawrance Thompson, *Robert Frost*, p. 463.

36 See *EF*, p. 11, where Eleanor Farjeon quotes a remark Thomas made to her: 'My wife could be the happiest woman on earth—and I won't let her.'

Chapter 3: BACK TO THE LAND

1   P. H. Thomas, *A Religion of This World.*

2   John Ruskin, *Unto This Last* (London, 1906 edn), pp. 167–8.

3   *ibid.*, p. 170.

4   Quoted in Armytage, *Heavens Below* (London, 1964), p. 332.

5   *The Open Road* (London, 1912), Vol. I, p. 294.

6   *Seed Time* (London), July 1895.

7   Edward Carpenter, *The Simplification of Life* (London, 1886), p. 29. Other information on Carpenter, particularly that relating to his political and sexual ideas, may be found in Sheila Rowbotham and Jeffrey Weeks, *Socialism and the New Life: The Personal and Sexual Politics of Edward Carpenter and Havelock Ellis* (London, 1977).

8   Edward Carpenter, *My Days and Dreams* (London, 1916), p. 145.

9   *Richard Jefferies*, p. 249.

10 Richard Jefferies, *The Story of My Heart* (London, 1883; Penguin edn, 1938), pp. 115–6.

11 On the whole, Morris's verse was more widely read and admired in his own time than were his political writings. Many young writers of the Edwardian and Georgian generations were inspired by Morris towards romantically socialist feelings and a wild and windy verse style; Rupert Brooke was an exception when he described Morris's verse as dull (see *Democracy and the Arts*, London, 1946).

12 W. B. Yeats, *Autobiographies* (London, 1955), p. 155.

13 See John Drinkwater, *Discovery* (London, 1932), p. 178.

14 *The Open Road* (1912) and *The Tramp* (1910) were short-lived magazines dedicated to the open-air life; *The Simple Life Limited* was the title of a novel by Ford Madox Ford, published under the pseudonym Daniel Chaucer in 1911.

15 See Armytage, *op. cit.*

16 *The Bedales Record*, 1913–14.

17   *The Letters of Rupert Brooke*, p. 501.
18   Quoted in *EF*, p. 161.
19   Virginia Woolf, *Night and Day* (1911), Ch. XV.
20   John Gawsworth (ed.), *Ten Contemporaries* (London, 1932), p. 19.
21   Arundel del Re, 'Georgian Reminiscences', *Studies in English Literature*, Vol. XII, No. 2 (Tokyo, 1932).
22   *The Story of My Heart, op. cit.*, p. 59.
23   *The Country* (London, 1913), p. 6.
24   Leslie Stephen, *Hours in a Library* (London, 1899), Vol. III, p. 175.
25   Thomas Hardy, *The Dorset Farm Labourer* (1884), p. 13.
26   See conversations recorded in Louis Mertins, *Robert Frost* (Norman, Oklahoma, 1965), p. 117.
27   John Barrell and John Bull (eds), *Penguin Book of Pastoral Verse* (1974), p. 4.
28   *The Country*, p. 55.

Chapter 4: A COUNTRY WRITER

1   Helen Thomas, introduction to *The Prose of Edward Thomas* (ed. Roland Gant, London, 1948), p. 12.
2   These scrapbooks are now in the care of University College, Cardiff (Arts Library) under the supervision of Professor R. G. Thomas, to whom I am indebted for permission to consult them. They show not only the much greater length of book reviews in pre-1914 newspapers, but also Thomas's meticulous habit of pasting up and dating all his press-cuttings. He reviewed chiefly for the *Daily Chronicle* but also for a range of other periodicals including *The Nation*, *The Morning Post*, *The Bookman* and *The English Review*. His attitude towards James Milne, literary editor of the *Daily Chronicle*, is revealed in the inclusion of a review by Milne also pasted into one of the scrapbooks, with the accompanying note: 'A specimen of a review by James Milne, Esq.' The review is of three books on South America, and reads in part: 'Mr MacDonald's book is brimful of first-hand information. It is a far cry to Patagonia, but we are clearly shown it has possibilities.' (*Daily Chronicle*, 20.12.11). This was the kind of jovial writing Thomas aimed to avoid. If Milne was aware of Thomas's contempt, he did not record it, recalling Thomas in his memoirs as 'a most likeable man and a gentleman, both sensitive and modest [who] hardly cared whether a review by him appeared with his name or without it' (*Memoirs of a Bookman*, London, 1934, p. 149).
3   See *The Autobiography of Arthur Ransome* (ed. Rupert Hart-Davis, London, 1976), Chs VII and VIII.
4   *ibid.*, p. 82.
5   Walter Pater, *Appreciations* (London, 1889), p. 11.
6   *ibid.*, p. 24.
7   *ibid.*, p. 10; see also Walter Pater, *Plato and Platonism* (London, 1893).
8   *Appreciations*, p. 18.
9   Anonymous review of *Rose Acre Papers* in *The Week's Survey*, 24.12.04, and

others contained in the Thomas press cuttings books at University College, Cardiff.

10 *WWE*, p. 101.
11 *ibid.*, p. 106.
12 *ibid.*, p. 60.
13 W. H. Davies, *Autobiography of a Super Tramp* (London, 1907), p. 208.
14 Quoted in R. J. Stonesifer, *W. H. Davies: A Critical Biography* (London, 1963), p. 50.
15 *ibid.*, p. 63.
16 *Daily Chronicle*, 21.10.05.
17 *GB*, p. 105.
18 For a full account of this incident, see Stonesifer, pp. 73–4.
19 *GB*, p. 107.
20 *ibid.*
21 *ibid.*, p. 124.
22 *ibid.*, p. 130.
23 See *GB*, p. 135.
24 Edward Garnett, 'Some Letters of Edward Thomas', *Athenaeum*, 16.4.20, p. 500.
25 Letter from Thomas to Garnett, 10.2.09, *ibid.*, p. 502.
26 Edward Garnett, *Athenaeum*, p. 501.
27 *ibid.*
28 *GB*, p. 126.
29 *WWE*, pp. 67–8.
30 *ibid.*, p. 69.
31 *ibid.*, p. 70.
32 *ibid.*, p. 71.
33 *GB*, p. 113.
34 Q. D. Leavis, 'Lives and Works of Richard Jefferies', *Scrutiny*, Vol. VI, 1938, reprinted in *A Selection from Scrutiny* (Cambridge, 1968), Vol. 2, p. 220.
35 *GB*, p. 156.
36 *Richard Jefferies*, p. 320.
37 *ibid.*, p. 326.
38 See *WWE*, p. 123: 'She was one of the family with whom I had lived at Margate, and was now about eighteen ... me she had known as Auntie Jenny.' For the girl's name, see the Note to the 1972 edition of *WWE*, p. 188.
39 See *WWE*, pp. 123–5 and *GB*, pp. 156–63.
40 *GB*, p. 156.
41 See *GB*, p. 160.
42 *Light and Twilight* (1911), p. 150.
43 *GB*, p. 165.
44 *ibid.*, p. 167.
45 See *GB*, p. 165.
46 *GB*, p. 174.
47 *ibid.*, p. 178.
48 *WWE*, p. 98.
49 *GB*, p. 183.

Chapter 5: THE DARK WOODS

1 *WWE*, p. 91.
2 *ibid.*, p. 108.
3 *GB*, pp. 89–90.
4 See *GB*, pp. 75 and 77.
5 *GB*, p. 162.
6 *EF*, p. 157.
7 James Guthrie, *To the Memory of Edward Thomas* (Pear Tree Press, 1937).
8 *GB*, p. 148.
9 *ibid.*
10 *GB*, p. 57.
11 *ibid.*, p. 180.
12 See *Athenaeum*, 16.4.20, pp. 500–2.
13 *GB*, p. 206.
14 *ibid.*, p. 205.
15 *ibid.*, p. 210.
16 *ibid.*, p. 211.
17 *ibid.*, p. 213.
18 *ibid.*, p. 215.
19 John Moore, *Life and Letters of Edward Thomas*, p. 171.
20 *ibid.*, p. 172.
21 *WWE*, pp. 148–50.
22 *Light and Twilight* (1911), p. 165.
23 See *WWE*, pp. 116–7.
24 *GB*, p. 222.
25 See David Garnett, *The Golden Echo* (London, 1953) for an account of this.
26 *EF*, p. 13.
27 *The Happy-Go-Lucky Morgans* (London, 1913), pp. 122–7.

Chapter 6: NEW FRIENDS, NEW FORMS

1 See *EF*, p. 44.
2 *ibid.*, p. 17.
3 *ibid.*, p. 43.
4 *GB*, p. 220.
5 *ibid.*, p. 223.
6 *Letters from W. H. Hudson to Edward Garnett* (London, 1925), p. 135.
7 Clifford Bax, *Some I Knew Well* (London, 1953), p. 178.
8 *EF*, p. ix.
9 See *ibid.*, p. x.
10 *ibid.*
11 *EF*, p. 17.
12 *WWE*, p. 140.
13 See *WWE*, p. 155.
14 *EF*, p. 28.
15 *ibid.*, p. 41.

16 *ibid.*, p. 46.
17 *ibid.*, p. 48.
18 *Childhood*, pp. 21–22.
19 The subtitle given to the book on publication: 'a fragment of autobiography' suggests that it was unfinished, but the letter to *EF* quoted above (see n. 16) shows that it was intended to cover the years up to 'about 1895' only.
20 John Moore, *Life and Letters*, p. 321.
21 For a full account of the history of Georgian Poetry, see Robert H. Ross, *The Georgian Revolt* (London, 1967) and Joy Grant, *Harold Monro and the Poetry Bookshop* (London, 1967).
22 *Quarterly Review*, October 1916.
23 F. R. Leavis, *New Bearings in English Poetry* (London, 1932), p. 15.
24 A. C. Bradley, *Poetry for Poetry's Sake* (Oxford, 1909).
25 See Christopher Hassall, *Rupert Brooke* (London, 1964), p. 373.
26 *The Letters of Rupert Brooke*, p. 541.
27 Quoted in introduction to *Collected Plays* (Penguin edn, 1952), p. 10.
28 Preface, *Poems* (Dublin, 1909), p. x.
29 *Letters of Rupert Brooke*, p. 328.
30 *ibid.*, p. 259.
31 Lascelles Abercrombie 'Poetry and Contemporary Speech' (English Association, 1914).
32 *GB*, p. 247.
33 John Drinkwater, *Prose Papers* (London, 1917), p. 183.
34 *Times Literary Supplement*, 11.3.15.
35 'Poetry and Contemporary Speech'.

Chapter 7: WRINGING RHETORIC'S NECK

1 See *The Autobiography of Arthur Ransome*, p. 87.
2 *EF*, p. 37. Lawrance Thompson (p. 464) gives 5 October as the date of the first meeting between Thomas and Frost, but it is clear from *EF* that the appointment was for the following day.
3 See *EF*, p. 38.
4 The Thomas-Frost correspondence is held in Dartmouth College Library, Hanover, New Hampshire.
5 *EF*, p. 51.
6 See *EF*, pp. 58–9.
7 Letter to Edward Garnett, 7.1.14, *Athenaeum* (23.4.20), p. 535.
8 For details of the Thomas-Frost relationship, see Lawrance Thompson, *Robert Frost*, Chs 32 and 33.
9 *ibid.*, *passim*. For Frost's poem on suicide, 'Despair', see p. 267, and for the incident with the revolver, see p. 308. The 'best way out is often through' is from the Introduction, p. xxii.
10 *ibid.*, pp. 463, 465–6.
11 *EF*, p. 61.
12 *ibid.*, p. 62.
13 See Cooke, p. 73.

14　Catherine Abercrombie, 'Memories of a Poet's Wife', *The Listener*, 15.11.56.
15　*Selected Letters of Robert Frost*, ed. Lawrance Thompson (London, 1965), p. 124.
16　See letter from Wilfrid Gibson to Edward Marsh, dated 24.4.14, in Marsh Letter Collection, Berg Collection, New York Public Library.
17　'This England', *The Nation*, 7.11.14.
18　For biographical information on Abercrombie see Jeffrey Cooper, *A Bibliography and Notes on the Work of Lascelles Abercrombie* (London, 1969).
19　John Gawsworth (ed.), *Ten Contemporaries*, p. 19.
20　Catherine Abercrombie, *The Listener*.
21　Abercrombie gave estimates of his income in a letter to Edward Marsh dated 5.9.14, in Marsh Letter Collection, Berg Collection, New York Public Library. Thomas's earnings are given in R. G. Thomas, *Edward Thomas*, p. 16.
22　*Times Literary Supplement*, 27.2.13.
23　For the history of *New Numbers* see Jan Marsh, 'Georgian Poetry and the Land', unpublished D.Phil dissertation, University of Sussex.
24　'This England', *op. cit.*
25　For details of Thomas's friendship with Brooke, see Christopher Hassall, *Rupert Brooke*, pp. 239–41.
26　'Rupert Brooke', *The English Review*, June 1915.
27　*Daily Chronicle*, 9.4.12.
28　See Christopher Hassall, *Edward Marsh: Patron of the Arts* (London, 1959), pp. 211, 422.
29　*The Letters of Rupert Brooke*, p. 459.
30　*Daily Chronicle*, 29.2.08.
31　*ibid.*, 18.4.08.
32　*ibid.*, 9.3.12.
33　See *The Letters of W. Dixon Scott*, ed. M. MacCrossan (London, 1932), letter dated 3.10.13.
34　See *GB*, p. 238.
35　*The Nation*, 13.6.14.
36　*Selected Letters of Robert Frost*, pp. 110–11.
37　*EF*, p. 90.
38　*English Review*, August 1914.
39　*Daily News*, 22.7.14.
40　*Walter Pater: A Critical Study* (1913).
41　*Algernon Charles Swinburne: A Critical Study* (1912). The publication dates of *Pater* and *Swinburne* suggest that the latter was written first; in fact, as a letter to Bottomley dated 22 March 1912 (*GB*, p. 220) makes clear, *Pater* was finished before *Swinburne*, and its publication was delayed.
42　*Morning Post*, 3.1.07.
43　Review of Yeats's *Plays for an Irish Theatre*, Vols 2 and 3, in *The Week's Survey*, n.d., pasted in the press cuttings album in University College Cardiff.
44　*Daily Chronicle*, 13.9.07.
45　*ibid.*, 7.6.09.
46　See Thomas's review of *Exultations* in *Daily Chronicle*, 23.11.09, which he

says contains 'very nearly nothing at all', and his letter dated 12 June 1909 to Bottomley (*GB*, p. 187) where he apologises for praising *Personae*.

47 See *A Literary Pilgrim in England* (London, 1917), 1928 Traveller's Library edn, p. 143.

48 *Morning Post*, 9.12.09.

49 See letter to Frost, 19.5.14, now in Dartmouth College Library, quoted in Cooke, p. 73, and *GB*, p. 228.

50 *GB*, p. 232. These 'Welsh pictures' are reprinted in the two posthumous collections of Thomas's essays, *Cloud Castle* (London, 1922) and *The Last Sheaf* (London, 1928).

51 See Gordon Bottomley, 'A Note on Edward Thomas', *The Welsh Review* (September 1945), p. 172, and *Letters from W. H. Hudson to Edward Garnett*, p. 135.

52 *EF*, p. 41.

53 Quoted in Harold Roy Brennan, 'The Poet of the Countryside: Edward Thomas', *The Cardinal* (Jan.–Feb. 1926).

54 Letter to Frost, 19.5.14, now in Dartmouth College Library, quoted in Cooke, p. 73.

55 *EF*, p. 81.

56 'Tipperary', *English Review*, October 1914.

57 *GB*, p. 238.

58 'It's a Long, Long Way', *English Review*, December 1914.

59 *Selected Letters of Robert Frost*, op. cit., p. 142.

60 See Lawrance Thompson, *Robert Frost*, pp. 467–8.

61 'War Poetry', *Poetry and Drama*, December 1914.

Chapter 8: IN IT AND NO MISTAKE

1 'The White House', prose sketch in manuscript notebook now in Lockwood Memorial Library, State University of New York at Buffalo, quoted in full in Cooke, pp. 163–6.

2 Almost all Thomas's poems are contained in surviving manuscript notebooks. The first, now in the Lockwood Memorial Library, Buffalo, contains five poems; the second, now in the British Museum, contains sixty-two poems; the third, now in the Bodleian, contains sixty-seven poems. Nearly all the poems are dated and a full chronology, with the exception of the handful of poems without precise dates, is set out in Cooke, 'Dates of the Poems in Order of Composition', Appendix I, pp. 243–7. I have followed this chronology when indicating the poems' dates of composition. However, although in general the poems did 'not ask or get much correction', most went through at least one working draft before completion and before being copied into the notebook (see Cooke, p. 250) and thus a few days might elapse between first and final drafts. In general, it seems safe to say that any given poem was 'completed' on the date given in the notebooks and Cooke's chronology.

For the titles of the poems, I have followed those given in *Collected Poems* (Faber, 1936; fifth impression, 1949, with the addition of the poem

'P.H.T.'). Titles were rarely given to the poems in the notebooks; many are known only by their opening words. *Edward Thomas: Complete Poems*, edited by R. G. Thomas (Oxford University Press, London, 1978), will contain definitive texts of the poems. According to Cooke, pp. 248–9, variant readings exist; in general, however, these appear to be slight, with significant variations affecting only a few poems. I have followed the texts given in the 1936 Faber edition (eleventh impression, 1974). The annotated edition prepared by Edna Longley and published under the title *Edward Thomas: Poems and Last Poems* (Macdonald and Evans Annotated Texts, London, 1973) places the poems for the first time in chronological order, although unaccountably omitting the very first poem 'Up in the Wind'. Textually it follows the Faber edition.

3 See Cooke, p. 171, where the text of 'Old Man's Beard' is quoted in juxta-position with the poem.
4 See *GB*, p. 263.
5 Letter to Frost, dated 15.12.14, now in Dartmouth College Library, quoted in Cooke, p. 82.
6 Letter to Harold Monro, dated 15.12.14, now in Lockwood Memorial Library, quoted in Cooke, p. 82.
7 See *EF*, p. 104.
8 *GB*, p. 241.
9 'The Other', together with four other poems, is left undated in the Cooke chronology, but it was apparently included in a packet of verse mailed to Frost at Dymock on 16 December 1914, now in Dartmouth College Library, which suggests that it was among Thomas's earliest poems.

Chapter 9: AN IDEAL ENGLAND

1   *EF*, p. 114.
2   *GB*, p. 243.
3   *EF*, p. 114.
4   *GB*, p. 245.
5   See *EF*, p. 117. 'Doomed hack' was Thomas's description of the writer Mr Torrance, one of the self-portraits in *The Happy-Go-Lucky Morgans*.
6   Other names considered included 'Edward Phillips' and 'Edward Marendaz'; see *EF*, pp. 118–9. Marendaz was rejected as being 'too un-English just now.'
7   See *EF*, p. 126.
8   See Cooke, p. 251, Appendix 2, 'A Note on the Manuscript Poems', where he states that 'A Private' exists in two early drafts written on 6 and 7 January 1915, with the printed version being a later reworking at an unknown date.
9   'Edward Thomas's Letters to W. H. Hudson', ed. James Guthrie, *London Mercury*, August 1920, p. 440.
10 *WWE*, p. 165.
11 See *EF*, p. 133.
12 See *GB*, p. 247.

13 See review of Frost's *North of Boston*, in *Daily News*, 14.7.14.
14 *GB*, p. 248.
15 *ibid.*, p. 251.
16 *EF*, p. 111.
17 *GB*, p. 247.
18 See Cooke, pp. 196–7 for a discussion of 'Swedes', and throughout the critical section of his book for other instances of prose ideas being later reworked in verse.
19 *EF*, p. 124.
20 *The Last Sheaf* (1928), p. 109.
21 See *EF*, p. 145.
22 Whether or not 'The Manor Farm' was based on a real place is speculation, but it is intriguing to find in *The Letters of W. H. Hudson to Edward Garnett* (1925), p. 33, the following extract, written in 1902 when Hudson was living at Selborne, Hampshire (not far from Thomas's later home at Steep): 'The village of Priors Dean where I went consists of a farmhouse, two or three cottages, and a church, very ancient, but no better than a cottage. By it grows a yew tree which might be a thousand years old; and that's all there is. A most lonely, silent, peaceful spot.' Could Thomas, who lived within walking distance of Priors Dean, have used it as the setting for 'The Manor Farm'?
23 *This England* (1915), pp. 111–2.

Chapter 10: COUNTRY AND COUNTRY

1 'This England', reprinted in *The Last Sheaf*, p. 221.
2 Rupert Brooke, 'An Unusual Young Man', *Letters from America* (London, 1916), pp. 173–8.
3 See *EF*, pp. 95–7.
4 See 'Edward Thomas's Letters to W. H. Hudson', *London Mercury* (August 1920), p. 440.
5 *GB*, p. 238.
6 *ibid.*, p. 248.
7 See *EF*, p. 128 and *GB*, p. 246.
8 See *EF*, p. 146.
9 'Edward Thomas's Letters to W. H. Hudson', *London Mercury*, p. 440.
10 *ibid.*
11 See letter to Jesse Berridge, quoted *GB*, p. 250.
12 *GB*, p. 249.
13 See Cooke, p. 222.
14 *GB*, p. 250.
15 See Cooke, p. 248.
16 *WWE*, p. 157.
17 *EF*, p. 152.
18 *ibid.*, p. 153.
19 See Cooke, p. 245.
20 *EF*, p. 153.

21   *ibid.*, p. 155.
22   See *EF*, p. 180.
23   See Rupert Brooke, *Collected Poems* (London, 1918), p. cxlix.
24   *EF*, p. 154.
25   R. G. Thomas, *Edward Thomas*, p. 15.
26   John Moore, *Life and Letters of Edward Thomas*, p. 330.

Chapter 11: WHATEVER IT IS I SEEK

1   W. H. Hudson, an authority on birds, doubted this at first—see *Letters from W. H. Hudson to Edward Garnett*, p. 191.
2   Walter de la Mare, Foreword to *Collected Poems* (1920), p. 12.
3   In the manuscript notebook they are dated 6, 7, 8 and 9 April respectively (see Cooke, p. 246) although from evidence in *EF* (p. 193) the first two were written some days earlier.
4   *GB*, p. 253.
5   *EF*, p. 192.
6   Two of the poems both Thomas and Bottomley wanted to appear in the *Annual* ('Lob' and 'Words') were prevented from doing so by their prior publication in an artistic magazine, *Form* (1916), of which Thomas's friend James Guthrie was literary editor and to whom he had promised the poems. Eight other poems were also first published by Guthrie, two in his own magazine *Root and Branch* and six in a handprinted booklet, *Six Poems* by Edward Eastaway (Pear Tree Press, 1916).
7   See *GB*, pp. 263–7 for the correspondence relating to the poems in the *Annual*.
8   *GB*, p. 269.
9   From a letter by John Freeman, it would appear that this may have been based on an actual experience. In the autumn of 1915 a storm brought down a large number of elm trees in the Essex countryside around Thomas's camp at Romford. See *John Freeman's Letters*, ed. Gertrude Freeman and Sir John Squire, (London, 1936), p. 177.
10   *EF*, p. 201.
11   *WWE*, p. 163.
12   For Helen Thomas's account of these events, see *WWE*, pp. 166–8.
13   *GB*, p. 269.
14   Few of the poems of this period were given titles, either by Thomas or by later editors. Most are known by shortened versions of their first lines, as 'When He Should Laugh' and 'How At Once'.
15   See *WWE*, p. 166.

Chapter 12: THE DARK HAUNTS ROUND

1   *EF*, p. 202.
2   See *EF*, p. 219, also Plate VI for the actual draft of the poem.
3   *EF*, p. 220.

4   See *WWE*, pp. 170–1.
5   See *EF*, p. 221.
6   See Cooke, pp. 177–82 for a long comparison of the prose passage and poem.
7   See Cooke, *passim*.
8   Letter to Frost, dated 19.10.16, now in Dartmouth College Library, quoted in Cooke, p. 92.
9   *ibid.*
10 See *EF*, p. 218.
11 *The Woodland Life* (1897), p. 61.
12 See *GB*, p. 274.
13 *EF*, p. 231.
14 See *WWE*, pp. 172–5.
15 *EF*, p. 237.
16 *ibid.*
17 *ibid.*
18 See *EF*, pp. 241–2.
19 See *WWE*, pp. 179–83.
20 *EF*, p. 240.
21 *EF*, p. 248.
22 *The Diary of Edward Thomas* (The Whittington Press, 1977), p. 13.
23 *ibid.*, pp. 25–6.
24 *EF*, p. 258.
25 See *GB*, p. 280.
26 See *GB*, p. 283.
27 John Moore, *Life and Letters of Edward Thomas*, p. 264.
28 There are conflicting accounts of the exact time and manner of Thomas's death, which are quoted in Cooke, pp. 268–70. The letter announcing his death to Helen from Thomas's fellow officer J. M. Thorburn states that it happened 'in the morning, by shell fire, in the observation post.' The subsequent letter from Major F. Lushington, in command of 244 Battery, says 'he died at a moment of victory from a direct hit by a shell.' (See *EF*, pp. 263–4, where the letter is quoted in full). By an odd coincidence, Eleanor Farjeon came to hear a week or so later that a sergeant from Thomas's company was in London, and she took Helen to meet him and hear in his words how Thomas died. The sergeant's words, as recalled by Eleanor, were: 'At the end of the day when the battle was over we had the Huns on the run, and the plain was full of our men shouting and dancing . . . Mr Thomas came up from the dug-out behind his gun and leaned in the opening filling his clay pipe. One of the Huns turned as he was running and shot a stray shot, and Mr Thomas fell. It was all over in an instant' (see *EF*, pp. 262–3). It would appear that Thomas was not hit directly by a shell, for his possessions, including his diary, his watch and his clay pipe, were returned to Helen and were unmarked except for a curious creasing of the diary's pages, 'like the scallops on a sea-shell' (see Myfanwy Thomas, Foreword, *The Diary of Edward Thomas*, p. viii). The pocket watch had stopped at about 7.30, which presumably gives the time of death; from all accounts this must have been 7.30 a.m., and the sergeant's version 'at the end of the day' being Eleanor's understanding of 'when the battle was

over'. Attacks on the Western Front commonly began some hours before daylight, so that the initial 'moment of victory' may well have been as early as 7.30.

29   *EF*, pp. 263–4.

POSTSCRIPT

1   See Edna Longley (ed.), *Edward Thomas: Poems and Last Poems*, Appendix A: 'Edward Thomas and Robert Frost'.
2   C. K. Stead, *The New Poetic* (London, 1964), p. 89.
3   See Chapter 7, note 47.
4   See Longley (ed.), *Poems and Last Poems*, p. 380.
5   See Maire A. Quinn, 'The Personal Past in the Poetry of Thomas Hardy and Edward Thomas', *The Critical Quarterly* (1974), i, p. 7.
6   See Donald Davie, *Thomas Hardy and British Poetry* (London, 1973).

Index